Turkish
PHRASE BOOK & DICTIONARY

Easy to use features

- Handy thematic colour coding
- Quick Reference Section—opposite page
- Tipping Guide—inside back cover
- Quick reply panels throughout

How best to use this phrase book

• We suggest that you start with the **Guide to pronunciation** (pp. 6–9), then go on to **Some basic expressions** (pp. 10–15). This gives you not only a minimum vocabulary, but also helps you get used to pronouncing the language.

• Consult the **Contents** pages (3–5) for the section you need. In each chapter you'll find travel facts, hints and useful information. Simple phrases are followed by a list of words applicable to the situation.

• Separate, detailed contents lists are included at the beginning of the extensive **Eating out** and **Shopping guide** sections (Menus, p. 39, Shops and services, p. 97).

• If you want to find out how to say something in Turkish, your fastest look-up is via the **Dictionary** section (pp. 165–189). This not only gives you the word, but is also cross-referenced to its use in a phrase on a specific page.

• If you want to learn more about constructing sentences, check the **Basic grammar** (pp. 159–163).

• Note the **colour margins** are indexed in Turkish and English to help both listener and speaker. And, in addition, there is also an **index in Turkish** for the use of your listener.

• Throughout the book, this symbol ☛ suggests phrases your listener might use to answer you. If you still can't understand, hand the phrase book to the Turkish-speaker to encourage pointing to an appropriate answer.

---

400 Alexander Park, Princeton, NJ 08540-6306, USA

Library of Congress Catalog Card No. 89-61139

Revised edition - 9th printing - May 1998 Printed in Spain

Contents

Travelling around 65

Sightseeing 80

Relaxing 86

Making friends 92

Shopping guide 97

Acknowledgments
We are particularly grateful to Zeynep Ersan and Hülya Uzer for their help in the preparation of this book, and to Dr. T.J.A. Bennett who devised the phonetic transcription.

Guide to pronunciation

This and the following chapter are intended to make you familiar with the phonetic transcription we have devised and to help you get used to the sounds of Turkish.

As a minimum vocabulary for your trip, we've selected a number of basic words and phrases under the title "Some basic expressions" (pages 10–15).

An outline of the spelling and sounds of Turkish

You'll find the pronunciation of the Turkish letters and sounds explained below, as well as the symbols we're using for them in the transcriptions. Note that Turkish has some diacritical letters – letters with special markings – which we don't have in English.

The imitated pronunciation should be read as if it were English except for any special rules set out below. It is based on Standard British pronunciation, though we have tried to take account of General American pronunciation also. Of course, the sounds of any two languages are never exactly the same; but if you follow carefully the indications supplied here you should be able to read our transcriptions in such a way as to make yourself understood.

Letters shown in bold print should be read with more stress (louder) than the others.

Consonants

Letter	Approximate pronunciation	Symbol	Example
b, d, f, l, m, n, p, t, z	as in English, but when pronouncing **d**, **n** and **t**, the tongue touches the upper teeth, not the gums behind them		

Letter	Approximate pronunciation	Symbol	Example	
c	like **j** in **j**am	j	**cep**	jehp
ç	like **ch** in **ch**ip	ch	**çocuk**	cho**jook**
g	1) before or after **a**, **ı**, **o**, **u**, as in **g**o	g	**gam**	gahm
	2) before or after **e**, **i**, **ö**, **ü**, it is followed by a **y**-sound as in an**g**ular	g^y	**göz**	g^yurz
ğ	1) when preceded and followed by **e, i, ö** or **ü**, usually a **y**-sound, as in law**y**er	y	**değer**	da**y**ehr
	2) otherwise indicates that the preceding vowel is lengthened		**dağ**	daa
h	always pronounced as in **h**it	h/hh	**hemen** **mahkeme**	**heh**mehn mahhkeh**meh**
j	like **s** in plea**s**ure	zh	**müjde**	mewzh**deh**
k	1) before or after **a**, **ı**, **o**, **u**, like **c** in **c**ool	k	**bakan**	bah**kahn**
	2) before or after **e**, **i**, **ö**, **ü**, it is followed by a **y**-sound, like **c** in **c**ure	k^y	**kürek**	k^yewrayk
r	with the tip of the tongue touching the gums just behind the teeth; at the end of a word, it often sounds almost like **sh** in **sh**ell	r	**kar**	**kahr**
s	always as in **s**o, never as in i**s**	s/ss	**su** **masa**	soo **mah**ssah
ş	like **sh** in **sh**ell	sh	**şimşek**	sheem**shehk**
v	often pronounced so weakly that it sounds more like a **w**	v	**yuva**	yoo**vah**
y	1) when at the beginning of a word or after a consonant, like **y** in **y**es	y	**yag**	yaa
	2) when **y** comes between **e**, **i**, **ö** or **ü** and a consonant, the vowel is lengthened		**öyle**	ur**leh**
	3) after a vowel, it becomes part of a diphthong			

Vowels

In Turkish, vowels are generally short but can be lengthened by **ğ** or **y**; or when used in some words borrowed from Persian or Arabic.

a	1) generally like a short version of the **a** in c**a**r, i.e. a sound between **a** in c**a**t and **u** in c**u**t	ah	**adam**	ah**dahm**
	2) when long, as in c**a**r	aa	**sağ**	saa
e	1) usually as in m**e**t	eh	**evet**	**eh**veht
	2) sometimes (especially when long) like **a** in late, but a pure vowel, not a diphthong	ay	**değil**	day**eel**
i	as in mach**i**ne	ee	**iğne**	ee**neh**
ı	a sound between **i** as in b**i**g and **u** as in b**u**g; with your lips spread as if to say **ee**, try to pronounce **u** as in p**u**t	ı	**kış**	kısh
o	1) as in tone, but a pure vowel, not a diphthong; sometimes as in h**o**t	o	**on** **nokta**	on nok**tah**
ö	like **ur** in f**ur** but shorter and with the lips a little rounded	ur*	**ömür**	urm**ewr**
u	as in p**u**ll	oo	**uzak**	oo**zahk**
ü	pronounce **ee** as in s**ee**, but round your lips, without moving your tongue	ew	**üç**	ewch

1) A circumflex accent (ˆ) over a vowel indicates that the preceding **g**, **k** or **l** is followed by a short y-sound, e.g. **Lâtin** (l[y]ah**tin**).

2) Elsewhere the circumflex indicates that a vowel is long.

* The **r** should not be pronounced when reading this transcription.

Diphthongs

ay	like **igh** in **sight**	ah^{y}	**bay**	bah^{y}
ey	like **ay** in **say**	eh^{y}	**bey**	beh^{y}
oy	like **oy** in **coy**	oy	**koy**	koy

Doubled consonants

These represent not two separate sounds, but a single, long one, like, for example, the **pp** in a rapid pronunciation of lam**pp**ost.

Stress

Stress – far less pronounced in Turkish than in English – is variable and depends partly on the position of the word in the sentence and on the suffixes present. As a *very* general guideline, stress often falls on alternate syllables. Also, the voice rises slightly on the last syllable.

Pronunciation of the Turkish alphabet

A	ah	**Ğ**	yoomooshahk g^{y}eh	**N**	neh	**U**	oo
B	beh	**H**	heh	**O**	o	**Ü**	ew
C	jeh	**I**	ı	**Ö**	ur	**V**	veh
Ç	cheh	**İ**	ee	**P**	peh	**Y**	yeh
D	deh	**J**	zheh	**R**	reh	**Z**	zeh
E	eh	**K**	k^{y}eh	**S**	seh		
F	feh	**L**	leh	**Ş**	sheh		
G	g^{y}eh	**M**	meh	**T**	teh		

Some basic expressions

Yes.	**Evet.**	ehveht
No.	**Hayır.**	**hah**^{y}ır
Please.	**Lütfen.**	**lewt**fehn
Thank you.	**Teşekkür ederim.**	tehshehk**k^{y}ewr** ehdehreem
Thank you very much.	**Çok teşekkür ederim.**	**chok** tehshehk**k^{y}ewr** ehdehreem
That's all right. (You're welcome.)	**Birşey değil.**	**beer**sheh^{y} day**eel**

Greetings *Selamlar*

Hello.	**Merhaba.**	**mehr**hahbah
Good morning.	**Günaydın.**	g^{y}ewnah^{y}**dın**
Good afternoon.	**İyi günler.**	eeyee g^{y}ewn**lehr**
Good evening.	**İyi akşamlar.**	eeyee ahk**shahm**lahr
Good night.	**İyi geceler.**	eeyee g^{y}ehjeh**lehr**
Goodbye.	**Allahaısmarladık.*** **Güle güle.****	ah**llah**hahısmahrlahdık. g^{y}ewleh g^{y}ewleh
See you later.	**Sonra görüşürüz.**	sonrah g^{y}urrewshewrewz
This is Mr ...	**Bu bay ...**	**boo** bah^{y}
This is Mrs ...	**Bu bayan ...**	**boo** bah^{y}ahn
This is Miss ...	**Bu bayan ...**	**boo** bah^{y}ahn
How do you do? (Pleased to meet you.)	**Memnun oldum.**	**mehm**noon **ol**doom
How are you?	**Nasılsınız?**	nah**ssıl**sınız
Very well, thanks. And you?	**Çok iyiyim, teşekkür ederim. Siz nasılsınız?**	chok eeyeeyeem tehshehk**k^{y}ewr** ehdehreem. seez nah**ssıl**sınız

* said by the one who is leaving.
** said by the one who remains.

How's life?	**Ne haber?**	**neh** hahbehr
Fine.	**İyiyim.**	eeyeeyeem
I beg your pardon?	**Efendim?**	eh**fehn**deem
Excuse me. (May I get past?)	**Affedersiniz.**	**ah**ffehdehrseeneez
Sorry!	**Özür dilerim!**	urzewr **dee**lehreem

Questions *Sorular*

Where?	**Nerede?**	**neh**rehdeh
How?	**Nasıl?**	**nah**ssıl
When?	**Ne zaman?**	**neh** zah**mahn**
What?	**Ne?**	**neh**
Why?	**Neden?**	**neh**dehn
Who?	**Kim?**	**k^{y}eem**
Which?	**Hangi?**	**hahng**^{y}ee
Where is ...?	**... nerededir?**	... **neh**rehdehdeer
Where are ...?	**... nerededir?**	... **neh**rehdehdeer
Where can I find/get ...?	**Nerede ... bulabilirim/alabilirim?**	**neh**rehdeh ... boolahbeeleer**eem**/ahlahbeeleer**eem**
Where can I rent ...?	**Nerede ... kiralayabilirim?**	**neh**rehdeh ... keerahlah^{y}ahbeeleer**eem**
How far?	**Ne uzaklıktadır?**	neh oozahklıktahdır
How long?	**Ne kadar zaman?**	neh kahdahr zah**mahn**
How much?	**Ne kadar?**	neh kahdahr
How many?	**Kaç tane?**	kahch **tah**neh
How much is it?	**Ne kadardır?**	**neh** kahdahrdır
When does ... open/close?	**Ne zaman ... açılır/kapanır?**	**neh** zah**mahn** ... achı**lır**/kahpah**nır**
What do you call this/that in Turkish?	**Bunun/Şunun Türkçesi ne?**	boonoon/shoonoon tewrkchehssee **neh**
What's that?	**Bu ne?**	boo neh
What does this/that mean?	**Bu/Şu ne demek?**	boo/shoo neh deh**mehk**
Is that right?	**Doğru mu?**	dawroo moo

Do you speak ...? *... biliyor musunuz?*

Do you speak English?	**İngilizce biliyor musunuz?**	eeng^{y}ee**leez**jeh beeleeyor **moo**ssoonooz
Does anyone here speak English?	**Burada biri İngilizce biliyor mu?**	boorahdah beeree eeng^{y}ee**leez**jeh beelee**yor** moo
I don't speak (much) Turkish.	**(İyi) Türkçe bilmem.**	(eeyee) **tewrk**cheh beelmehm
Could you speak more slowly?	**Daha yavaş konuşur musunuz?**	**dah**hah yah**vahsh** konoo**shoor moo**ssoonooz
Could you repeat that?	**Şunu tekrar edebilir misiniz?**	shoonoo tehkrahr ehdehbee**leer mee**sseeneez
Could you spell it?	**Heceler misiniz?**	hehjehlehr **mee**sseeneez
Please write it down.	**Lütfen yazar mısınız.**	**lewt**fehn yahzahr **mı**ssınız
Can you translate this for me?	**Benim için bunu tercüme edebilir misiniz?**	behneem eecheen boonoo tehrjewmeh ehdehbee**leer mee**sseeneez
Could you point to the ... in the book?	**Lütfen ... kitapta gösterir misiniz?**	**lewt**fehn ... k^{y}ee**tahp**tah g^{y}urs**teh**reer **mee**sseeneez
word	**kelimeyi**	k^{y}ehlee**meh**^{y}ee
phrase	**deyimi**	**deh**^{y}eemee
sentence	**cümleyi**	jewm**leh**^{y}ee
Just a minute.	**Bir dakika.**	beer dah**k^{y}ee**kah
I'll see if I can find it in this book.	**Bakayım kitapta var mı?**	bahkah^y**ım** k^{y}ee**tahp**tah **vahr** mı
I understand.	**Anlıyorum.**	ahnlı**yo**room
I don't understand.	**Anlamıyorum.**	ahn**lah**mı**yo**room
Do you understand?	**Anlıyor musunuz?**	ahnlı**yor moo**ssoonooz

Can/May ...? *Rica edebilir mi ...?*

Can I have ...?*	**... rica edebilir miyim?**	... reejah ehdehbee**leer** meeyeem

* The verb 'can' when it stands alone cannot be translated by a direct equivalent in Turkish. Instead, the suffix *-ebilir* is used together with the main verb when asking a question. This suffix cannot be used in the answer, so one must answer with the main verb, and politeness must be expressed in the tone of voice: e.g. Can you give me a book? Yes, I give *or*, I don't give.

Can we have ...?	**... rica edebilir miyiz?**	... reejah ehdehbee**leer** meeyeez
Can you show me ...?	**Bana ... gösterebilir misiniz?**	**bah**nah ... g^{y}urstehrehbee**leer mee**sseeneez
Can you tell me ...?	**Bana ... söyleyebilir misiniz?**	**bah**nah ... surleh^{y}ehbee**leer mee**sseeneez
Can you help me?	**Yardım edebilir misiniz?**	**yahr**dım ehdehbee**leer mee**sseeneez
Can I help you?	**Yardım edebilir miyim?**	**yahr**dım ehdehbee**leer mee**yeem
Can you direct me to ...?	**... yolunu gösterebilir misiniz?**	... yoloonoo g^{y}urstehrehbee**leer mee**sseeneez

Wanting *... istemek*

I'd like ...	**... istiyorum.**	... eestee**yo**room
We'd like ...	**... istiyoruz.**	... eestee**yo**rooz
What do you want?	**Ne istiyorsunuz?**	**neh** eestee**yor**soonooz
Please give me ...	**Lütfen ... bana veriniz.**	**lewt**fehn ... **bah**nah **veh**reeneez
Please bring me ...	**Lütfen bana ... getiriniz.**	**lewt**fehn **bah**nah ... g^{y}eh**tee**reeneez
Please show me ...	**Lütfen bana ... gösteriniz.**	**lewt**fehn **bah**nah ... g^{y}ur**steh**reeneez
I'm looking for ...	**... arıyorum.**	... ahrı**yo**room
I'm hungry.	**Acıktım.**	ahjık**tım**
I'm thirsty.	**Susadım.**	soossah**dım**
I'm tired.	**Yorgunum.**	yor**goo**noom
I'm lost.	**Kayboldum.**	**kah**^{y}boldoom
It's important.	**Önemlidir.**	urnehm**lee**deer
It's urgent.	**Aceledir.**	ahjeh**leh**deer

It is/There is ... *... dir/vardır*

It is ...	**... dir.**	... deer
Is it ...?	**... mıdır?**	... mıdır
It isn't.	**... değildir.**	... day**eel**deer

Here it is.	**Burada.**	**boo**rahdah
Here they are.	**Buradalar.**	**boo**rahdahlahr
There it is.	**Orada.**	**o**rahdah
There they are.	**Oradalar.**	**o**rahdahlahr
There is/are ...	**... vardır.**	... vahrdır
Is/Are there ...?	**... var mı?**	... **vahr** mı
There isn't/aren't ...	**... yoktur.**	... yoktoor
There isn't/aren't any.	**Hiç yoktur.**	heech yoktoor

Some opposites *Karşıtlar*

big/small	**büyük/küçük**	bewyewk/k^{y}ewchewk
quick/slow	**çabuk/yavaş**	chah**book**/yah**vahsh**
hot/cold	**sıcak/soğuk**	sı**jahk**/**saw**ook
full/empty	**dolu/boş**	do**loo**/bosh
easy/difficult	**kolay/zor**	ko**lah**^{y}/zor
heavy/light	**ağır/hafif**	aaır/hah**feef**
open/shut	**açık/kapalı**	ah**chık**/kah**pah**lı
right/wrong	**doğru/yanlış**	daw**roo**/yahn**lısh**
old/new	**eski/yeni**	ehs**k^{y}ee**/yeh**nee**
old/young	**ihtiyar/genç**	eehtee**yahr**/g^{y}ehnch
next/last	**gelecek/son**	g^{y}ehlehjehk/son
beautiful/ugly	**güzel/çirkin**	g^{y}ew**zehl**/cheer**k^{y}een**
free (vacant)/occupied	**serbest/meşgul**	sehrbehst/meshgool
good/bad	**iyi/kötü**	eeyee/k^{y}ur**tew**
better/worse	**daha iyi/daha kötü**	dahhah eeyee/dahhah k^{y}ur**tew**
early/late	**erken/geç**	ehr**k^{y}ehn**/g^{y}ehch
cheap/expensive	**ucuz/pahalı**	oo**jooz**/pah**hah**lı
near/far	**yakın/uzak**	yah**kın**/oo**zahk**
here/there	**burada/orada**	**boo**rahdah/**o**rahdah

Quantities *Miktar*

a little/a lot	**biraz/çok**	**beerahz/chok**
few/a few	**az/birkaç**	ahz/**beer**kahch
much/too much	**çok/pek çok**	chok/pehk chok
many/too many	**çok/pek çok**	chok/pehk chok
more/less	**daha çok/daha az**	**dah**hah chok/**dah**hah ahz
more than/less than	**... dan daha çok/ ... dan daha az**	dahn dahhah chok/ dahn dahhah ahz

enough/too	**yeter/daha**	yeh**tehr**/**dah**hah
some/any	**biraz/hiç**	**bee**rahz/heech

A few more useful words *Birkaç önemli kelime*

at	**-da/-de**	dah/deh
on	**üstünde**	ewstewndeh
in	**içinde**	ee**cheen**deh
to	**-e/-a/-ye/-ya**	eh/ah/yeh/yah
after	**sonra**	**son**rah
before	**önce**	**urn**jeh
for	**için**	**ee**cheen
from	**-den/-dan**	**dehn/dahn**
with	**ile**	**ee**leh
without	**-siz/-sız**	seez/sız
through	**içinden**	eecheen**dehn**
towards	**doğru**	**daw**roo
until	**kadar**	kah**dahr**
during	**esnasında**	ehsnahssındah
next to	**yanında**	yahnındah
near	**yakın**	yahkın
behind	**arkada**	ahrkahdah
between	**arasında**	ahrahssındah
since	**beri**	behree
above	**üstünde**	ewstewndeh
below/under	**altında**	ahltındah
inside	**içeride**	eechehreedeh
outside	**dışarıda**	dıshahrıdah
up	**yukarda**	yookahrdah
upstairs	**yukarı katta**	yookahrı kahttah
down	**aşağıda**	ahshaaıdah
downstairs	**aşağı katta**	ahshaaı kahttah
and	**ve**	veh
or	**veya**	veh[y]ah
not	**değil**	dayeel
never	**hiç**	heech
nothing	**hiç birşey**	heech beershay
none	**hiç biri**	heech beeree
very	**çok**	chok
too (also)	**-da/de**	dah/deh
yet	**henüz**	hehnewz
soon	**yakında**	yahkındah
now	**şimdi**	sheemdee
then	**sonra**	sonrah
perhaps	**belki**	behlk[y]ee
only	**sadece**	sahdehjeh

Arrival

Passport control	*Pasaport kontrolü*	
Here's my passport.	**İşte pasaportum.**	**eesh**teh **pah**ssah**por**toom
I'll be staying ...	**... kalacağım.**	... kahlah**jaa**ım
a few days	**Birkaç gün**	beer**kahch** g^yewn
a week	**Bir hafta**	beer **hahf**tah
a month	**Bir ay**	beer **ah**^{y}
I don't know yet.	**Henüz bilmiyorum.**	**heh**newz **beel**mee**yo**room
I'm here on holiday.	**Burada izindeyim.**	**boo**rahdah eezeendeh^{y}eem
I'm here on business.	**Burada iş için bulunuyorum.**	**boo**rahdah eesh ee**cheen** booloonoo**yo**room
I'm just passing through.	**Transit geçiyorum.**	**trahn**seet g^yehchee**yo**room

If things get difficult:

I'm sorry, I don't understand.	**Özür dilerim anlamıyorum.**	urzewr deelehreem ahn**lah**mıyo**room**
Is there anyone here who speaks English?	**Burada İngilizce bilen biri var mı?**	**boo**rahdah eeng^{y}eeleezjeh bee**lehn** **bee**ree **vahr** mı

GÜMRÜK
CUSTOMS

After collecting your baggage at the airport (*hava alanı*-hahvah alahnı) you have a choice: follow the green arrow if you have nothing to declare, or leave via the doorway marked with a red arrow if you do have something to declare.

vergiye tabi eşya	**vergiden muaf eşya**
goods to declare	nothing to declare

The chart below shows what you can bring in duty-free: **

	Cigarettes	Cigars	Tobacco	Spirits (liquor)	Wine
	400	50	200 gr.	5 l. *	
* In opened bottles, 3 litres of which may be whisky.					

Valuable items including jewellery, tape recorders, transistor radios and similar objects should be registered in your passport on entry, to ensure they can be taken out when you leave.

I have nothing to declare.	**Deklare edecek birşeyim yok.**	**deh**klahreh ehdeh**jehk** beer**sheh**ʸeem **yok**
I have ...	**... var.**	... vahr
a carton of cigarettes	**Bir karton sigaram**	**beer** kahr**ton** seegah**rahm**
a bottle of whisky	**Bir viski şişesi**	beer **vees**kee sheeshehssee
It's for my personal use.	**Bu özel ihtiyacım için.**	**boo** urzehl eehhteeyahjım eecheen

Pasaportunuz, lütfen.	Your passport, please.
Deklare edecek birşeyiniz var mı?	Do you have anything to declare?
Lütfen bu çantayı açın.	Please open this bag.
Bunun için gümrük ödemeniz lâzım.	You'll have to pay duty on this.
Başka bagajınız var mı?	Do you have any other luggage?

** All allowances subject to change without notice.

Baggage – Porter *Bagaj – Hamal*

Porter!	**Hamal!***	hah**mahl**
Please take this ...	**Lütfen ... alın.**	**lewt**fehn ... **ah**lın
luggage suitcase bag	**bu bagajı** **bu bavulu** **bu çantayı**	**boo** bah**gah**zhı **boo bah**vooloo **boo chahn**tah[y]ı
That's mine.	**Şu benimkidir.**	shoo behneemk[y]eedeer
Take this luggage ...	**Bu bagajı ... götürün.**	**boo** bah**gah**zhı ... g[y]urtewrewn
to the bus to the taxi	**otobüse** **taksiye**	oto**bews**seh **tahk**seeyeh
How much is that?	**Şu ne kadar?**	shoo neh kahdahr
Where are the luggage trolleys (carts)?	**Bagaj arabaları nerede?**	bah**gahzh** ah**rah**bahlahrı **neh**rehdeh

Changing money *Kambiyo*

Banks are open from Monday to Friday, between 8.30 or 9.00 and 17.00 or 17.30, with an hour's break for lunch around midday. You can normally change money until 16.00.

Where's the currency exchange office?	**Kambiyo bürosu nerededir?**	**kahm**beeyo bew**ros**soo **neh**rehdehdeer
Where can I cash some traveller's cheques (checks)?	**Traveller's çeklerimi nerede bozdurabilirim?**	'travellers' chehkleh**ree**mee **neh**rehdeh bozdoorah-beeleereem
I'd like to change some dollars/pounds.	**Dolar/Sterlin çevirmek istiyorum.**	dolahr/stehrleen chehveer-mehk eesteeyoroom
Can you change this into lire?	**Bunu liraya çevirebilir misiniz?**	boonoo leerah[y]ah chehveerehbeeleer meesseeneez
What's the exchange rate?	**Kambiyo kuru nedir?**	**kahm**beeyo **koo**roo **neh**deer

* You'll also hear people calling out 'Lütfen!' to attract the porter's attention.

BANK CURRENCY, see page 129

Where is ...? *... nerede?*

Where is the ...?	**... nerededir?**	... **neh**rehdehdeer
booking office	**Bilet gişesi**	bee**leht** g^{y}ee**sheh**ssee
bus stop	**Otobüs durağı**	oto**bewss** doo**raa**ı
newsstand	**Bayi**	bah^{y}ee
restaurant	**Restoran**	**rehs**torahn
station	**İstasyon**	eestahss**yon**
tourist office	**Turizm bürosu**	too**reezm** bew**ro**ssoo
Where's the nearest currency exchange office?	**En yakın kambiyo bürosu nerededir?**	ehn yah**kın** **kahm**beeyo bew**ro**ssoo **neh**rehdehdeer
How do I get to the station?	**İstasyona nasıl gidebilirim?**	eestahssyonah **nah**ssıl g^{y}eedehbee**lee**reem
Is there a bus into town?	**Şehir merkezine bir otobüs gidiyor mu?**	sheh**heer** mehr**k^{y}eh**zeeneh **beer** oto**bewss** g^{y}eedee**yor** moo
Where can I get a taxi?	**Nerede bir taksi bulabilirim?**	**neh**rehdeh beer **tahk**see boolahbee**lee**reem
Where can I hire a car?	**Nerede bir araba kiralayabilirim?**	**neh**rehdeh beer ahrahbah k^{y}eerahlah^{y}ahbee**lee**reem

Hotel reservation *Otel rezervasyonu*

Do you have a hotel guide?	**Bir otel listeniz var mı?**	beer o**tehl** lees**teh**neez **vahr** mı
Could you reserve a room for me at a hotel/guest house?	**Bir otelde/pansiyonda bir oda ayırtabilir misiniz?**	beer o**tehl**deh/pahnsee**yon**dah beer **o**dah ah^{y}ırtahbeeleer **mee**sseeneez
in the centre	**merkez'de**	mehr**k^{y}ehz**deh
near the railway station	**istasyon yakınlarında**	eestahss**yon** yahkınlah**rın**dah
a single room	**bir tek yataklı oda**	beer **tehk** yah**tahk**lı odah
a double room	**bir çift yataklı oda**	beer **cheeft** yah**tahk**lı odah
not too expensive	**pek pahalı olmayan**	pehk pah**hah**lı **ol**mah^{y}ahn
Where is the hotel/guest house?	**Otel/Pansiyon nerede?**	o**tehl**/pahnsee**yon** **neh**rehdeh
Do you have a street map?	**Bir şehir planınız var mı?**	beer sheh**heer** plah**nı**nız **vahr** mı

HOTEL/ACCOMMODATION, see page 22

Car hire (rental) *Araba kiralama*

To hire a car, the driver must have a valid driving licence, and an International Driving Licence is recommended. Depending on the company and the car, the minimum age is 19, 21, 25 or 28. A deposit is usually required unless you pay by credit card. If another person is going to drive the car you should let the company know, otherwise the insurance is void.

I'd like to hire (rent) a car.	**Bir araba kiralamak istiyorum.**	beer ahrahbah k^{y}eerahlah**mak** eestee**yo**room
A(n) ... car.	**... bir araba.**	... beer ahrahbah
small	**Küçük**	k^{y}ew**chewk**
medium	**Orta büyüklükte**	**or**tah bewyewk**lewk**teh
large	**Büyük**	**bewy**ewk
automatic	**Otomatik vitesli**	oto**mah**teek vee**tehs**lee
I'd like it for a day/week.	**Bir gün/Bir hafta için istiyorum.**	**beer** g^{y}ewn/**beer hahf**tah ee**cheen** estee**yo**room
Are there any week-end arrangements?	**Hafta sonu indirimi var mı?**	**hahf**tah **so**noo eendeereemee vahr mı
Do you have any special rates?	**İndirimli tarifeniz var mı?**	eendeereemlee tahree-fehneez **vahr** mı
How much does it cost per day/week?	**Günlük/Haftalık fiyatı ne kadardır?**	g^{y}ewn**lewk**/hahftah**lık** feeyahtı **neh** kah**dahr**dır
Is mileage included?	**Kilometre ücreti dahil mi?**	k^{y}eelo**meh**treh ewj**reh**tee **dah**heel mee
What's the charge per kilometre?	**Kilometre başına ücret nedir?**	k^{y}eelo**meh**treh bah**shı**nah ewj**reht** neh**deer**
I want to hire the car here and leave it in ...	**Arabayı burada kiralamak ve ... de/da bırakmak istiyorum.**	ahrahbah^{y}ı **boo**rahdah k^{y}eerahlahmahk veh ... deh/dah bırahkmahk eestee**yo**room
I'd like fully comprehensive insurance.	**Tam kasko sigorta istiyorum.**	**tahm kah**sko see**gor**tah eestee**yo**room
How much is the deposit?	**Depozito ne kadardır?**	deh**po**zeeto **neh** kahdahr-dır
I have a credit card.	**Kredi kartım var.**	**kreh**dee **kahr**tım vahr
Here's my driving licence.	**İşte ehliyetim.**	**eesh**teh ehh**lee**yeh-teem

CAR, see page 75

Taxi *Taksi*

Taxis are metered. Have the address written down to avoid struggling to explain directions to drivers, who usually only speak Turkish. At night, you'll be hooted at by one taxi after another; it's their way of indicating that they are free. Tipping is up to you, but as rates are low and drivers usually helpful, you can always add a little.

Where can I get a taxi?	**Nerede bir taksi bulabilirim?**	**neh**rehdeh beer **tahk**see boolahbeelee**reem**
Please get me a taxi.	**Bana bir taksi çağırın, lütfen.**	bahnah beer **tahk**see **chaa**ırın **lewt**fehn
How much is it to ...?	**... a/e ücret ne kadardır?**	... ah/eh ewjreht neh kahdahrdır
How far is it to ...?	**Orası ... a/e ne kadar uzak?**	orahssı ... ah/eh **neh** kahdahr oozahk
Take me to ...	**Beni ... götürün.**	**beh**nee ... **g^{y}ur**tewrewn
this address	**bu adrese**	**boo** ahd**reh**sseh
the airport	**hava alanına**	hah**vah** ahlahnınah
the town centre	**şehir merkezine**	sheh**heer** mehr**k^{y}eh**zeeneh
the ... Hotel	**... Oteline**	... o**teh**leeneh
the railway station	**istasyona**	eestahss**yo**nah
Turn ... at the next corner.	**Gelecek köşeden ... dönünüz.**	g^{y}ehlehjehk k^{y}ursheh-dehn ... durnewnewz
left/right	**sola/sağa**	**so**lah/**saa**ah
Go straight ahead.	**Doğru gidin.**	**daw**ru g^{y}ee**deen**
Please stop here.	**Lütfen burada durun.**	**lewt**fehn **boo**rahdah doo**roon**
I'm in a hurry.	**Acelem var.**	ahjeh**lehm vahr**
Could you drive more slowly?	**Daha yavaş kullanabilir misiniz?**	**dah**hah yahvahsh kool-lahnahbee**leer mee**sseeneez
Could you help me carry my luggage?	**Bagajlarımı taşımama yardım eder misiniz?**	bahgahzh**lah**rımı tahshı-**mah**mah yahr**dım** eh**dehr mee**sseeneez
Could you wait for me?	**Lütfen beni bekler misiniz.**	**lew**tfehn **beh**nee behk**lehr mee**sseeneez
I'll be back in 10 minutes.	**10 dakikada dönerim.**	**on** dah**k^{y}ee**kahdah dur**neh**reem

TIPPING, see inside back-cover

Hotel — Other accommodation

The Turkish Ministry of Culture and Tourism has rated some hotels, motels and guest houses from luxury to fourth class. Those with top ratings offer the maximum comfort on a par with international standards. Many other establishments are checked by municipal authorities, particularly on the Aegean coast.

Otel (o**tehl**)
Most big towns have either first- or second-class hotels. Luxury establishments are almost all confined to Ankara, Istanbul, Bursa, Izmir, Antalya and Adana

Motel (mo**tehl**)
These fall into three categories. Rooms are nearly always equipped with shower, toilet and a radio. Some include air-conditioning and a fridge. Normally they sleep two people, but extra beds can usually be put in for children

Pansiyon (pahnsee**yon**)
Guest houses offer a more intimate glimpse of Turkish life. Breakfast is included in the price, and there may be a kitchen where you can cook and share a fridge. Toilets and bathrooms are usually communal

Tatil köyleri (**tah**teel k^{y}ur**leh**ree)
Holiday villages in seaside areas, classed A and B, provide furnished flats, sometimes with cooking facilities. They all have shopping facilities close at hand and most have a swimming pool

Gençlik yurdu (g^{y}ehnchleek yoordoo)
Youth hostels are open to holders of International Student Travel Conference (ISTC) or International Youth Hostel Federation (IYHF) cards and visitors with 'student' or 'teacher' on their passport

Can you recommend a hotel/guest house?	**Bana bir otel/bir pansiyon tavsiye edebilir misiniz?**	bahnah beer o**tehl**/beer pahnsee**yon tahv**seeyeh ehdehbee**leer mee**sseeneez
Is there a youth hostel nearby?	**Yakında bir gençlik yurdu var mı?**	yah**kın**dah beer g^{y}ehnchleek **yoor**doo **vahr** mı

Checking in – Reception *Kayıt – Resepsiyon*

My name is ...	**Adım ...dır**	ah**dım** ...dır
I have a reservation.	**Rezervasyonum var.**	rehzehrvahsyonoom **vahr**
We've reserved two rooms.	**İki odayı rezerve ettik.**	eek^{y}ee **o**dah^{y}ı reh**zehr**veh **eh**tteek
Here's the confirmation.	**İşte konfirmasyon.**	**eesh**teh konfeermahs**yon**
Do you have any vacancies?	**Boş odanız var mı?**	bosh odahnız **vahr** mı
I'd like a ... room.	**... bir oda istiyorum.**	... beer **o**dah eesteey**o**room
single	**Tek yataklı**	**tehk** yah**tahk**lı
double	**Çift yataklı**	**cheeft** yah**tahk**lı
I'd like a room ...	**... bir oda istiyorum.**	... beer **o**dah eesteey**o**room
with twin beds	**İki yataklı**	**eek**^{y}ee yah**tahk**lı
with a double bed	**Çift kişilik**	**cheeft** k^{y}eesheeleek
with a bath	**Banyolu**	**bahn**yoloo
with a shower	**Duşlu**	**doosh**loo
with a balcony	**Balkonlu**	**bahl**konloo
with a view	**Manzaralı**	**mahn**zahrahlı
at the front/back	**Ön/Arka tarafta**	urn/ahrkah tah**rahf**tah
overlooking the sea	**Denize bakan**	dehneezeh bahkahn
It must be quiet.	**Sakin bir yer olsun.**	**sahk**^{y}een beer yehr **ol**soon
Is there ...?	**... var mı?**	... **vahr** mı
air conditioning	**Soğuk hava tertibatı**	saw**ook** **hah**vah tehrtee**bah**tı
heating	**Isıtma**	**ıssıt**mah
a radio/television in the room	**Odada radyo/televizyon**	odahdah **rahd**yo/tehlehveez**yon**
a laundry service	**Çamaşır servisi**	chah**mah**shır sehr**vee**ssee
room service	**Oda servisi**	odah sehr**vee**ssee
hot water	**Sıcak su**	sı**jahk** soo
running water	**Lavabo**	lahvahbo
a private toilet	**Odanın içinde tuvalet**	odahnın eecheendeh **too**vahleht

KİRALIK ODA	DOLU
ROOMS TO LET	NO VACANCIES

CHECKING OUT, see page 31

Could you put an extra bed/a cot in the room?	**Odaya bir yatak/ çocuk için bir yatak daha koyabilir misiniz?**	odahyah beer yaht**ahk**/ **cho**jook ee**cheen** beer yahtahk **dah**hah koyah-beel**eer mee**sseeneez

How much? *Ne kadar?*

What's the price ...?	**... fiyatı ne kadardır?**	... feeyahtı **neh** kahdahrdır
per night	**Bir gecelik**	beer gʸeh**jeh**leek
per week	**Bir haftalık**	beer **hahf**tahlık
for bed and breakfast	**Yatak ve kahvaltı için**	yahtahk veh kahhvahltı eecheen
excluding meals	**Yemek hariç**	yeh**mehk hah**reech
for full board (A.P.)	**Tam pansiyon için**	tahm pahnsee**yon** ee**cheen**
for half board (M.P.A.)	**Yarım pansiyon için**	**yah**rım pahnsee**yon** ee**cheen**
Does that include ...?	**Buna ... dahil mi?**	boonah ... **dah**heel mee
breakfast	**kahvaltı**	kahhvahltı
service	**servis**	sehrvees
value-added tax (VAT)*	**KDV (katma değer vergisi)**	kahdehveh (kahtmah dayehr vehrgʸeessee)
Is there any reduction for children?	**Çocuklar için indirim var mı?**	cho**jook**lahr eecheen eendeereem **vahr** mı
Do you charge for the baby?	**Bebek için ücret alıyor musunuz?**	behbehk eecheen ewjreht ahlıyor **moo**ssoonooz
That's too expensive.	**Çok pahalı.**	**chok** pahhahlı
Don't you have anything cheaper?	**Daha ucuz birşeyiniz yok mu?**	**dah**hah oojooz **beer**shahʸ-eeneez **yok** moo

How long? *Ne kadar zaman?*

We'll be staying ...	**... kalacağız.**	... kahlahjaaız
overnight only	**Sadece bir gece**	sahdehjeh beer gʸehjeh
a few days	**Birkaç gün**	**beer**kahch gʸewn
a week (at least)	**Bir hafta (en azından)**	beer **hahf**tah (ehn ahzındahn)
I don't know yet.	**Henüz bilmiyorum.**	**heh**newz **beel**mee**yo**room

* Americans note: a type of sales tax in England.

Decision *Karar*

May I see the room?	**Odayı görebilir miyim?**	odah^{y}ı g^{y}urrehbee**leer** meeyeem
That's fine. I'll take it.	**İyi. Alıyorum.**	eeyee. ahlı**yo**room
No, I don't like it.	**Hayır, beğenmedim.**	**hah**^{y}ır bayehnmehdeem
It's too ...	**Çok ...**	chok
cold/hot	**soğuk/sıcak**	**saw**ook/sı**jahk**
dark/small	**karanlık/küçük**	kahrahnlık/**k^{y}ew**chewk
noisy	**gürültülü**	g^{y}ewrewltewlew
I asked for a room with a bath.	**Banyolu bir oda istemiştim.**	**bahn**yoloo beer **o**dah eestehmeeshteem
Do you have anything ...?	**... birşeyiniz var mı?**	... **beer**sheh^{y}eeneez vahr mı
better	**Daha iyi**	**dah**hah eeyee
bigger	**Daha büyük**	**dah**hah bewyewk
cheaper	**Daha ucuz**	**dah**hah oojooz
quieter	**Daha sakin**	**dah**hah sahk^{y}een
Do you have a room with a better view?	**Daha iyi manzaralı bir odanız var mı?**	**dah**hah eeyee mahnzahrahlı **beer** odahnız **vahr** mı

Registration *Kayıt*

Upon arrival at a hotel or guest house you'll be asked to fill in a registration form (*kayıt formu* – kah^{y}ıt formoo).

Soyadı/Adı	Last name/First name
Mahalle/Sokak/Numara	Home town/Street/Number
Tabiyet/Meslek	Nationality/Occupation
Doğum tarihi/Doğum yeri	Date/Place of birth
Pasaport numarası	Passport number
Yer/Tarih	Place/Date
İmza	Signature

What does this mean?	**Bu ne demektir?**	boo **neh** dehmehk**teer**

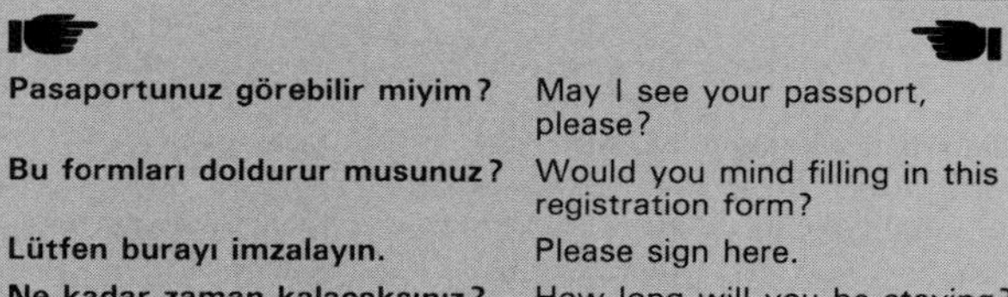

Pasaportunuz görebilir miyim?	May I see your passport, please?
Bu formları doldurur musunuz?	Would you mind filling in this registration form?
Lütfen burayı imzalayın.	Please sign here.
Ne kadar zaman kalacaksınız?	How long will you be staying?

What's my room number?	**Oda numaram kaç?**	**o**dah noomahrahm kahch
Will you have our luggage sent up?	**Bagajımızı yukarı gönderir misiniz?**	bahgahzhımızı yookahrı g^{y}urndeh**reer mee**sseeneez
Where can I park my car?	**Arabamı nereye park edebilirim?**	ahrahbahmı **neh**reh^{y}eh pahrk ehdehbeelee**reem**
Does the hotel have a garage?	**Otelin garajı var mı?**	oteh**h**leen gahrahzhı **vahr** mı
I'd like to leave this in your safe.	**Bunu kasanıza bırakmak istiyorum.**	**boo**noo kahssahnızah bırahk**mahk** eestee**yo**room

Hotel staff *Otelde personel*

hall porter	**kapıcı**	kahpıjı
maid	**oda temizlikçisi**	odah tehmeezleekcheessee
manager	**müdür**	mewdewr
page (bellboy)	**belboy**	behlboy
porter	**hamal**	hah**mahl**
receptionist	**resepsiyon şefi**	rehsehpseeyon shehfee
switchboard operator	**santral memuresi**	sahntrahl mehmoorehssee
waiter	**garson**	gahrson
waitress	**kadın garson**	kahdın gahrson

When calling the waiter or waitress say *'Lütfen bakar mısınız'*, which is the equivalent of 'would you serve us, please?'

General requirements *Genel sorular*

The key to room ..., please.	**... odanın anahtarı, lütfen.**	... odahnın ahnahhtahrı **lewt**fehn
Will you wake me at ..., please?	**Lütfen beni saat ... de uyandırır mısınız?**	**lewt**fehn behnee sahaht ... **deh** ooyahndırır mıssınız
Is there a bath on this floor?	**Bu katta banyo var mı?**	**boo** kahttah **bahn**yo **vahr** mı
What's the voltage here?	**Burada voltaj nedir?**	**boo**rahdah voltahzh **neh**deer
Where's the shaver socket (outlet)?	**Tıraş makinesının prizi nerededir?**	tırahsh mahk^{y}eenehssının preezee **neh**rehdehdeer
Can you find me a ...?	**Bana ... bulabilir misiniz?**	**bah**nah ... boolah**bee**leer **mee**sseeneez
babysitter	**bir çocuk bakıcısı**	beer cho**jook** bahkıjıssı
secretary	**bir sekreter**	beer sehkrehtehr
typewriter	**bir yazı makinesi**	beer yah**zı** mahk^{y}ee-nehssee
May I have a/an/some ...?	**... istiyorum.**	... eestee**yo**room
ashtray	**Bir küllük**	beer k^{y}ewllewk
bath towel	**Bir banyo havlusu**	beer **bahn**yo hahvloossoo
(extra) blanket	**Bir battaniye (daha)**	beer bahttahneeyeh (dahhah)
envelopes	**Birkaç mektup zarfı**	**beer**kahch mehk**toop** zahrfı
(more) hangers	**(Daha) Askı**	(**dah**hah) ahskı
hot water bottle	**Termofor**	**tehr**mofor
ice cubes	**Buz kübü**	booz k^{y}ewbew
needle and thread	**İğne ve iplik**	eeneh veh eepleek
(extra) pillow	**Bir yastık (daha)**	beer yahsstık (**dah**hah)
reading lamp	**Bir başucu lambası**	beer **bah**shoojoo lahm-bahssı
soap	**Sabun**	sahboon
writing paper	**Yazı kağıdı**	yah**zı** kaaıdı
Where's the ...?	**... nerededir?**	... **neh**rehdehdeer
dining room	**Yemek salonu**	yehmehk sahlonoo
emergency exit	**İmdat çıkışı**	eemdaht chıkıshı
lift (elevator)	**Asansör**	ahssahnsurr
Where are the toilets?	**Tuvalet nerededir?**	**too**vahleht **neh**rehdehdeer

BREAKFAST, see page 38

Telephone – Post (mail) *Telefon – Posta*

Can you get me Izmir 123-45-67?	**İzmir 1234567 bağlar mısınız?**	**eez**meer 1234567 baalahr **mı**ssınız
Do you have stamps?	**Posta pulu var mı?**	**pos**tah pooloo **vahr** mı
Would you post this for me, please?	**Lütfen bunu benim için postalar mısınız?**	**lewt**fehn **boo**noo behneem eecheen **pos**tahlahr **mıs**sınız
Is there any post (mail) for me?	**Benim için posta var mı?**	behneem ee**cheen pos**tah **vahr** mı
Are there any messages for me?	**Bana mesaj var mı?**	**bah**nah mehssahzh **vahr** mı
How much is my telephone bill?	**Telefon hesabım ne kadar?**	**teh**lehfon hehssahbım **neh** kahdahr

Difficulties *Zorluklar*

The ... doesn't work.	**... çalışmıyor.**	... chah**lısh**mı**yor**
air conditioning	**Soğuk hava tertibatı**	**saw**ook hahvah tehrtee-bahtı
fan	**Vantilâtör**	vahnteelaaturr
heating	**Isıtma**	ıssıtmah
light	**Işık**	ıshık
radio	**Radyo**	**rah**dyo
television	**Televizyon**	tehlehveez**yon**
The tap (faucet) is dripping.	**Musluk damlıyor.**	mooslook **dahm**lıyor
There's no hot water.	**Sıcak su gelmiyor.**	sı**jahk** soo g^y^ehlmee**yor**
The wash basin is blocked.	**Lavabo tıkalı.**	lahvahbo tı**kah**lı
The window is jammed.	**Pencere sıkışmış.**	pehnjehreh sıkıshmısh
The light doesn't work.	**Elektrik kesik.**	ehlehktreek k^y^eh**sseek**
The bulb is burned out.	**Ampul yanmış.**	ahmpool **yahn**mısh
My room hasn't been prepared.	**Odam hazırlanmamış.**	odahm hahzırlahnmahmısh

POST OFFICE AND TELEPHONE, see page 132

The ... is broken.	**... bozuk.**	... bozook
blind	**Kepenk**	k^{y}ehpehnk
lamp	**Lamba**	**lahm**bah
plug	**Fiş**	feesh
shutter	**Panjur**	pahnzhoor
switch	**Elektrik düğmesi**	ehlehktreek dewmehssee
Can you get it repaired?	**Tamir ettirebilir misiniz?**	tahmeer ehtteerehbee**leer** **mee**sseeneez

Laundry – Dry cleaner's *Çamaşırhane – Kuru temizleyici*

I'd like these clothes ...	**Bu elbiseleri ... istiyorum.**	boo ehlbeessehlehree ... eesteey**o**room
cleaned	**temizletmek**	tehmeezleht**mehk**
ironed/pressed	**ütületmek**	ewtewleht**mehk**
washed	**yıkatmak**	yıkaht**mahk**
When will they be ready?	**Ne zaman hazır olur?**	**neh** zahmahn hahzır oloor
I need them ...	**... lâzım.**	... laazım
today	**Bugün**	**boo**g^{y}ewn
tonight	**Bu akşam**	**boo** ahk**shahm**
tomorrow	**Yarına**	**yah**rınah
before Friday	**Cumadan önce**	joomahdahn **urn**jeh
as soon as possible	**Bir an önce**	beer ahn **urn**jeh
Can you ... this?	**Bunu ... misiniz?**	**boo**noo ... **mee**sseeneez
mend	**onarabilir**	onahrahbee**leer**
patch	**yamayabilir**	yahmah^{y}ahbee**leer**
stitch	**dikebilir**	deek^{y}ehbee**leer**
Can you sew on this button?	**Bu düğmeyi dikebilir misiniz?**	**boo** dewmeh^{y}ee deek^{y}ehbee**leer** **mee**sseeneez
Can you get this stain out?	**Bu lekeyi çıkarabilir misiniz?**	**boo** lehkeh^{y}ee chıkahrah-bee**leer** **mee**sseeneez
Is my laundry ready?	**Çamaşırlarım hazır mı?**	chahmahshırlahrım hahzır mı
This isn't mine.	**Bu benim değil.**	**boo** behneem dayeel
There's something missing.	**Birşey eksik.**	**beer**shay **ehk**seek
There's a hole in this.	**Bunda bir delik var.**	**boon**dah beer dehleek **vahr**

Hairdresser – Barber *Kuaför – Berber*

Is there a hairdresser/beauty salon in the hotel?	**Otelde kuaför/ güzellik salonu var mı?**	o**tehl**deh kooahfurr/ g^{y}ewzehlleek sahlonoo **vahr** mı
Can I make an appointment for Thursday?	**Perşembe gününe bir randevu alabilir miyim?**	pehrshehmbeh g^{y}ewnewneh beer **rahn**dehvoo ahlahbee**leer** meeyeem
I'd like a cut and blow dry.	**Saç kesme ve fönleme istiyorum.**	sahch k^{y}ehsmeh veh furnlehmeh eestee**yo**room
I'd like a haircut, please.	**Lütfen saçımı kesin.**	**lewt**fehn sahchımı k^{y}ehsseen
bleach	**renk açma**	rehnk ahchmah
blow dry	**fönleme**	furnlehmeh
colour rinse	**şampuanla boyama**	shahmpooahnlah boyahmah
dye	**boyama**	boyahmah
face pack	**yüz maskesi**	yewz mahsk^{y}ehssee
manicure	**manikür**	mahneek^{y}ewr
permanent wave	**perma**	pehrmah
shampoo and set	**mizampli**	meezahmplee
with a fringe (bangs)	**kâküllü**	kaak^{y}ewllew
I'd like a shampoo for ... hair.	**... saç için bir şampuan istiyorum.**	... sahch eecheen beer shahmpooahn eestee**yo**room
normal/dry/ greasy (oily)	**Normal/Kuru/ Yağlı**	**nor**mahl/**koo**roo/**yaa**lı
Do you have a colour chart?	**Renk kataloğunuz var mı?**	rehnk kahtahlawoonooz **vahr** mı
Don't cut it too short.	**Çok kısa kesmeyin.**	chok kıssah k^{y}ehsmeh^{y}een
A little more off the ...	**... biraz daha kısa.**	... bee**rahz dah**hah kıssah
back	**Arkadan**	ahrkahdahn
neck	**Boyundan**	boyoondahn
sides	**Kenarlardan**	k^{y}ehnahrlahrdahn
top	**Üstünden**	ewstewndehn
I don't want any hairspray.	**Sprey istemiyorum, lütfen.**	spreh^{y} ees**teh**mee**yo**room **lewt**fehn
Please don't use any oil.	**Briyantin sürmeyin.**	bree**yahn**teen sewr**meh**^{y}een

DAYS OF THE WEEK, see page 151

I'd like a shave.	**Sakal tıraşı olmak istiyorum.**	sahkahl tırahshı olmahk eesteе**yo**room
Would you trim my ..., please?	**Lütfen ... kısaltın.**	**lewt**fehn ... kıssahltın
beard	**sakalımı**	sahkahlımı
moustache	**bıyığımı**	bıyıımı
sideboards (sideburns)	**favorilerimi**	fahvoreelehreemee

Checking out *Hareket*

May I have my bill, please?	**Lütfen hesabı istiyorum.**	**lewt**fehn hehssahbı eestee**yo**room
I'm leaving early in the morning.	**Yarın sabah erken-den hareket ediyorum.**	**yah**rın sahbah ehrk^{y}ehn-dehn hahrehk^{y}eht ehdee**yo**room
Please have my bill ready.	**Lütfen hesabımı hazırlayın.**	**lewt**fehn hehssahbımı hahzırlah^{y}ın
We'll be checking out around noon.	**Öğleye doğru hare-ket ediyoruz.**	urleh^{y}eh **daw**roo hah-rehk^{y}eht ehdee**yo**rooz
I must leave at once.	**Hemen hareket etmeliyim.**	**heh**mehn hahrehk^{y}eht ehtmehleeyeem
Is everything included?	**Herşey dahil mi?**	hehrsheh^{y} dahheel mee
Can I pay by credit card?	**Kredi kartı ile ödeyebilir miyim?**	krehdee kahrtı eeleh urdeh^{y}ehbee**leer mee**yeem
I think there's a mis-take in the bill.	**Sanırım bu hesapta bir hata yaptınız.**	sahnırım boo hehssahptah beer hahtah yahptınız
Can you get us a taxi?	**Bize bir taksi çağırır mısınız?**	beezeh beer **tahk**see chaaırır **mı**ssınız
Would you have our luggage brought down?	**Bagajlarımızı aşağı taşıtır mısınız?**	bahgahzhlahrımızı ahshaaı tahshı**tır mı**ssınız
Here's the forwarding address.	**İşte gideceğimiz yerin adresi.**	eeshteh g^{y}eedehjayeemeez yehreen ahdreh**ssee**
You have my home address.	**Ev adresim sizde var.**	ehv ahdrehsseem seezdeh **vahr**
It's been a very enjoyable stay.	**Burada çok hoş zaman geçirdik.**	**boo**rahdah chok hosh zah-mahn g^{y}ehcheerdeek

TIPPING, see inside back-cover

Camping *Kamping*

Campsites registered with the Ministry of Culture and Tourism are limited in number but offer showers and toilets, kitchen and laundry facilities, a shop and electricity. They are open April/May to October. Especially recommended are the sites operated by the Mocamp-Kervansaray.

Is there a camp site near here?	**Yakında kamping yeri var mı?**	yahkındah kahmpeeng yehree vahr mı
Can we camp here?	**Burada kamp yapabilir miyiz?**	**boo**rahdah kahmp yahpahbee**leer mee**yeez
Do you have room for a tent/caravan (trailer)?	**Çadır/Karavan için yeriniz var mı?**	**chah**dır/**kah**rahvahn eecheen yehreeneez **vahr** mı
What's the charge ...?	**... ücreti ne kadardır?**	... ewjrehtee neh kahdahrdır
per day/person	**Günlük/Bir kişi için**	g^y^ewnlewk/beer k^y^eeshee eecheen
for a car	**Bir araba için**	beer ahrahbah eecheen
for a tent	**Bir çadır için**	beer **chah**dır ee**cheen**
for a caravan	**Bir karavan için**	beer **kah**rahvahn eecheen
Is tourist tax included?	**Turist vergisi dahil mi?**	tooreest vehrg^y^eessee **dah**heel mee
Is/Are there (a) ...?	**... var mı?**	... **vahr** mı
drinking water	**İçme suyu**	eechmeh sooyoo
electricity	**Elektrik**	ehlehk**treek**
playground	**Oyun alanı**	oyoon ahlahnı
restaurant	**Restoran**	**rehs**torahn
shopping facilities	**Alışveriş imkânı**	ahlıshvehreesh eemkaanı
swimming pool	**Yüzme havuzu**	yewzmeh ahvoozoo
Where are the showers/toilets?	**Duş/Tuvalet nerede?**	doosh/**too**vahleht **neh**rehdeh
Where can I get butane gas?	**Bütangaz nerede bulabilirim?**	bew**tahn**gahz **neh**rehdeh boolahbeelee**reem**
Is there a youth hostel near here?	**Yakında gençlik yurdu var mı?**	yahkındah g^y^ehnchleek yoordoo vahr mı

KAMP YAPMAK YASAKTIR CAMPING FORBIDDEN	KARAVAN GİREMEZ NO CARAVANS

CAMPING EQUIPMENT, see page 106

Eating out

In Turkey you will find any number of eating establishments to suit your mood. Whether you want a noisy, romantic or an elegant evening, you should be able to find something to suit.

Appearances are not always to be trusted and you may find excellent food hiding behind a drab exterior.

Lokanta/Restaurant (lo**kahn**tah/**reh**storahn) If a place calls itself a restaurant then it is often geared to the business trade, with a certain number of international dishes. Lokantas tend to serve mainly Turkish food, sometimes with a tourist menu, always varied.

Balık lokantası (bahlık lo**kahn**tahssı) Fish restaurants, found all along the coast and in port cities. Fine selection of fresh fish and seafood as well as splendid variety of *meze*.

Kebapçi (k^{y}ehbahpji) A restaurant serving grilled meats of different kinds – kebabs.

Köfteci (**k^{y}urf**tehjee) A restaurant specializing in *köfte*, a type of grilled croquette made of minced lamb. It can either be fried or shaped into a ball and cooked in stock with rice. Often served with a string bean salad and garnished with onions and hard-boiled eggs.

Hazır yemek (hahzır yeh**mehk**) Type of fast-food restaurant specialising in a number of dishes that have been prepared beforehand and only need reheating. The menu will include soup, rice, and meat and vegetable dishes.

İşkembeci (eesh**k^{y}ehm**behjee) Specialists in *İşkembe çorbası* – mutton tripe soup.

Pideci (**pee**dehjee) The closest thing to a pizzeria. Serves flat bread (*pide*) hot out of the oven and garnished with minced meat, tomatoes and/or cheese.

Tatlıcı (tahtlıjı)	Restaurant serving wide variety of puddings and local pastries. Also serves light chicken lunches.
Kuru yemiş (kooroo yehmeesh)	Shop selling dried fruit, nuts, cereals and chocolate.
Büfe (bewfeh)	Snack stands selling sandwiches, chicken dishes, soft drinks and other snacks.
Gazino (gah**zee**no)	Family restaurant where you can choose between a light supper or full meal, often with some form of entertainment such as music and dancing.

Turkish cuisine *Türk mutfağı*

Turkish cooking is characterized by its grilled meats, savoury stuffed vegetables and pastry desserts steeped in syrup. Shish kebabs, stuffed vine leaves and baklava are among the many dishes enjoyed all around the world.

Though large cities have a selection of foreign restaurants, you shouldn't pass up the opportunity of sampling the simple but tasty local dishes. They represent a style of cooking that is echoed throughout the Mediterranean region.

If you seem at all unsure about the menu (if there is one), don't be surprised if the waiter leads you right into the kitchen. You can just choose from the dozen or so dishes. This practice is very common throughout the country except in high class restaurants.

Moslem law restrains the drinking of alcohol. Nevertheless, you'll probably be able to order beer, wine or *rakı* (aniseed liqueur) with your meal in most restaurants. Moslem law also forbids the eating of pork, but you may find it on offer in tourist-oriented restaurants.

Meal times *Yemek saatleri*

Lunch (*öğle yemeği*) is normally served between midday and around 2 p.m., while dinner (*akşam yemeği*) is served from 7 to 10 p.m.

Ne istersiniz?	What would you like?
Bunu tavsiye ederim.	I recommend this.
Ne içersiniz?	What would you like to drink?
... yoktur.	We don't have ...
... ister misiniz?	Would you like ...?

Hungry? *Aç mısınız?*

I'm hungry/I'm thirsty.	**Acıktım/Susadım.**	ahjık**tım**/soossah**dım**
Can you recommend a good restaurant?	**İyi bir lokanta tavsiye edebilir misiniz?**	eeyee beer lo**kahn**tah tahv**see**yeh ehdehbee**leer** **mee**sseeneez
Are there any inexpensive restaurants around here?	**Buralarda çok pahalı olmayan lokantalar var mı?**	boorahlahrdah chok pahhahlı olmah^{Y}ahn lokahntahlahr vahr mı
I'd like to try some Turkish food.	**Türk yemeği tatmak istiyorum.**	**tewrk** yehmayee taht**mahk** eestee**yo**room
Where can I get a snack?	**Hafif bir yemek nerede bulabilirim?**	hahfeef beer yehmehk **neh**rehdeh boolahbeeleer**eem**

If you want to be sure of getting a table in a popular restaurant, it's better to telephone and book in advance.

I'd like to reserve a table for 4.	**Dört kişi için bir masa ayırtmak istiyorum.**	**durrt** k^{Y}eeshee eecheen beer mahssah ah^{Y}ırt**mahk** eestee**yo**room
I'd like to reserve a table for ...	**... için bir masa ayırtmak istiyorum.**	... eecheen beer mahssah ah^{Y}ırtmak eestee**yo**room
this evening	**Bu akşam**	**boo** ahkshahm
lunch	**Öğle yemeği**	urleh yehmayee
tomorrow	**Yarın**	**yah**rın
We'll come at 8.	**Saat 8 de geliriz.**	sahaht 8 deh g^{Y}ehleereez
My name is ...	**Adım ...**	ah**dım**

Could we have a table ...?	**... bir masa verir misiniz?**	... beer mahssah veh**reer** **mee**sseeneez
in the corner	**Köşede**	k^{y}urshehdeh
by the window	**Pencere tarafında**	**pehn**jehreh tahrahfındah
outside	**Dışarıda**	dıshahrıdah
on the terrace	**Terasta**	tehrahstah
in a non-smoking area	**Sigara içilmeyen tarafta**	seegahrah eecheelmeh^{y}ehn tahrahftah

Asking and ordering *Sormak ve ısmarlamak*

Waiter/Waitress!	**Lütfen bakar mısınız!**	**lewt**fehn bah**kahr** **mı**ssınız
I'd like something to eat/drink.	**Yemek/İçmek için birşey istiyorum.**	yehmehk/eechmehk eecheen **beer**sheh^{y} eestee**yo**room
May I have the menu, please?	**Menüyü verir misiniz, lütfen?**	mehnewyew veh**reer** **mee**sseeneez **lewt**fehn
Do you have any local dishes?	**Yerli yemekleriniz var mı?**	yehrlee yehmehklehreeneez **vahr** mı
What do you recommend?	**Ne tavsiye edersiniz?**	**neh** tahvseeyeh ehdehrseeneez
Could I have a look in the kitchen?	**Mutfağa bir bakabilir miyim?**	mootfaaah beer bahkahbee**leer** meeyeem
Do you have anything ready quickly?	**Çabuk hazır olan birşeyiniz var mı?**	chahbook hahzır olahn beersheh^{y}eeneez vahr mı
I'm in a hurry.	**Acelem var.**	ahjeh**lehm** vahr
Could we have a/an ..., please?	**... verir misiniz, lütfen?**	... veh**reer** **mee**sseeneez lewtfehn
ashtray	**Küllük**	k^{y}ewllewk
cup	**Fincan**	feenjahn
fork	**Çatal**	chahtahl
glass	**Bardak**	bahrdahk
knife	**Bıçak**	bıchahk
napkin (serviette)	**Peçete**	pehchehteh
plate	**Tabak**	tahbahk
spoon	**Kaşık**	kahshık
May I have some ...?	**... verir misiniz?**	... veh**reer** **mee**sseeneez
bread	**Ekmek**	ehkmehk
butter	**Tereyağ**	tehreh^{y}aa

lemon	**Limon**	leemon
mustard	**Hardal**	hahrdahl
oil	**Yağ**	yaa
pepper	**Karabiber**	kahrahbeebehr
salt	**Tuz**	tooz
seasoning	**Baharat**	bah**hah**raht
sugar	**Şeker**	shehk^{y}ehr
vinegar	**Sirke**	seerk^{y}eh

Some useful expressions for those with special requirements:

I'm on a special diet.	**Perhizdeyim.**	pehrheezdeh^{y}eem
I don't drink alcohol.	**İçki içmiyorum.**	eechk^{y}ee **eech**meey**o**room
I mustn't eat food containing ...	**... yemekleri yememeliyim.**	... yehmehklehree yehmehmehleeyeem
flour/fat salt/sugar	**Unlu/Yağlı** **Tuzlu/Şekerli**	oonloo/yaalı toozloo/shehk^{y}ehrlee
Do you have ... for diabetics?	**Şeker hastaları için ... var mı?**	shehk^{y}ehr hahstahlahrı eecheen ... **vahr** mı
cakes fruit juice a special menu	**pastanız** **meyva suyunuz** **özel menünüz**	pahstahnız meh^{y}vah sooyoonooz urzehl mehnewnewz
Could I have ... instead of dessert?	**Tatlı yerine ... alabilir miyim?**	tahtlı yehreeneh ... ahlahbee**leer** meeyeem
Can I have an artificial sweetener?	**Sakarin verir misiniz?**	sahkahreen veh**reer** **mee**sseeneez

And ...

Do you have any vegetarian dishes?	**Etsiz yemeğiniz var mı?**	ehtseez yehmayeeneez **vahr** mı
I'd like some more.	**Biraz daha istiyorum.**	beerahz dahhah eesteeyoroom
Can I have more ..., please?	**... daha alabilir miyim, lütfen?**	... **dah**hah ahlahbee**leer** meeyeem **lewt**fehn
Just a small portion.	**Küçük bir porsiyon.**	k^{y}ew**chewk** beer porsee**yon**
Nothing more, thanks.	**Yeter, teşekkür ederim.**	**yeh**tehr tehshehkk**k^{y}ewr** ehdehreem
Where are the toilets?	**Tuvaletler nerededir?**	**too**vahlehtlehr **neh**reh-dehdeer

Breakfast *Kahvaltı*

In most places you'll find that a continental breakfast, with rolls, jam and honey, is the norm. If the breakfast is authentically Turkish then there will probably also be a few black olives and some sheep's cheese on your plate.

I'd like breakfast, please.	**Kahvaltı istiyorum, lütfen.**	kahhvahltı eesteeyoroom lewtfehn
I'll have a/an/some ...	**... alırım.**	... ahlırım
boiled egg	**Haşlanmış yumurta**	hahshlahnmısh yoomoortah
soft/hard	**Az pişmiş/Çok pişmiş**	ahz peeshmeesh/chok peeshmeesh
eggs	**Yumurta**	yoomoortah
fruit juice	**Meyva suyu**	meh^{y}vah sooyoo
grapefruit	**Greyfrut suyu**	greh^{y}froot sooyoo
orange	**Portakal suyu**	portahkahl sooyoo
ham and eggs	**Jambon ve yumurta**	zhahmbon veh yoomoortah
jam	**Reçel**	rehchehl
marmalade	**Portakal reçeli**	portahkahl rehchehlee
toast	**Kızarmış ekmek**	kızahrmısh ehkmehk
yoghurt	**Yoğurt**	yawoort
May I have some ...?	**... alabilir miyim?**	... ahlahbee**leer** meeyeem
bread	**Ekmek**	ehkmehk
butter	**Tereyağ**	tehrehyaa
cheese	**Peynir**	peh^{y}neer
coffee	**Kahve**	kahhveh
decaffeinated	**Kafeinsiz**	kahfeheenseez
black/with milk	**Koyu/Sütlü**	koyoo/sewtlew
honey	**Bal**	bahl
hot chocolate	**Sütlü kakao**	sewtlew kahkaho
milk	**Süt**	sewt
cold/hot	**Soğuk/Sıcak**	sawook/sıjahk
olives	**Zeytin**	zeh^{y}teen
pepper	**Karabiber**	kahrahbeebehr
rolls	**Küçük ekmek**	k^{y}ew**chewk** ehkmehk
salt	**Tuz**	tooz
tea	**Çay**	chah^{y}
with milk	**Sütlü**	sewtlew
with lemon	**Limonlu**	leemonloo
(hot) water	**(Sıcak) Su**	(sıjahk) soo

What's on the menu? *Menüde ne var?*

Large restaurants and those used to tourists will display a menu outside. However, many restaurants, particularly local ones, will have no menu. In order to find out what's available you will have to ask or go into the kitchen and look.

Under the headings below you'll find alphabetical lists of dishes that might be offered on a Turkish menu with their English equivalent. You can simply show the book to the waiter. If you want some fruit, for instance, let *him* point to what's available on the appropriate list. Use pages 36 and 37 for ordering in general.

Reading the menu *Menüyü okumak*

A la kart	A la carte
15 dakika bekleme	15 minutes wait
Fiks menü	Fixed-price menu
Mevsime göre	When in season

Starters (Appetizers) *Antreler*

Probably the best way of getting to know Turkish food is by replacing one of your evening meals with a selection of starters known as *meze*. Vegetarians need not worry about going hungry as vegetable and pulse dishes are a mainstay of Turkish cuisine.

Try dips made of mashed beans, vegetables stuffed with meat or more vegetables, and tasty seafood morsels.

I'd like a starter.	**Antre istiyorum.**	ahn**treh** eestee**yo**room
What do you recommend?	**Ne tavsiye edersiniz?**	**neh tahv**seeyeh ehdehrseeneez

ançuez	**ahn**chooehz	anchovies
arnavut ciğeri	ahrnah**voot** jeeehree	spiced mutton liver
beyin tavası	beh^{y}**een** tahvahssı	fried lamb brains
çiroz salatası	chee**roz** sahlahtahssı	cured mackerel salad
deniz mahsulleri kokteyli	deh**neez** mahhssoollehree kokteh^{y}lee	seafood cocktail
dil	deel	ox tongue
füme/haşlama	**few**meh/hahshlahmah	smoked/boiled
enginar	ehng^{y}eenahr	marinated artichoke
havyar	hahvyahr	caviar
humus	hoomoos	chick pea dip
istakoz (ızgara)	eestahkoz (ızgahrah)	(grilled) lobster
istiridye	eesteereedyeh	oysters
kılıç balığı füme	kı**lıch** bahlııı fewmeh	smoked swordfish
kuru fasulye piyaz	koo**roo** fahssoolyeh peeyahz	butter bean salad
kuzu	koo**zoo**	lamb
ciğeri	jeeehree	liver
beyin salatası	beh^{y}**een** sahlahtahssı	brain salad
lâkerda	laak^{y}ehrdah	salted tuna

mersin balığı füme	**mehr**seen bahlıııı fewmeh	smoked sturgeon
midye	**meed**yeh	mussels
pavurya	pah**voor**yah	crab
sardalya	sahrdahlyah	sardines
tarama	tahrahmah	creamed red caviar
ton balığı	**ton** bahlıııı	tuna fish (tinned)
turşu	toorshoo	pickled vegetables
zeytin	zeh^{y}teen	olives

cacık (jahjık) — diced cucumbers with a dressing of yoghurt, olive oil and garlic

çerkez tavuğu (**chehr**k^{y}ehz tahvoooo) — Circassian chicken; minced chicken mixed with chopped walnuts, chilli peppers and bread

çiğ köfte (chee k^{y}urfteh) — spicy meat balls with cracked wheat

fava (fahvah) — mashed fava beans in olive oil with onions and dill

midye dolması (**meed**yeh dolmahssı) — minced mussels with rice and onion, served on the half shell

midye tavası (**meed**yeh tahvahssı) — mussels boiled in white wine and then rolled in batter and deep fried. Served with *tarator* sauce

mercimekli köfte (mehrjeemehklee k^{y}urfteh) — lentil balls with cracked wheat, onions, herbs and spices

mücver (mewjvehr) — pancakes filled with fried courgettes

pastırma (pahstırmah) — dried beef cured with red chillies

patates köftesi (pah**tah**tehss k^{y}urftehssee) — potatoes mashed with eggs, formed into balls and fried

tavuk köftesi (tahvook k^{y}urftehssee) — minced chicken, onions and bread, rolled into balls and fried

taze börülce salatası (tahze burrewljeh sahlahtahssı) — black-eyed beans in a bread, garlic, pistachio and lemon sauce

zeytinyağlı dolmalar (zeh^{y}teenyaalı dolmahlahr) — aubergine, vine leaves or green peppers stuffed with rice, raisins and pistachios, served chilled

Salads *Salatalar*

You'll find salads made from both cooked and raw vegetables, and dressed very simply with a vinaigrette made from lemon juice and olive oil. The dressing may often be sharper than its European equivalent and will probably be strongly flavoured with garlic.

What salads do you have?	**Salata olarak neler var?**	sahlahtah olahrahk **neh**lehr vahr
çoban salatası	cho**bahn** sahlahtahssı	cucumber and tomato salad
domates salatası	do**mah**tehss sahlahtahssı	tomato salad
havuç salatası	hah**vooch** sahlahtahssı	carrot salad
karışık salata	kahrı**shık** sahlahtah	mixed salad
karışık turşu	kahrı**shık** toorshoo	pickled vegetables
kereviz salatası	kʸehreh**veez** sahlahtahssı	celery salad
marul salatası	mah**rool** sahlahtahssı	romaine lettuce salad
mevsim salatası	mehv**seem** sahlahtahssı	salad of the season
mercimek salatası	mehrjee**mehk** sahlahtahssı	lentil salad
pancar salatası	pahn**jahr** sahlahtahssı	beetroot salad
patlıcan salatası	pahtlı**jahn** sahlahtahssı	aubergine (eggplant) salad
piaz	peeahz	haricot bean salad
rus salatası	**roos** sahlahtahssı	diced vegetable salad
yeşil salata	yeh**sheel** sahlahtah	green salad
yoğurtlu ıspanak salatası	yawoortloo ıspahnahk sahlahtahssı	spinach salad with yoghurt

Egg dishes and omelets *Yumurtalı yemekler ve omletler*

I'd like an omelet.	**Bir omlet istiyorum.**	beer **om**leht eestee**yo**room
çılbır	chılbır	poached eggs with yoghurt
haşlanmış yumurta	hahshlahnmısh yoomoortah	boiled eggs
omlet	**om**leht	omelet
mantarlı omlet	mahntahr**lı** omleht	mushroom omelet
maydanozlu omlet	mahʸdahnoz**loo** omleht	parsley omelet
peynirli omlet	pehʸneer**lee** omleht	cheese omelet

Soup *Çorba*

I'd like some soup.	**Çorba istiyorum.**	chorbah eesteeyoroom
What do you recommend?	**Ne tavsiye edersiniz?**	**neh** tahvseeyeh ehdehrseeneez
bezelye çorbası	beh**zehl**yeh chorbahssı	pea soup
borç	borch	beetroot soup
domates çorbası	do**mah**tehss chorbahssı	tomato soup
domatesli pirinç çorbası	do**mah**tehslee peereench chorbahssı	tomato and rice soup
ekmek çorbası	ehkmehk chorbahssı	bread soup
erişteli çorba	ehreeshtehlee chorbah	noodle soup
et suyu (konsome)	eht sooyoo (konsomeh)	consomme
gratine soğan çorbası	grahteeneh sawahn chorbahssı	French onion soup
irmik çorbası	eermeek chorbahssı	semolina soup
kırmızı mercimek çorbası	kırmızı mehrjeemehk chorbahssı	red lentil soup
kremalı domates çorbası	**kreh**mahlı do**mah**tehss chorbahssı	cream of tomato soup
mercimek çorbası	mehrjeemehk chorbahssı	lentil soup
sebze çorbası	sehbzeh chorbahssı	vegetable soup
soğuk et suyu	sawook eht sooyoo	chilled consomme
tavuk suyu	tahvook sooyoo	chicken consomme
taze mısır çorbası	tahzeh mıssır chorbahssı	corn soup
un çorbası	oon chorbahssı	flour soup

balık çorbası (bahlık chorbahssı) — rich fish soup, coloured with saffron and flavoured with vinegar, lemon, mint, cinnamon and thickened with egg yolks

düğün çorbası (dewewn chorbahssı) — 'wedding soup'; lamb soup flavoured with lemon juice and thickened with beaten eggs

havuç corbası (hahvooch chorbahssı) — carrot soup made with vegetable stock and thickened with flour, milk and egg whites

işkembe çorbası (eeshk^{y}ehmbeh chorbahssı) — mutton tripe soup; made of vinegar, garlic, red pepper and often eggs; Turks say it's a good remedy for a hangover

ıspanak çorbası (ıspahnahk chorbahssı) — thick spinach soup with egg yolks and lemon juice, garnished with parsley and dill

yayla çorbası (**yah**^{y}lah chorbahssı) — chicken and yoghurt soup with rice; rice cooked in chicken stock to which yoghurt and beaten egg yolks are added. Served with a little mint sauteed in butter

Fish and seafood *Balık ve deniz hayvanları*

When they tell you the fish is fresh, they mean it. You will enjoy a magnificent choice of fish, usually prepared in the simplest manner (basted with oil, and grilled) to allow the natural good flavours to dominate. In Istanbul the smart fish restaurants are at Tarabya on the Bosphorus, but they're good anywhere in the city and along the coast. Seafood is delicious, but it's also expensive.

I'd like some fish.	**Balık istiyorum.**	bahlık eesteeyoroom
What kinds of seafood do you have?	**Deniz hayvanlarından neler var?**	dehneez hahʸvahnlahrın-dahn nehlehr vahr

alabalık	ahlahbahlık	trout
barbunya	bahr**boon**yah	red mullet
çiroz	cheeroz	salted dried mackerel
dil balığı	deel bahlıı	sole
gümüş	gʸewmewsh	sand smelt
hamsi	**hahm**see	fresh anchovy/ sprats
ıstakoz	ıs**tah**koz	lobster
istavrit	eestahvreet	horse mackerel
kalkan	kahlkahn	turbot
karagöz	kahrahgʸurz	black bream
karides	kʸeh**ree**dehss	prawns
kefal	kʸehfahl	grey mullet
kılıç balığı	kılıch bahlıı	swordfish
lâkerda	laakʸehrdah	salted tuna
levrek	lehvrehk	sea bass
lüfer	lewfehr	bluefish
mercan	mehrjahn	red sea bream
mersin balığı	mehrseen bahlıı	sturgeon
midye	**meed**yeh	mussels
pavurya	pahvooryah	crab
pisi	peessee	plaice
sardalya	sahr**dahl**yah	sardines
sazan	sahzahn	carp
som balığı	som bahlıı	salmon
tekir	tehkʸeer	striped mullet
ton balığı	ton bahlıı	tuna fish (tinned)
torik	toreek	large tuna
turna	**toor**nah	pike
uskumru	ooskoomroo	mackerel
yılan balığı	y**ılahn** bahlıı	eel

Fish on a skewer is very popular, look out for the word *şiş* on the menu preceded by the type of fish used. Most fish is grilled; one particularly tasty dish is sardines wrapped in vine leaves before grilling.

çınarçık usulu balık (chınahrjık oossooloo bahlık)	swordfish, seabass and prawns fried, served garnished with mushrooms and flavoured with brandy
kefal pilakisi (k^{y}ehfahl pee**lah**-k^{y}eessee)	mullet cooked in olive oil with vegetables and served cold
kılıç şiş (kılıch sheesh)	chunks of swordfish skewered and charcoal grilled with bay leaves, tomatoes and green peppers
lüfer fırın (lewfehr fırın)	bluefish baked with parsley, served chilled and garnished with olives, lemon, gherkins, carrots and hard-boiled eggs
uskumru dolması (ooskoomroo dol-mahssı)	mackerel skins carefully filled with a stuffing of onions, walnuts, hazelnuts, raisins, mixed spices and herbs as well as mackerel flesh. The small package is sewn up, rolled in eggs, flour and breadcrumbs, and fried
uskumru pilakisi (ooskoomroo **peelah**-k^{y}eessee)	mackerel fried in olive oil with potatoes, celery, carrots and garlic. Served cold

baked	**fırında**	fırındah
braised	**pilâki**	peelaak^{y}ee
fried	**tavada kızarmış**	tahvah**dah** kızahrmısh
deep fried	**yağda kızarmış**	yaa**dah** kızahrmısh
grilled	**ızgara**	**ız**gahrah
marinated	**salamura**	sahlah**moo**rah
poached	**haşlama**	hahshlahmah
sauteed	**tavası**	tahvahssı
smoked	**füme**	fewmeh
steamed	**buğulama**	boolahmah
stewed	**yahni**	yahnee
cold	**pilakisi**	peelahk^{y}eessee
raw	**çiğ**	cheeee
stuffed	**dolması**	dolmahssı
with mayonnaise	**mayonezli**	**mah**^{y}onehzlee

Meat *Et*

What kind of meat is this?	**Bu ne tür bir etdir?**	boo neh tewr beer ehtdeer
I'd like some ...	**... istiyorum.**	... eesteeyoroom
beef/pork veal/lamb	**Sığır/Domuz** **Dana/Kuzu**	sıır/domooz dahnah/koozoo

antirikot	ahnteereekot	(beef) ribsteak
baş	bahsh	head
beyin	beh^{y}een	brains
biftek	beeftehk	steak
böbrek	burbrehk	kidneys
bonfile	**bon**feeleh	(beef) steak
ciğer	jeeehr	liver
dana rozbif	dahnah rozbeef	roast veal
düğün eti	dewewn ehtee	mutton stew
fileto	feelehto	fillet
göğüs	g^{y}urewsh	breast
haşlama	hahshlahmah	stew
içli köfte	eechlee k^{y}urfteh	stuffed mutton croquettes
kıyma	kıymah	minced meat
köfte	k^{y}urfteh	veal and mutton burger
kuru köfte	kooroo k^{y}urfteh	fried meatballs
kuzu fırında	koozoo fırındah	roast leg of lamb
kuzu pirzolası	koozoo peerzolahssı	lamb chops
pirzola	peerzolah	chop
sığır kızartması	sıır kızahrtmahssı	roast beef

baked	**fırında**	fırındah
boiled	**haşlama**	hahshlahmah
broiled	**ızgara**	ızgahrah
casserole	**tencerede pişmiş**	tehnjehreh**deh** peeshmeesh
fried	**tavada kızarmış**	tahvah**dah** kızahrmısh
grilled	**ızgara**	ızgahrah
roasted	**kızarmış**	kızahrmısh
stewed	**yahni**	yahnee
spit roasted	**çevirme**	chehveermeh
stuffed	**dolma**	dolmah
underdone (rare)	**az pişmiş**	**ahz** peeshmeesh
medium	**orta pişmiş**	or**tah** peeshmeesh
well done	**iyi pişmiş**	ee**yee** peeshmeesh

Arnavut ciğeri (ahrnahvoot jeeehree) — Albanian-style spicy fried liver with onions

çiğ köfte (**chee** k^{y}urfteh) — raw meatballs; a mixture of minced meat, pounded wheat and chilli powder

döner kebap (durnehr k^{y}ehbahp) — leg of lamb roasted on a vertical spit from which thin slices are cut and served on a bed of rice

etli yaprak dolması (**eht**lee yahprahk dolmahssı) — vine leaves stuffed with a rice and meat mixture

hünkâr beğendi (hewnkaar bayehndee) — minced lamb served on an eggplant purée; literally 'His Majesty enjoys it'

kadın budu köfte (kahdın boodoo k^{y}urfteh) — 'lady's thigh'; seasoned lamb and rice croquettes, first simmered and then fried

kuzu dolması (koozoo dolmahssı) — lamb stuffed with savoury rice, liver and pistachios

kuzu güveç (koozoo g^{y}ewvehch) — lamb stew with onions, garlic, potatoes, tomatoes, bay leaves and dill, cooked slowly in a clay oven

kuzu kapama (koozoo kahpahmah) — leg of lamb cooked with onions, spring onions and herbs, simmered until tender

şiş kababı (sheesh kahbahbı) — shish kebab; marinated cubes of meat threaded on a skewer with quartered tomatoes, onions and sweet peppers, and grilled over a fire perfumed with herbs

şiş köfte (sheesh k^{y}urfteh) — minced lamb croquettes threaded on a skewer and grilled over a charcoal fire

terbiyeli köfte (tehrbeeyehlee k^{y}urfteh) — meatballs poached in salted water until tender and then dropped into a light egg and lemon sauce, served with rice

yoğurtlu kebab (yawoortloo k^{y}ehbahb) — cubes of grilled meat on a bed of toasted bread, pureed tomatoes and seasoned yoghurt

yoğurtlu paça (yawoortloo pahchah) — simmered sheep's feet sliced over a layer of fried bread and garnished with seasoned yoghurt and paprika butter

yumurta köftesi (yoomoortah k^{y}urftehssee) — minced meat croquettes stuffed with hard-boiled eggs. Eaten hot with rice and a tomato sauce, or cold

Game and poultry *Av hayvanları ve kümes hayvanları*

I'd like some game.	**Av eti istiyorum.**	ahv ehtee eesteeyoroom
What's in season?	**Ne mevsimi?**	neh mehvseemee
What do you recommend?	**Ne tavsiye edersiniz?**	neh tahvseeyeh ehdehrseeneez
bıldırcın	bıldırjın	quail
çil	cheel	partridge
çulluk	choollook	woodcock
hindi	heendee	turkey
keklik	kʸehkleek	red partridge
piliç	peeleech	chicken
sülün	sewlewn	pheasant
tavşan	tahvshahn	hare
yabani domuz	yahbahnee domooz	wild boar
yabani kaz	yahbahnee kahz	wild goose
yabani ördek	yahbahnee urdehk	wild duck

bıldırcın şişte (bıldırjın sheeshteh) — halves of quail marinated in olive oil and then cooked over a charcoal fire

çerkez tavuğu (chehrkʸehz tahvoo-oo) — Circassian chicken; boiled chicken served on a bed of rice with a nut sauce. Eaten hot or cold

çulluk kızartması (choollook kızahrt-mahssı) — woodcocks cooked in a wine sauce with tomatoes and onions

hindi dolması iç pilâvı (heendee dolmahssı eech peelaavı) — stuffed turkey with seasoned rice

kâğıtta piliç (kaaıttah peeleech) — chicken baked in a parchment envelope

kaz kızartması (kahz kızahrtmahssı) — roast goose

piliç haşlama (şarapta) (peeleech hahshlahmah shahrahptah) — browned chicken simmered in wine until tender; walnuts are added just before serving

tavşan tencerede (tahvshahn tehnjeh-rehdeh) — hare stew; hare cooked in tomatoes, vinegar, onions and seasoning until all the liquid is absorbed and only a little oil remains

tavuk jölesi (tahvook zhurlehssee) — pieces of deboned boiled chicken suspended in a clear chicken jelly, garnished with parsley and almonds

Vegetables *Sebzeler*

What vegetables do you recommend?	**Sebze olarak ne tavsiye edersiniz?**	sehbzeh olahrahk neh tahv**see**yeh eh**dehr**seeneez
I'd prefer some salad.	**Salata tercih ederim.**	sahlahtah tehrjeeh ehdeh**reem**
bakla	bahklah	fava beans
bamya	**bahm**yah	okra
bezelye	beh**zehl**yeh	peas
biber	beebehr	peppers
Brüksel lahanası	**brewk**sehl lahhahnahssı	Brussels sprouts
çalı fasulyesi	chahlı fahssoolyehssee	string beans
domates	do**mah**tehss	tomatoes
enginar	ehng^{y}eenahr	artichoke
fasulye	fah**ssool**yeh	beans
havuç	hahvooch	carrots
hindiba	heendeebah	wild chicory
hıyar	hıyahr	cucumber
ıspanak	ıspahnahk	spinach
kabak	kahbahk	courgette (zucchini)
karnıbahar	kahrnıbahhahr	cauliflower
kereviz	k^{y}ehrehveez	celery
kırmızı biber	kırmızı beebehr	paprika
kuşkonmaz	kooshkonmahz	asparagus
lâhana	**laa**hahnah	cabbage
mantar	mahntahr	mushrooms
marul	mahrool	lettuce
mercimek	mehrjeemehk	lentils
mısır	mıssır	sweet corn
nohut	nohoot	chick peas
pancar	pahnjahr	beetroot
patates	pah**tah**tehss	potatoes
patlıcan	pahtlıjahn	aubergine (eggplant)
pancar turşusu	pahnjahr toorshoossoo	pickled beetroot
pırasa	pırahssah	leeks
roka	rokah	watercress
şalgam	shahlgahm	turnip
sakızkabağı	sah**kız**kahbaaı	marrow
soğan	sawahn	onions
tatlı biber	tahtlı beebehr	sweet peppers
taze soğan	tahzeh sawahn	spring onions
turp	toorp	radish
turşu	toorshoo	pickled vegetables
yaz türlüsü	yahz toorloossoo	stewed summer vegetables
yeşil fasulye	yehsheel fahssoolyeh	green beans

fasulye pilakisi (fah**ssool**yeh peelah-k^{y}eessee)	navy beans cooked in olive oil with celeriac, potatoes, garlic, carrots and spring onions. Eaten cold
imam bayıldı (eemahm bah^{y}ıldı)	a Turkish speciality, literally 'the priest fainted'. Aubergines stuffed with an onion, tomato, parsley and garlic filling, and cooked in olive oil. Eaten cold
kabak musakkası (kahbahk moossah-kkahssı)	moussaka using courgettes instead of aubergines. Alternating layers of fried courgettes and spiced minced meat with tomatoes. Eaten hot
patlıcan beğendi (pahtlıjahn bayehndee)	grilled aubergine mashed and added to butter and flour. Just before serving grated cheese is added and the dish is sprinkled with parsley
türlü (tewrlew)	mixed vegetables and pulses cooked in water and olive oil, seasoned with salt and a little sugar. Served hot
yoğurtlu bakla (yawoortloo bahklah)	fava beans in olive oil with onions, dill, mint and fresh onions. Eaten cold with yoghurt
zeytinyağlı kızartmalar (zeh^{y}teenyaalı kızahrt-mahlahr)	fried vegetables with a yoghurt or tomato sauce

Turkish cooking is renowned for its variety of vegetables that are served stuffed. There are two principal types of stuffing; either with a tomato-onion-garlic-olive oil filling or one containing minced meat, tomatoes, onions and cheese.

If, as well as the word *dolma*, you see the word *zeytinyağlı* this means that raisins and pistachios will probably also be included in the filling. These *dolma* may be eaten hot or cold and are usually served with yoghurt.

biber dolması	beebehr dolmahssı	stuffed peppers
domates dolması	do**mah**tehss dolmahssı	stuffed tomatoes
kabak dolması	kahbahk dolmahssı	stuffed courgettes
lâhana dolması	**laa**hahnah dolmahssı	stuffed cabbage leaves
patlıcan dolması	pahtlıjahn dolmahssı	stuffed aubergines (eggplant)
yaprak dolması	yahprahk dolmahssı	stuffed vine leaves

Vegetables may be served:

baked	**fırında**	fırındah
boiled	**haşlama**	hahshlahmah
chopped	**kıyılmış**	kıyılmısh
creamed	**kremalı**	krehmahlı
diced	**doğranmış**	dawrahnmısh
fried	**tavada kızarmış**	tahvah**dah** kızahrmısh
grilled	**ızgara**	ızgahrah
roasted	**kızarmış**	kızahrmısh
stewed	**yahni**	yahhnee
stuffed	**dolma**	dolmah

Rice, potatoes and pasta *Pilav, patates ve hamur işleri*

Potatoes are not used much in traditional Turkish cookery, although you will find chips making an appearance on the menu. Both pasta and rice, on the other hand, are staples in the Turkish diet. Rice is served either plain or with other ingredients in the form of a *pilav*, while pasta is served almost as in Italy.

arpa şehriyesi fırında	ahrpah shehhreeyehs-see fırındah	baked oat noodles
bulgur pilavı	boolgoor peelahvı	cracked wheat pilav
domatesli pilav	do**mah**tehslee peelahv	tomato pilav
erişte	ehreeshteh	vermicelli
kıymalı makarna	kıymahlı mah**kahr**nah	macaroni with minced meat
makarna	mah**kahr**nah	macaroni
mantı	mahntı	ravioli
tavuklu pilav	tahvookloo peelahv	chicken pilav
tereyağlı pilav	tehreh^{y}aalı peelahv	butter pilav
patates	pah**tah**tehss	potatoes
kızartması	kızahrtmahssı	chips (french fries)
köftesi	k^{y}urftehssee	croquettes

iç pilav (eech peelahv) fried chicken or goose liver pilav with pine nuts, raisins and tomatoes

kuzu pilav (koozoo peelahv) lamb pilav with onions, pine nuts and raisins, spiced with cinnamon

patlıcanlı pilav (pahtlıjahnlı peelahv) aubergine pilav. Fried cubes of aubergine buried in rice flavoured with olive oil

Cheese *Peynir*

It isn't customary to have a cheese course in Turkey, nor does cheese play a particularly important part in the Turkish kitchen. You will find some imitations of European cheeses. Below are listed a few Turkish ones:

beyaz peynir (beh^{y}ahz peh^{y}neer)	white sheep's milk cheese, not unlike Greek feta cheese
çerkez peyniri (**cheh**rk^{y}ehz peh^{y}-neeree)	buffalo cheese, like mozzarella
kaşar peyniri (kahshahr peh^{y}neeree)	firm yellowish cheese, can be eaten either:
eski (ehsk^{y}ee)	mature
taze (tahzeh)	fresh
tulum peyniri (tooloom peh^{y}neeree)	salty, dry goat's milk cheese that is cured in a goatskin bag

Herbs and spices *Otlar ve baharatlar*

çam fıstığı	cham fıstııı	pine kernels
ceviz	jehveez	walnuts
çöreotu	churehotoo	black cumin
dereotu	dehrehotoo	dill
fındık	fındık	hazelnuts
fıstık	fıstık	pistachios
hardal	hahrdahl	mustard
karabiber	kahrahbeebehr	black pepper
karışık baharatlar	kahrıshık bahhahraht-lahr	allspice
kekik	k^{y}ehk^{y}eek	thyme
kimyon	k^{y}eemyon	cumin
kişniş	k^{y}eeshneesh	coriander
kırmızı biber	kırmızı beebehr	chilli pepper
maydanoz	mah^{y}dahnoz	parsley
nane	nahneh	mint
sarmısak	sahrmıssahk	garlic
susam	soossahm	sesame
tuz	tooz	salt
ufak hindistancevizi	oofahk heendeestahn-jehveezee	nutmeg
üzüm	ewzewm	raisins
zeytinyağı	zeh^{y}teenyaaı	olive oil

Fruit *Meyve*

In summer you'll find a wonderful variety of fruit in the markets and restaurants. If it's hot the fruit will be served on large platters surrounded with ice to keep it cool.

Do you have any fruit?	**Meyvenız var mı?**	meh^{y}vehnız **vahr** mı
I'd like a fruit salad.	**Meyve salatası istiyorum.**	meh^{y}veh sahlahtahssı eesteeyoroom

ahududu	ahhoodoodoo	raspberries
amerikan fıstığı	ahmahreekahn feestııı	peanuts
ananas	ahnahnahss	pineapple
armut	ahrmoot	pear
ayva	ah^{y}vah	quince
badem	bahdehm	almond
bektaşi üzümü	behktahshee ewzew-mew	gooseberries
böğürtlen	burewrtlehn	blackberries
ceviz	jehveez	walnuts
çilek	cheelehk	strawberries
dut	doot	mulberries
elma	ehlmah	apple
erik	ehreek	plums
fındık	fındık	hazelnuts
hindistancevizi	heendeestahnjehveezee	coconut
hurma	hoormah	dates
incir	eenjeer	figs
karpuz	kahrpooz	water melon
kavun	kahvoon	melon
kayısı	kah^{y}ıssı	apricot
kiraz	k^{y}eerahz	cherries
kuru erik	kooroo ehreek	prunes
kuru üzüm	kooroo ewzewm	raisins
limon	leemon	lemon
mandalina	mahndahleenah	tangerine
mango	mahngo	mango
misket limonu	meesk^{y}eht leemonoo	lime
muz	mooz	banana
nar	nahr	pomegranate
portakal	portahkahl	orange
ravent	rahvehnt	rhubarb
şeftali	shehftahlee	peach
siyah frenküzümü	seeyah frehnk^{y}ewzew-mew	blackcurrants
üzüm	ewzewm	grapes

Desserts *Tatlılar*

Turks have a sweet tooth and are famous for their syrupy desserts like *baklava*. Some desserts bear titillating names like 'sweetheart's lips', 'lady's navel', or 'vizier's finger'. But if you'd like something plain and relatively unsweetened, ask for *krem karamel* (creme caramel).

I'd like a dessert, please.	**Bir tatlı istiyorum, lütfen.**	beer tahtlı eesteeyoroom lewtfehn
What do you recommend?	**Ne tavsiye edersiniz?**	neh tahvseeyeh ehdehrseeneez
Something light, please.	**Hafif birşey, lütfen.**	hahfeef beerschehy lewtfehn
Just a small portion.	**Sadece küçük bir porsiyon.**	sahdehjeh kyewchewk beer porseeyon

frape	frahpeh	milkshake
güllaç tatlısı muhallebi	gyewllahch tahtlıssı moohahllehbee	rose-flavoured pudding
irmik helvası	eermeek hehlvahssı	semolina-sugar confection
karışık dondurma	kahrıshık dondoormah	assorted ice cream
karışık hamur tatlıları	kahrıshık hahmoor tahtlılahrı	assorted pastries
kaymaklı ve sütlü dondurma	kahymahklı veh sewtlew dondoormah	ice cream
kazan dibi	kahzahn deebee	pudding with caramelized bottom
komposto	komposto	stewed fruit
krem şokola	krehm shokolah	chocolate pudding
krem karamel	krehm kahrahmehl	creme caramel
krep süzet	krehp sewzeht	jam-filled pancakes
meyvelı dondurma	mehyvehlı dondoormah	sorbet (sherbet)
meyvelı tartlet	mehyvehlı tahrtleht	fruit tart
meyvelı turta	mehyvehlı toortah	fruit cake
meyve salatası (likörlü/kremalı)	mehyveh sahlahtahssı (leekyurlew/krehmahlı)	fruit salad (with liqueur/cream)
peşmelba	pehshmehlbah	peach melba
revâni	rehvaanee	semolina pudding
strudel	stroodehl	apple strudel
sufle	soofleh	souffle
turtalar	toortahlahr	tarts
yoğurt	yawoort	yoghurt

aşure (ahshooreh)	dried fruit, nuts, seeds, chick peas and vegetables cooked together in a thick syrup, served cold
baba tatlısı (bahbah tahtlıssı)	ring-shaped cake soaked in syrup, with custard or nuts in the central hole
baklava (bahklahvah)	layers of very fine fillo pastry interspersed with chopped nuts and doused with sweet syrup, eaten cold
börek (burrehk)	strips of pastry that are either knotted or twisted through a slit in the strip and then deep-fried briefly before rolling in sugar. Delicious and very light
bülbül yuvası (bewlbewl yoovahssı)	'nightingale's nest'; similar to baklava, pastry filled with a pistachio and walnut puree and served with a sorbet
dilber dudağı (deelbehr doodaaı)	pastry filled with pistachios and other nuts
dondurma kaymaklı (dondoormah kah^{y}-mahklı)	milk ice cream with a creamy and slightly elastic texture; made with starch from saleb root and mastic
ekmek kadayıfı (ehkmehk kahdah^{y}ıfı)	a golden-brown bread soaked in a syrup of honey, rose water, sugar and lemon juice. Often served spread with a thick layer of clotted cream and decorated with pistachios
kabak tatlısı (kahbahk tahtlıssı)	pumpkin served with nuts and a sugary syrup
lokum (lokoom)	Turkish delight available in a variety of different flavours, including pistachio, almond and coconut
muhallebi (moo**hah**llehbee)	wobbly milk custard thickened with flour and flavoured with cinnamon, served cold.
şekerpare (shehk^{y}ehrpahreh)	baked biscuits with hot syrup
sütlaç (sewtlahch)	milk and rice pudding dusted with cinnamon, eaten hot or cold
tavuk göğsü (tahvook g^{y}ursew)	finely-chopped chicken breast poached in milk and flavoured with cinnamon
tel kadayıfı (**tehl** kahdah^{y}ıfı)	batter poured through a sieve onto a hot plate to form thin strands of pastry, coated with butter and baked, then doused with syrup

Wine *Şarap*

Because drinking alcohol is restricted for Moslems, wine isn't commonly drunk in Turkey. It's possible that you won't find any wine in small villages outside tourist resorts. Nevertheless, wine production in Turkey goes back to ancient times. Only a very small part of the grapes cultivated in Turkey are used to produce wine, and much of it is exported. Generally of a good quality, the best Turkish wine – particularly white – comes from the area around Izmir, while other vineyards are found in Thrace, around the Marmara coast and in Anatolia. Here are a few Turkish wines:

Adabağ	ah**dah**baa	red
Kalebağ	kah**leh**baa	red
Tekel Gaziantep	tehk^{y}ehl gahzeeahntehp	red dessert wine
Tekel Misbağ İzmir	tehk^{y}ehl meesbaa **eez**meer	dry white

And a few table wines:

Çubuk	**choo**book	red, dry white
Güzel Marmara	g^{y}ewzehl **mahr**mahrah	red, medium dry to dry white

I'd like a bottle of white/red wine.	**Bir şişe beyaz şarap/kırmızı şarap istiyorum.**	**beer** sheesheh beh^{y}ahz shahrahp/kırmızı shahrahp eestee**yo**room
half a bottle	**yarım şişe**	yahrım sheesheh
a carafe	**bir sürahi**	beer sewrahhee
half a litre	**yarım litre**	yahrım leetreh
a glass	**bir bardak**	beer bahrdahk

red	**kırmızı**	kırmızı
white	**beyaz**	beh^{y}ahz
sparkling	**köpüklü**	k^{y}urpewklew
dry	**sek**	sehk
light	**hafif**	hah**feef**
medium dry	**orta**	ortah
sweet	**tatlı**	tahtlı
chilled	**soğutulmuş**	sawootoolmoosh
at room temperature	**oda ısısında**	odah ıssıssındah

Where does this wine come from?	**Bu şarap nereden geliyor?**	boo shahrahp **neh**rehdehn gʸehleeyor
What's this wine called?	**Bu şarabın adı nedir?**	boo shahrahbın ahdı **neh**deer
I don't want anything too sweet.	**Fazla tatlı birşey istemiyorum.**	fahzlah tahtlı beershehʸ ees**teh**meeyoroom
Please bring me another ...	**Bir ... daha getirin, lütfen.**	beer ... dahhah gʸehteereen **lewt**fehn
glass/carafe/bottle	**bardak/sürahi/şişe**	bahrdahk/sewrahhee/sheesheh
I'd like some champagne, please.	**Şampanya istiyorum, lütfen.**	shahm**pahn**yah eestee**yo**room **lewt**fehn

Rakı

Raki (87 proof) is without doubt the national drink. It is made from distilled grapes with aniseed, and is usually drunk diluted with water which turns this clear spirit milky.

For the really adventurous, follow the example of Turkish soldiers who mix together equal portions of beer and raki.

I'd like a glass of raki, please.	**Bir bardak rakı istiyorum, lütfen.**	**beer** bahrdahk rahkı eestee**yo**room **lewt**fehn

Beer *Bira*

You may be surprised to discover that beer is perhaps the nation's most popular drink. Try some of these:

Efes-Pilsen	**eh**fehss**peel**sehn	lager with a strong hoppy flavour
Tekel beyaz	tehkʸehl behʸahz	lager
Tekel siyah	tehkʸehl seeyah	dark beer
I'd like a glass/bottle of beer, please.	**Bir bardak/şişe bira istiyorum, lütfen.**	**beer** bahrdahk/sheesheh **bee**rah eestee**yo**room **lewt**fehn
A cold beer, please.	**Soğuk bir bira, lütfen.**	sawook beer **bee**rah **lewt**fehn
Do you have any ... beer?	**... biranız var mı?**	... **bee**rahnız **vahr** mı
light/dark	**Beyaz/Siyah**	behʸahz/seeyah

Other alcoholic drinks *Başka alkollü içkiler*

Although Turkey is a Muslim country there is a state-run Turkish Monopolies company, Tekel, which either distributes home-produced alcohol or imports it. Imported alcohol tends to be very expensive so it's worth asking the price before ordering. But Tekel does produce a few spirits like gin (*cin*), vodka (*votka*), whisky (*viski*), and brandy (*kanyak*) – the latter either regular or five-star. There are also a number of locally-produced fruit brandies, however, these are very sweet.

Are there any local specialities?	**Özel bir içkiniz var mı?**	urzehl beer eechk^{y}eeneez **vahr** mı
I'd like to try a glass of ..., please.	**Bir ... istiyorum, lütfen.**	beer ... eesteeyoroom **lewt**fehn
A (double) whisky, please.	**Bir (duble) viski, lütfen.**	beer (**doob**leh) **veesk**^{y}ee **lewt**fehn

glass	**bardak**	bahrdahk
bottle	**şişe**	sheesheh
single (shot)	**tek**	tehk
double (shot)	**duble**	**doob**leh

brandy	**konyak/kanyak**	**kon**yahk/**kahn**yahk
five star	**beş yıldız**	behsh yıldız
gin and tonic	**cin-tonik**	jeen-**to**neek
liqueur	**likör**	leek^{y}**urr**
port	**porto**	porto
rum	**rom**	rom
sherry	**şeri**	**sheh**ree
vermouth	**vermut**	**vehr**moot
vodka	**votka**	**vot**kah
neat (straight)	**sek**	sehk
on the rocks	**buzlu**	boozloo
with water/soda	**sulu/sodalı**	sooloo/sodahlı

ŞEREFE
(shehrehfeh)
CHEERS!

Nonalcoholic drinks *Alkolsüz içkiler*

If you don't want anything alcoholic, you'll find a satisfying variety of soft drinks to try. These range from the fizzy bottled drinks like Coca-cola and Pepsi to fruit juices and mineral water. Although tap water is safe to drink, it is heavily chlorinated – mineral water is a cheap pleasant-tasting alternative.

There are also a number of traditional drinks like *ayran*, a refreshing drink made of yoghurt mixed with mineral water and a pinch of salt, *şira*, unfermented grape juice, and *boza*, a calorie-packed sourish drink made from fermented millet. It is best bought from cake shops where it's served sprinkled with cinnamon, but can only be bought in winter.

Although coffee is the drink that one associates with Turkey, in fact, tea is the early morning drink, and the one most often drunk during the day. You should also try some of the available herbal infusions; mint is particularly refreshing.

I'd like a/an...	**... istiyorum**	... eestee**yo**room
Do you have any ...?	**... var mı?**	... **vahr** mı
fruit juice	**Meyve suyu**	meh^{Y}**veh** sooyoo
apple	**Elma**	ehlmah
grapefruit	**Greyfrut**	greh^{Y}froot
lemon	**Limon**	leemon
orange	**Portakal**	portahkahl
pineapple	**Ananas**	ahnahnahss
tomato	**Domates**	do**mah**tehss
lemonade	**Limonata**	leemo**nah**tah
milk	**Süt**	sewt
milkshake	**Frape**	frahpeh
mineral water	**Maden suyu**	mahdehn sooyoo
fizzy	**Gazlı**	gahzlı
still	**Sade**	sahdeh
soda water	**Soda**	sodah
tea	**Çay**	chah^{Y}
with milk	**Sütlü**	sewt**lew**
with lemon	**Limonlu**	leemon**loo**
iced tea	**Buzlu çay**	booz**loo** chah^{Y}
tonic water	**Tonik**	**to**neek
(iced) water	**(Buzlu) Su**	(booz**loo**) soo

Coffeehouse *Kahvehane*

The coffeehouse is an institution in Turkey. Usually rather modest establishments, they're ubiquitous in towns, and there's at least one coffeehouse in even the tiniest hamlet. Traditionally it is a male gathering place, but as Western visitors, women probably won't be much remarked on.

You will see men vigorously discussing politics, the weather, football or otherwise solving the problems of the world over a cup of strong coffee or tea. You'll probably be stared at out of curiosity, and some Turks may want to strike up a conversation with you.

You cannot usually get food in a coffeehouse, unless a street vendor happens to be passing by with some sesame rolls or pasties, but in many places you can have a water pipe (*nargile*) prepared for you. This is smoked very slowly rather like an Indian peace pipe by passing the mouthpiece around a small group.

Can you prepare a hubble-bubble pipe for me?	**Bana bir nargile hazırlar mısınız, lütfen?**	bahnah beer nahrg[y]eeleh hahzırlahr mıssınız lewtfehn

This is obviously the place to try a cup of the world-renowned Turkish coffee. It is prepared by boiling ground coffee and water together in individual containers. The contents are then tipped into a small cup – grounds and all. Let the grounds settle for a minute or so and then only drink about half the cup. You should let the waiter know in advance how sweet you like it, as the sugar is mixed in with the coffee. Note that neither milk nor cream is served.

coffee without sugar	**sade kahve**	sah**deh** kahhveh
slightly sweetened	**az şekerli kahve**	**ahz** shehk[y]ehrlee kahhveh
sweet	**orta şekerli kahve**	ortah shehk[y]ehrlee kahhveh
very sweet	**çok şekerli kahve**	**chok** shehk[y]ehrlee kahhveh

Complaints *Şikayetler*

There is a plate/glass missing.	**Bir tabak/bardak eksik.**	**beer** tahbahk/bahrdahk ehkseek
I don't have a knife/fork/spoon.	**Bıçağım/Çatalım/Kaşığım yok.**	bıchaaım/chahtahlım/kahshıım yok
That's not what I ordered.	**Bunu ısmarlamamıştım.**	boonoo ısmahrlahmahmıshtım
I asked for ...	**... ısmarlamıştım.**	... ısmahrlahmıshtım
There must be a mistake.	**Bir hata olacak.**	beer hahtah olahjahk
May I change this?	**Bunu değiştirebilir miyim?**	boonoo dayeeshteerehbee**leer** meeyeem
I asked for a small portion (for the child).	**(Çocuk için) Küçük porsiyon ısmarlamıştım.**	(cho**jook** eecheen) k^{y}ew**chewk** porseeyon ısmahrlahmıshtım
The meat is ...	**Et ...**	eht
overdone	**çok pişmiş**	**chok** peeshmeesh
underdone	**az pişmiş**	**ahz** peeshmeesh
too rare	**çiğ**	**cheeee**
too tough	**çok sert**	**chok** sehrt
This is too ...	**Bu çok ...**	boo chok
bitter/salty	**acı/tuzlu**	ahjı/toozloo
spicy/sour	**baharatlı/ekşi**	bahhahrahtlı/ehkshee
sweet	**tatlı**	tahtlı
I don't like this.	**Bunu beğenmedim.**	boonoo bayehnmehdeem
The food is cold.	**Yemek soğuk.**	yehmehk sawook
This isn't fresh.	**Bu taze değil.**	boo tahzeh dayeel
What's taking so long?	**Bu kadar uzun süren nedir?**	**boo** kahdahr oozoon sewrehn nehdeer
Have you forgotten our drinks?	**Içkilerimizi unuttunuz mu?**	eechk^{y}eelehreemeezee oonoottoonooz moo
The wine doesn't taste right.	**Şarapta bir gariplik var.**	shahrahptah beer gahreepleek vahr
This isn't clean.	**Bu temiz değil.**	boo tehmeez dayeel
Would you ask the head waiter to come over?	**Şef garsonu çağırır mısınız?**	shehf gahrsonoo **chaa**ırır mıssınız

The bill *Hesap*

Service charges are normally included in the bill, but if not you should add around 10 per cent for the waiter. In some cases tipping may offend, if the tip is declined forcefully enough, don't insist. There is no cover charge in Turkey. Credit cards may be used in an increasing number of restaurants. However, these are limited to large cities and tourist resorts at the moment.

Could I have the bill, please?	**Hesabı alabilir miyim, lütfen.**	hehssahbı ahlahbee**leer** meeyeem **lewt**fehn
I'd like to pay.	**Ödemek istiyorum.**	urdehmehk eestee**yo**room
We'd like to pay separately.	**Ayrı ödemek isteriz.**	ah^{y}rı urdehmehk eestehreez
I think there's a mistake in this bill.	**Bu hesapta bir hata var galiba.**	boo hehssahptah beer hahtah vahr gahleebah
What is this amount for?	**Bu miktar ne içindir?**	boo meektahr neh eecheendeer
Is service included?	**Servis dahil mi?**	sehrveess dahheel mee
Is everything included?	**Herşey dahil mi?**	**hehr**sheh^{y} dahheel mee
Do you accept traveller's cheques?	**Travelers çek kabul ediyor musunuz?**	'traveller's' chehk kahbool ehdeeyor **moo**ssoonooz
Can I pay with this credit card?	**Bu kredi kartı ile ödeyebilir miyim?**	boo **kreh**dee kahrtı eeleh urdeh^{y}ehbee**leer** meeyeem
Thank you. This is for you.	**Teşekkür ederim. Bu da sizin için.**	tehsheh**kk^{y}ewr** ehdehreem. boo dah seezeen eecheen
Keep the change.	**Üstü kalsın.**	ewstew kahlsın
That was delicious.	**Nefis idi.**	**neh**feess eedee
We enjoyed it, thank you.	**Hoşumuza gitti, teşekkür ederiz.**	hoshoomoozah g^{y}eettee tehsheh**kk^{y}ewr** ehdehreez

SERVİS DAHİL
SERVICE INCLUDED

TIPPING, see inside back cover

Snacks – Picnic *Hafif yemekler – Piknik*

There is no shortage of snacks in Turkey, served from small shops full of fruit and nuts, roadside stalls, on the quay by the sea and even directly from the boat.

If you're doing a tour of villages on the Bosphorus then you'll certainly come across boats that come into the harbour having already gutted and grilled their catch ready to sell to the public. If you're lucky you'll also come across a type of mussel kebab sold at seaside stalls, which is made up of deep-fried mussels threaded on to a skewer.

In villages and towns you'll see people strolling around holding on to rolled cornets of paper containing fruit and nuts. You can buy, among others, grilled and salted pistachios and roasted chick peas (*leblebi*). Near Bodrum you should be able to get iced almonds to refresh you.

If you're after something a little more solid try some tripe soup, corn on the cob, or one of the many pies filled with spinach, cheese or meat.

The obvious choice for a takeaway is a *döner kebap*, slices of mutton tucked into a bread pouch with onions and a little salad.

işkembe çorbası	eeshk^{y}ehmbeh chorbahssı	tripe soup
ıspanaklı kuru börek	ıspahnahk**lı** kooroo burrehk	spinach pie
karadeniz pidesi	kahrahdehneez **pee**dehssee	Turkish-style pizza
kıymalı börek	kıymah**lı** burrehk	minced meat pie
peynirli börek	peh^{y}neer**lee** burrehk	cheese pie
salatalık	sahlahtahlık	seasoned peeled cucumber
simit	seemeet	sesame seed rolls
su böreği kıymalı	**soo** burrayee kıymahlı	minced meat pie
su böreği peynirli	**soo** burrayee peh^{y}neerlee	cheese pie, steamed then baked
talaş kebabı	tahlahsh k^{y}ehbahbı	meat pie made with chunks of meat
tavuklu börek	tahvook**loo** burrehk	chicken pie

Here's a basic list of food that might come in useful when shopping for a picnic.

I'll have one of those, please.	**Şunlardan bir tane istiyorum, lütfen.**	shoonlahrdahn **beer** tahneh eesteeyoroom **lewt**fehn
May I have a/an/ some ...?	**... alabilir miyim.**	... ahlahbee**leer** meeyeem
apples	**Elma**	ehlmah
bananas	**Muz**	mooz
biscuits (Br.)	**Birkaç bisküvi**	**beer**kahch beesk^{y}ewvee
beer	**Bira**	**bee**rah
bread	**Biraz ekmek**	**bee**rahz ehkmehk
butter	**Tereyağ**	tehreh^{y}aa
cake	**Bir pasta**	beer **pah**stah
cheese	**Peynir**	peh^{y}neer
chips (Am.)	**Çips**	cheeps
chocolate bar	**Çikolata**	**chee**kolahtah
cookies	**Birkaç bisküvi**	**beer**kahch beesk^{y}ewvee
crisps	**Çips**	cheeps
dried fruit	**Kuru meyve**	kooroo meh^{y}veh
eggs	**Yumurta**	yoomoortah
gherkins (pickles)	**Turşu**	toorshoo
grapes	**Üzüm**	ewzewm
hamburger	**Hamburger**	hahmboorgehr
hot dog	**Sosis**	sosseess
ice cream	**Bir dondurma**	beer dondoormah
lemon	**Limon**	leemon
milk	**Süt**	sewt
mustard	**Hardal**	hahrdahl
nuts	**Fındık**	fındık
oranges	**Portakal**	portahkahl
pastries	**Birkaç tatlı**	**beer**kahch tahtlı
pepper	**Biber**	beebehr
pie	**Bir börek**	**beer** burrehk
roll	**Birkaç küçük ekmek**	**beer**kahch k^{y}ewchewk ehkmehk
salami	**Salam**	sahlahm
salt	**Tuz**	tooz
sandwich	**Bir sandviç**	**beer** sahndveech
sausage	**Sosis**	sosseess
soft drink	**Alkolsüz içki**	ahlkolsewz eechk^{y}ee
sugar	**Şeker**	shehk^{y}ehr
tea	**Çay**	chah^{y}
tomatoes	**Domates**	do**mah**tehss
yoghurt	**Yoğurt**	yawoort

Travelling around

Plane *Uçak*

Is there a flight to Antalya?	**Antalya'ya uçuş var mı?**	ahntahlyah**yah** oo**choosh** **vahr** mı
Is it a direct flight?	**Bu bir direkt uçuş mudur?**	boo beer dee**rehkt** oo**choosh** moo**door**
When's the next flight to Ankara?	**Ankara'ya ilk uçak ne zaman?**	ahnkahrah**yah** eelk oo**chahk** **neh** zahmahn
Is there a connection to Adana?	**Adana'ya bağlantı var mı?**	ahdahnah**yah** baalahnt**ı** vahr mı
I'd like a ticket to Samsun.	**Samsun'a bir bilet istiyorum.**	sahmsoo**nah** beer bee**leht** eestee**yo**room
single	**gidiş**	g^{y}eedeesh
return	**gidiş-dönüş**	g^{y}eedeesh-durnewsh
first class	**birinci mevki**	beereen**jee** **mehvk**^{y}ee
economy	**turist mevki**	too**reest** **mehvk**^{y}ee
What time do we take off?	**Uçak saat kaçta kalkar?**	oo**chahk** sah**aht** **kahch**tah **kahl**kahr
What time do I have to check in?	**Bagajların kaydını saat kaçta yapmam gerek?**	bahgahzhlah**rın** **kah**^{y}dını sah**aht** **kahch**tah yahp**mahm** g^{y}eh**rehk**
Is there a bus to the airport?	**Hava alanına giden bir otobüs var mı?**	hahvah **ah**lahnı**nah** g^{y}ee**dehn** beer oto**bewss** vahr mı
What's the flight number?	**Uçuş numarası kaçtır?**	oo**choosh** noomahrah**ssı** **kahch**tır
What time do we arrive?	**Saat kaçta varırız?**	sah**aht** **kahch**tah vahrırız
I'd like to ... my reservation.	**Rezervasyonumu ... istiyorum.**	rehzehrvahsyonoo**moo** ... eestee**yo**room
cancel	**iptal etmek**	eep**tahl** eht**mehk**
change	**değiştirmek**	dayeeshteer**mehk**
confirm	**konfirme etmek**	konfeermeh ehtmehk

VARIŞ
ARRIVAL

HAREKET
DEPARTURE

To the bus/railway station *Otogara/Tren istasyonuna*

Where is the ...?	**... nerededir?**	... nehrehdehdeer
bus station railway station	**Otogar** **İstasyon**	oto**gahr** eestahss**yon**
Can I get there on foot?	**Yürüyerek gidebilir miyim?**	yewrewyehrehk g^y^eedeh-bee**leer** mee**yeem**
Taxi!	**Taksi!**	**tahk**see
Take me to the bus station.	**Beni otogara götürün.**	beh**nee** otogah**rah** g^y^urtewrewn
How much is that?	**Ne kadardır?**	neh kah**dahr**dır

Coach (long-distance bus) *Şehirlerarası otobüs*

A comprehensive network of buses serves all parts of Turkey. They are cheap, faster than trains, and comfortable if you take a modern air-conditioned vehicle. Tickets can be bought from agents, but the cheapest prices will be offered at the bus station itself, if you are prepared to queue up for them.

In Istanbul, coaches and minibuses leave from Topkapi Otogari, the central bus station. The station is divided into two sections, the Trakya Otogari for buses going west, and the Anadolu Otogari for eastbound buses.

When is the ... bus to Emirgan?	**Emirgân'a ... otobüs ne zaman?**	ehmeergaanah ... oto**bewss neh** zahmahn
first/last/next	**ilk/son/gelecek**	eelk/son/g^y^ehleh**jehk**
What's the fare to Erzurum?	**Erzurum'a yolculuk kaça?**	**ehr**zooroo**mah** yoljoo**look** kah**chah**
Do I have to change buses?	**Aktarma yapmam gerekir mi?**	ahktahr**mah yahp**mahm g^y^ehreh**k^y^eer** mee
Does the coach stop in Taksim?	**Otobüs Taksim'de duruyor mu?**	oto**bewss tahk**seemdeh dooroo**yor** moo
What time does the coach arrive in Troy?	**Truva'ya otobüs kaçta varıyor?**	troovahyah oto**bewss** **kahch**tah vahrı**yor**
How long does the journey take?	**Yolculuk ne kadar zaman sürer?**	yoljoo**look** neh kahdahr zahmahn sewrehr
Can we stop, please?	**Durabilir miyiz, lütfen?**	doorahbee**leer** mee**yeez** **lewt**fehn

Train *Tren*

The Turkish State Railways (TCDDY) run fast, comfortable trains, but only on certain routes. Among the best are the *Mavi Tren* (Blue Train), which runs daily between Istanbul and Ankara (7½ hours), and the *Boğaziçi Ekspresi*, also daily between Istanbul and Ankara (9½ hours, and slower than the bus). Istanbul has two railway stations: Sirkeci Gari for westbound trains and Haydarpasa Gari for eastbound trains.

ekspres (ehksprehss)	fast train, usually first class only with couchettes, sleeping- and restaurant cars
mototren (mototrehn)	long distance stopping train
yolcu treni (**yol**joo trehnee)	local stopping train, best avoided

Where's the ...? *... nerededir?*

Where's the ...?	**... nerededir?**	... **neh**rehdehdeer
bar	**Bar**	bahr
booking office	**Bilet gişesi**	bee**leht** g[y]ee**sheh**ssee
information office	**Danışma bürosu**	dahnısh**mah** bew**ro**ssoo
lost property (lost and found) office	**Kayıp eşya bürosu**	kah[y]**ıp** ehshyah bew**ro**ssoo
newsstand	**Gazete bayii**	gahzehteh **bah**[y]eeee
platform 7	**Peron 7**	peh**ron** 7
reservations office	**Rezervasyon bürosu**	rehzehrvahss**yon** bew**ro**ssoo
restaurant	**Restoran**	rehsto**rahn**
snack bar	**Snack bar**	snahck bahr
ticket office	**Bilet gişesi**	bee**leht** g[y]ee**sheh**ssee
tourist office	**Turizm bürosu**	too**reezm** bew**ro**ssoo
waiting room	**Bekleme salonu**	behkleh**meh** sahlonoo
Where are the toilets?	**Tuvaletler nerededir?**	**too**vahlehtlehr **neh**rehdehdeer

GİRİŞ	ENTRANCE
ÇIKIŞ	EXIT
PERONA	TO THE PLATFORMS

When is the ... train to Eskisehir?	**Eskişehir'e ... tren ne zaman?**	ehskeeshehhee**reh** ... trehn **neh** zahmahn
first/last/next	**ilk/son/gelecek**	eelk/son/g^{y}ehleh**jehk**
What time does the train to Izmir leave?	**İzmir'e tren saat kaçta hareket ediyor?**	eezmee**reh** trehn sa**haht** **kahch**tah hahrehk^{y}eht ehdee**yor**
How much is it to Erzurum?	**Erzurum'a yolculuk ne kadar?**	ehrzooroo**mah** yoljoo**look** **neh** kahdahr
Is it a through train?	**Bu tren ekspres midir?**	boo trehn ehksprehss meedeer
Is there a connection to Manisa?	**Manisa'ya bağlantı var mı?**	mahneessah**yah** **baa**lahntı vahr mı
Do I have to change trains?	**Aktarma yapmam gerekli mi?**	ahktahrmah yahpmahm g^{y}ehrehk**lee** mee
Is there enough time to change?	**Aktarma yapmak için zaman yeterli mi?**	ahktahrmah yahpmahk eecheen zahmahn yehtehr**lee** mee
Is the train running on time?	**Tren zamanında kalkar mı?**	trehn zahmahnındah kahl**kahr** mı
What time does the train arrive in Manisa?	**Tren Manisa'ya saat kaçta varıyor?**	trehn mahneessah**yah** sa**haht** **kahch**tah vahrıyor
Is there a dining car/sleeping car on the train?	**Trende restoran vagon/yataklı vagon var mı?**	trehn**deh** rehstorahn vahgon/yahtahk**lı** vahgon vahr mı
Does the train stop in Yesilyurt?	**Tren Yeşilyurt'da durur mu?**	trehn yehsheelyoortdah dooroor moo
Which platform does the train from Ankara arrive at?	**Ankara treni hangi perona geliyor?**	**ahn**kahrah treh**nee** hahng^{y}ee pehronah g^{y}ehleeyor
Which platform does the train to Aydin leave from?	**Aydın treni hangi perondan hareket ediyor?**	**ah**^{y}dın trehnee hahng^{y}ee pehrondahn hahrehk^{y}eht ehdeeyor
I'd like a timetable.	**Bir tren tarifesi istiyorum.**	beer trehn tahreefehssee eestee**yo**room

SİGARA İÇİLEN
SMOKER

SİGARA İÇİLMEYEN
NON-SMOKER

Bu tren ekspresdir.	It's a through train.
...'de aktarma yapmanız gerekir.	You have to change at ...
7 numaralı peron ...dır.	Platform 7 is ...
orada/yukarı katta **solda/sağda**	over there/upstairs on the left/on the right
Manisa'ya saat ...de bir tren var.	There is a train to Manisa at ...
Treniniz 8 numaralı perondan hareket edecek.	Your train will leave from platform 8.
... dakika gecikme var.	There'll be a delay of ... minutes.
Birinci mevki, trenin ön tarafında/ortasında/arkada.	First class at the front/in the middle/at the back of the train.

Tickets *Biletler*

I'd like a ticket to Bandirma.	**Bandırma'ya bir bilet istiyorum.**	bahn**dır**mah**yah** beer bee**leht** eesteey**yo**room
single (one-way)	**gidiş**	g^{y}eedeesh
return (roundtrip)	**gidiş-dönüş**	g^{y}eedeesh-durnewsh
first class	**birinci mevki**	beereenjee **mehvk^{y}ee**
second class	**ikinci mevki**	eek^{y}eenjee **mehvk^{y}ee**
with a supplement	**fark ile**	fahrk ee**leh**

Reservation *Rezervasyon*

I'd like to reserve a ...	**Bir ... rezerve etmek istiyorum.**	beer ... rehzehrveh eht-mehk eestee**yo**room
seat (by the window)	**(pencere kenarında) yer**	(**pehn**jehreh kehnahrındah) yehr
berth	**kuşet**	koo**sheht**
upper	**yukarıda**	yookahrı**dah**
middle	**ortada**	ortah**dah**
lower	**aşağıda**	ahshaaı**dah**
berth in the sleeping car	**yataklı vagonda kuşet**	yahtahklı vahgondah koo**sheht**

All aboard *Trende*

Is this the right platform for the train to Ankara?	**Ankara treni için doğru peronda mıyız?**	**ahn**kahrah trehnee ee**cheen daw**roo pehrondah mıyız
Is this the train to Mersin?	**Mersin treni bu mudur?**	mehrseen trehnee **boo** moodoor
Excuse me. Could I get past?	**Affedersiniz. Geçebilir miyim?**	ahffeh**dehr**seeneez. g^{y}ehchehbee**leer** meeyeem
Is this seat taken?	**Bu yerin sahibi var mı?**	boo yehreen sahheebee vahr mı
I think that's my seat.	**Sanırım burası benim yerim.**	sahnırım boorah**ssı** behneem yehreem
Would you let me know before we get to Izmir?	**İzmir'e varınca bana haber verir misiniz?**	**eez**meereh vahr**ın**jah bahnah hahbehr vehreer **mee**sseeneez
What station is this?	**Bu hangi istasyon, acaba?**	boo **hahng**^{y}ee eestahss**yon** ahjah**bah**
How long does the train stop here?	**Tren burada ne kadar zaman durur?**	trehn boorahdah **neh** kahdahr zahmahn dooroor
When do we get to Denizli?	**Denizli'ye ne zaman varıyoruz?**	dehneezlee**yeh neh** zahmahn vahrı**yo**rooz

BİRİNCİ MEVKİ	İKİNCİ MEVKİ
FIRST CLASS	SECOND CLASS

Sleeping *Uyumak*

Are there any free compartments in the sleeping car?	**Yataklı vagonda boş kompartman var mı?**	yahtahkl**ı** vahgon**dah** bosh kompahrtmahn vahr mı
Where's the sleeping car?	**Yataklı vagon nerededir?**	yahtahkl**ı** vahgon **neh**rehdehdeer
Where is my berth?	**Kuşetim nerede acaba?**	koosheh**teem neh**rehdeh ahjah**bah**
I'd like a lower berth.	**Aşağıda uyumak isterim.**	ahshaaı**dah** ooyoomahk eestehreem

Would you make up our berths?	**Kuşetlerimizi hazırlar mısınız?**	kooshehtlehreemeezee hahzır**lahr** **mı**ssınız
Would you wake me at 7 o'clock?	**Beni saat 7 de uyandırır mısınız?**	behnee sahaht 7 deh ooyahndırır **mı**ssınız

Eating *Yemek yemek*

On long distance journeys there will be a buffet car on the train. Normally, the meals are not only good, but are also excellent value.

Where's the dining car?	**Restoran vagon nerededir?**	rehsto**rahn** vahgon **neh**rehdehdeer
First/Second call for dinner.	**Yemek için birinci/ ikinci çağrı.**	yeh**mehk** ee**cheen** bee-reenjee/eek[y]eenjee chaarı

Baggage and porters *Bagaj ve hamal*

Porter!	**Hamal!***	hah**mahl**
Can you help me with my luggage?	**Bagajımı taşımama yardım edebilir misiniz?**	bahgahzhımı tahshımah-mah yahrdım ehdehbee-**leer** **mee**sseeneez
Where are the luggage trolleys (carts)?	**Bagaj arabaları nerededir?**	bahgahzh ahrahbahlahrı **neh**rehdehdeer
Where's the left-luggage office (baggage check)?	**Bagaj deposu nerededir?**	bahgahzh dehpo**ssoo** **neh**rehdehdeer
I'd like to leave my luggage.	**Bagajımı vermek istiyorum.**	bahgahzhımı vehr**mehk** eestee**yo**room
I'd like to register my luggage.	**Bagajımı teslim etmek istiyorum.**	bahgahzhımı tehsleem ehtmehk eestee**yo**room

BAGAJ TESLİMİ

REGISTERING (CHECKING) BAGGAGE

* You'll also hear people calling out 'Lütfen!' to attract the porter's attention.

Bus *Otobüs*

I'd like a booklet of tickets.	**Bir bilet karnesi istiyorum.**	beer bee**leht** kahrnehssee eestee**yo**room
I'd like a Blue Card.	**Mavi kart istiyorum.**	**mah**vee kahrt eestee**yo**room
Which bus goes to the town centre?	**Şehir merkezine hangi otobüs gider?**	sheh**heer** mehrk^{y}ehzee**neh** **hahn**g^{y}ee oto**bewss** g^{y}eedehr
Where can I get a bus to ...?	**... e/a giden otobüsü nerede bulabilirim?**	... eh/ah g^{y}eedehn otobew**ssew** **neh**rehdeh **boo**lahbeeleereem
Which bus do I take to Taksim?	**Taksim'e gitmek için hangi otobüse binmeliyim?**	**tahk**seemeh g^{y}eet**mehk** ee**cheen** hahng^{y}ee otobew**sseh** beenmeh-leeyeem
Where's the bus stop?	**Otobüs durağı nerededir?**	oto**bewss** dooraaı **neh**reh-dehbeer
When is the ... bus to Florya?	**Florya'ya ... otobüs ne zaman?**	**flor**yahyah ... oto**bewss** **neh** zahmahn
first/last/next	**ilk/son/gelecek**	eelk/son/g^{y}ehleh**jehk**
How much is it to the park?	**Parka gitmek için ücret ne kadar?**	pahrkah g^{y}eetmehk eecheen ewjreht **neh** kahdahr
Do I have to change buses?	**Aktarma yapmam gerekir mi?**	ahktahrmah yahpmahm g^{y}ehrehk^{y}eer mee
How many bus stops are there to the Blue Mosque?	**Sultanahmet'e kaç durak var?**	sooltahnahhmehteh kahch doorahk vahr
Can you tell me when to get off?	**Ne zaman inmem gerektiğini söyler misiniz?**	**neh** zahmahn eenmehm g^{y}ehrehk**tee**eenee surlehr **mee**sseeneez
I want to get off at the Mosque.	**Camide inmek istiyorum.**	**jah**meedeh eenmehk eestee**yo**room

OTOBÜS DURAĞI
BUS STOP

Dolmuş

Dolmus are shared taxis - a midway solution between taxis and buses. In the city, official stops are marked with a 'D', otherwise just wait until a car (very often a big old American make or a minibus) slows down, enquire *'Dolmuş?'* and name your destination.

Dolmus run prescribed routes but unfortunately there are no printed timetables nor route maps. When giving the driver the fare, always specify for how many people you are paying.

Dolmus?	**Dolmuş?**	dol**moosh**
Are you going to Yildiz park?	**Yıldız parkına gidiyor musunuz?**	yıldız pahrkınah g[y]eedee-yor **moo**ssoonooz
Is the Blue Mosque on a dolmus route?	**Sultanahmet camii yolunuzun üzerinde mi?**	sooltahnahhmeht **jah**-meeee yoloonoozoon ewzehreen**deh** mee

And when paying:

For 2/3, please.	**Buradan iki/üç tane alır mısınız.**	**boo**rahdahn eek[y]ee/ewch tahneh ahlır **mı**ssınız

Underground (subway) *Metro*

At present Istanbul has only a very short underground system consisting of two stations. However, plans are under way to build a system that will be a cross between an underground railway and tram network.

Where's the underground station?	**Metro istasyonu nerededir?**	**meh**tro eestahssyo**noo** **neh**rehdehdeer

Boat service *Vapurlar*

There is no better way of seeing the Bosphorus than taking a ferry from Eminönü in Old Istanbul and making a series of stops in villages along the way. For coastal services and cruises, reserve ahead of time through the Turkish Maritime Lines, which have agents at the quays in all Turkish ports.

When does the next boat for Samsun leave?	**Samsuna gelecek vapur ne zaman hareket ediyor?**	**sahm**soonah g^{y}ehleh**jehk** vahpoor **neh** zahmahn hahrehk^{y}eht ehdeeyor
Where's the embarkation point?	**İskele nerededir?**	eesk^{y}ehleh **neh**rehdehdeer
How long does the crossing take?	**Karşıya geçiş ne kadar zaman sürer?**	kahrshıyah g^{y}ehcheesh **neh** kahdahr zahmahn sewrehr
I'd like to take a cruise.	**Bir vapur gezisi yapmak istiyorum.**	beer vah**poor** g^{y}ehzeessee yahp**mahk** eestee**yo**room
I'd like a ticket to Üsküdar.	**Üsküdara bir vapur bileti istiyorum.**	ewskewdahrah beer vah**poor** beelehtee eestee**yo**room
boat	**vapur**	vah**poor**
cabin	**kamara**	kahmahrah
single	**tek yataklı kamara**	tehk yahtahklı kahmahrah
double	**çift yataklı kamara**	cheeft yahtahklı kahmahrah
deck	**güverte**	g^{y}ew**vehr**teh
ferry	**araba vapuru**	ahrahbah vahpooroo
hydrofoil	**deniz otobüsü**	dehneez otobewssoo
life belt/boat	**cankurtaran simidi/sandalı**	**jahn**koortahrahn seemeedee/sahndahlı
life jacket	**cankurtaran yeleği**	**jahn**koortahrahn yehlayee
port	**liman**	leemahn
ship	**gemi**	g^{y}ehmee

Bicycle hire *Bisiklet kiralama*

I'd like to hire a bicycle.	**Bir bisiklet kiralamak istiyorum.**	beer beesseekleht k^{y}eerahlahmahk eestee**yo**room

Other means of transport *Başka nakil araçları*

cable car	**teleferik**	tehlehfehreek
helicopter	**helikopter**	hehleekoptehr
moped	**küçük motosiklet**	k^{y}ewchewk motosseekleht
motorcycle/scooter	**motosiklet**	motosseekleht

Or perhaps you prefer:

to hitchhike	**otostop yapmak**	otostop yahpmahk
to walk	**yürümek**	yewrewmehk

Car *Araba*

On entering Turkey by car you must have the car registered in your passport and your passport stamped. The use of seatbelts is compulsory and you must carry *two* red-reflector warning triangles, as well as a first-aid kit.

You will find the roads around Istanbul and main tourist areas well-maintained. Elsewhere it's a different story. If you are involved in an accident, however slight, the police must be informed.

Where's the nearest filling station?	**En yakın benzin istasyonu nerededir?**	ehn yah**kın** behn**zeen** eestahssyo**noo neh**reh-dehdeer
Fill it up, please.	**Doldurun, lütfen.**	dol**doo**roon **lewt**fehn
Could you give me ... litres of petrol (gasoline)?	**... litre benzin verir misiniz?**	... leet**reh** behn**zeen** vehreer **mee**sseeneez
super (premium)/ regular/diesel	**süper/normal/ motorin**	sewpehr/normahl/ motoreen
Please check the ...	**... kontrol edebilir misiniz, lütfen.**	... kontrol ehdehbee**leer mee**sseeneez **lewt**fehn
battery	**Aküyü**	ahkewyew
brake fluid	**Hidrolik yağını**	heedroleek yaaını
oil/water	**Yağı/Suyu**	**yaa**ı/soo**yoo**
Would you check the tyre pressure?	**Lâstikleri kontrol eder misiniz?**	laasteeklehree kontrol eh**dehr mee**sseeneez
1.6 front, 1.8 rear.	**Ön taraf 1,6, arkalar 1,8.**	urn tahrahf 1,6 ahrkah-lahr 1,8
Please check the spare tyre, too.	**Yedek lâstiği de kontrol edin, lütfen.**	yehdehk laas**tee**ee deh kontrol ehdeen **lewt**fehn
Can you mend this puncture (fix this flat)?	**Bu lâstiği yamayabilir misiniz?**	boo laas**tee**ee yahmah[y]ahbee**leer mee**sseeneez
Would you change the ..., please?	**Lütfen ... değiştirir misiniz?**	**lewt**fehn ... dayeesh-teereer **mee**sseeneez
bulb	**ampulu**	ahmpoo**loo**
fan belt	**v-kayışını**	vehkah[y]ıshını
spark plugs	**bujiyi**	boozheeyee

CAR HIRE, see page 20

tyre	**lâstiği**	laas**tee**ee
wipers	**cam sileceğini**	**jahm** seelehjayeenee
Would you clean the windscreen (windshield)?	**Ön camı temizler misiniz?**	urn jahmı tehmeez**lehr mee**sseeneez

Asking the way – Street directions *Yol sormak*

Can you tell me the way to ...?	**... yolunu göstere-bilir misiniz?**	... yoloo**noo** gʸurstehreh-bee**leer mee**sseeneez
In which direction is ...?	**... ne yönde?**	... **neh** yurndeh
How do I get to ...?	**...'e nasıl gide-bilirim?**	...eh nahssıl gʸeedehbee-leereem
Are we on the right road for ...?	**... için doğru yolda mıyız?**	... ee**cheen** dawroo yoldah mıyız
How far is the next village?	**Gelecek köy ne kadar uzaklıkta?**	gʸehlehjehk kʸur **neh** kahdahr oozahklıktah
How far is it to ... from here?	**Buradan ...a/e ne var?**	boorahdahn ...ah/eh **neh** vahr
Is there a motorway (expressway)?	**Bir otoyol var mı?**	beer otoyol vahr mı
How long does it take by car/on foot?	**Araba ile/Yürüyerek ne kadar zaman sürer?**	ahrahbah eeleh/yewrew-yehrehk neh kahdahr zahmahn sewrehr
Can I drive to the centre of town?	**Şehir merkezine kadar araba kullana-bilir miyim?**	sheh**heer** mehr**kʸeh**zeeneh kahdahr ahrahbah kool-lahnahbee**leer** meeyeem
Is traffic allowed in the town centre?	**Şehir merkezinde trafik serbest mi?**	sheh**heer** mehr**kʸeh**zeen-deh trah**feek** sehrbehst mee
Can you tell me where ... is?	**...'in, nerede oldu-ğunu bana söyler misiniz?**	...een nehrehdeh ol**doo**oonoo bah**nah** sur-lehr **mee**sseeneez
How can I find this place/address?	**Bu yeri/Bu adresi nasıl bulabilirim?**	boo yehree/boo ahdrehs-see **nah**ssıl boolahbeelee-reem
Can you show me on the map where I am?	**Nerede bulunduğumu haritada gösterir misiniz?**	**neh**rehdeh booloon**doo**-oomoo hahreetahdah-gʸurstehreer **mee**sseeneez

Yanlış yoldasınız.	You're on the wrong road.
Doğru gidin.	Go straight ahead.
Orada ileride solda/ sağda.	It's down there on the left/right.
...ın karşısında/...ın arkasında	opposite/behind ...
...ın yanında/...den/dan sonra	next to/after ...
kuzey/güney/doğu/batı	north/south/east/west
İlk/İkinci kavşağa kadar gidin.	Go to the first/second crossroads (intersection).
Trafik ışıklarında sola dönün.	Turn left at the traffic lights.
Gelecek köşede sağa dönün.	Turn right at the next corner.
İzmir'e giden yolu alın.	Take the Izmir road.
Tek yönlü sokak.	It's a one-way street.
Bursa'ya geri dönmelisiniz.	You have to go back to Bursa.
'Ankara' levhasını takip edin.	Follow signs for Ankara.

Parking *Park etmek*

Is there a car park nearby?	**Yakında bir park yeri var mı?**	yah**kı**ndah beer pahrk yehree vahr mı
May I park here?	**Burada park edebilir miyim?**	boorahdah pahrk ehdeh-beeleer meeyeem
How long can I park here?	**Burada ne kadar zaman park ede-bilirim?**	boorahdah **neh** kahdahr zahmahn pahrk ehdehbee-leereem
What's the charge per hour?	**Saatlik ücreti ne kadar?**	sahahtleek ewjrehtee **neh** kahdahr

PARK YAPMAYINIZ
NO PARKING

Breakdown – Road assistance *Arıza – Yol yardım*

Where's the nearest garage?	**En yakın garaj nerededir?**	ehn yah**kın** gahrahzh **neh**rehdehdeer
My car has broken down.	**Arabam arızalandı.**	ahrah**bahm** ahrızahlahndı
May I use your phone?	**Telefonunuzu kullanabilir miyim?**	tehlehfonoonoozoo koollahnahbeeleer meeyeem
I've had a breakdown at ...	**...'da/de arabam arızalandı.**	...dah/deh ahrahbahm ahrızahlahndı
Can you send a mechanic?	**Bir araba tamircisi gönderir misiniz?**	beer ahrah**bah tah**meerjeessee g^{y}urndehreer **mee**sseeneez
My car won't start.	**Arabam çalışmıyor.**	ahrah**bahm** chahlıshmıyor
The battery is dead.	**Akü boş.**	ahk^{y}**ew** bosh
I've run out of petrol (gasoline).	**Benzinim bitti.**	behnzeeneem bee**ttee**
I have a flat tyre.	**Lâstiğim patlak.**	laas**tee**eem paht**lahk**
The engine is overheating.	**Motor ısınıyor.**	motor ıssınıyor
There's something wrong with the ...	**... bozuk.**	... bo**zook**
brakes	**Frenler**	frehnlehr
carburettor	**Karbüratör**	kahrbewrahturr
exhaust pipe	**Egzoz**	ehgzoz
radiator	**Radyatör**	rahdyahturr
wheel	**Tekerlek**	tehk^{y}ehrlehk
Can you send a breakdown van (tow truck)?	**Bir kurtarma aracı gönderir misiniz?**	beer koortahrmah ahrah**jı** g^{y}urndehreer **mee**sseeneez
Can you give me an estimate?	**Masraf konusunda bir tahmin yapabilir misiniz?**	mahsrahf konoo**ssoon**dah beer tahhmeen yahpahbeeleer **mee**sseeneez

Accident – Police *Kaza – Polis*

Please call the police.	**Lütfen polis çağırın.**	**lewt**fehn po**leess chaa**ırın
There's been an accident. It's about 2 km. from ...	**...'e yaklaşık 2 km mesafede bir kaza oldu.**	...eh yahklahshık 2 k^{y}eelomehtreh meh**ssah**fehdeh beer kahzah **ol**doo

Where's there a telephone?	**Nerede bir telefon var?**	**neh**rehdeh beer tehlehfon vahr
Call a doctor/an ambulance quickly.	**Çabuk bir doktor/ bir ambülans çağırın.**	chah**book** beer doktor/ beer ahmbew**lahns** **chaa**ırın
There are people injured.	**Yaralılar var.**	yahrahlı**lahr** vahr
Here's my driving licence.	**İşte ehliyetim.**	eeshteh ehhleeyeh**teem**
What's your name and address?	**Soyadınız ve adresiniz nedir?**	soyahdınız veh ahdrehsseeneez **neh**deer
What's your insurance company?	**Sigorta şirketiniz, lütfen?**	see**gor**tah sheerk[y]eh-teeneez **lewt**fehn

Road signs *Trafik işaretleri*

ASGARI HIZ	Minimum speed
AZAMİ PARK 1 SAAT	Parking allowed for 1 hour
BAŞKA YOLA VERME	Diversion (detour)
BOZUK YOL/SATIH	Poor surface
DARALAN KAPLAMA	Road narrows
DİKKAT	Caution
DÖNEL KAVŞAK	Roundabout
DÖNEMEÇ	Bend
DUR	Stop
DURMAK YASAKTIR	No stopping
DÜŞÜK BANKET	Low verge
GEÇMEK YASAK	No overtaking (passing)
İNŞAAT	Road works (men working)
IŞIKLI İŞARET	Traffic signals
KAYGAN YOL	Slippery road
KAVŞAK	Junction
OKUL	School
PARK YAPILMAZ	No parking
ÖNCELİK VERMEK	Give way (yield)
SAĞA DÖNÜLMEZ	No right turn
TAŞIT GİREMEZ	No entry
TEHLİKE	Danger
TEHLİKELİ EĞİM	Dangerous hill
TEHLİKELİ VİRAJ	Dangerous bend (curve)
VİRAJ	Bend
YAVAŞ	Slow down
YAYA	Pedestrians

Sightseeing

Where's the tourist office?	**Turizm bürosu nerededir?**	too**reezm** bewro**ssoo** **neh**rehdehdeer
What are the main points of interest?	**Görülmeye değer şeyler nelerdir?**	g^{y}urrewlmeh^{y}eh dayehr sheh^{y}lehr neh**lehr**deer
We're here for ...	**... buradayız.**	... **boo**rahdah^{y}ız
only a few hours	**Sadece birkaç saatliğine**	**sah**dehjeh beer**kahch** sahahtleeeeneh
a day	**Bir günlüğüne**	beer g^{y}ewnlewewneh
a week	**Bir haftalığına**	beer hahftah**lıı**nah
Can you recommend a sightseeing tour/an excursion?	**Bir şehir turu/Bir gezinti tavsiye edebilir misiniz?**	beer sheh**heer** too**roo**/ beer g^{y}ehzeentee tahvseeyeh ehdehbeeleer **mee**sseeneez
Where do we leave from?	**Nereden hareket edeceğiz?**	**neh**rehdehn hahrehk^{y}eht ehdehjayeez
Will the bus pick us up at the hotel?	**Otobüs bizi otelden alacak mı?**	oto**bewss** beezee otehldehn ahlah**jahk** mı
How much does the tour cost?	**Turun fiyatı ne kadardır?**	too**roon** feeyahtı **neh** kahdahrdır
What time does the tour start?	**Tur saat kaçta başlar?**	toor sah**aht** **kahch**tah **bahsh**lahr
Is lunch included?	**Öğle yemeği ücrete dahil mi?**	urleh yehma**yee** ewjreh**teh** dah**heel** mee
What time do we get back?	**Ne zaman geri döneceğiz?**	**neh** zahmahn g^{y}ehree durnehjayeez
Do we have free time in ...?	**...de/da serbest zamanımız olacak mı?**	...deh/dah sehrbehst zahmahnımız olah**jahk** mı
Is there an English-speaking guide?	**İngilizce bilen bir rehber var mı?**	eeng^{y}ee**leez**jeh beelehn beer **rehh**behr vahr mı
I'd like to hire a private guide for ...	**... için bir turist rehberi istiyorum.**	... ee**cheen** beer too**reest** rehhbehree eestee**yo**room
half a day	**Yarım gün**	yahrım g^{y}ewn
a day	**Bir gün**	beer g^{y}ewn

Where is/Where are the ...?	**... nerededir?**	... **neh**rehdehdeer
art gallery	**Sanat galerisi**	sah**naht** gahlehree**ssee**
bazaar	**Çarşı**	chahrshı
botanical gardens	**Botanik bahçesi**	botahneek bahhchehssee
building	**Bina**	bee**nah**
business district	**Ticaret merkezi**	teejahreht mehrk^{y}ehzee
castle	**Şato**	**shah**to
cathedral	**Katedral**	kahtehdrahl
cave	**Mağara**	maaahrah
cemetery	**Mezarlık**	mehzahr**lık**
city centre	**Şehir merkezi**	sheh**heer** mehrk^{y}ehzee
city walls	**Surlar**	soorlahr
church	**Kilise**	k^{y}eeleesseh
concert hall	**Konser salonu**	kon**sehr** sahlonoo
convent	**Manastır**	mah**nahs**tır
court house	**Mahkeme**	mahhk^{y}eh**meh**
downtown area	**Şehir merkezi**	sheh**heer** mehrk^{y}ehzee
exhibition	**Sergi**	sehrg^{y}ee
factory	**Fabrika**	fahbreekah
fair	**Fuar**	fooahr
flea market	**Bit pazarı**	beet pahzahrı
fortress	**Kale**	kah**leh**
fountain	**Çeşme**	chehsh**meh**
gardens	**Park**	pahrk
gate	**Büyük kapı**	bewyewk kahpı
harbour	**Liman**	lee**mahn**
lake	**Göl**	g^{y}url
library	**Kütüphane**	k^{y}ewtewp**hah**neh
market	**Pazar**	pahzahr
memorial	**Anıt**	ah**nıt**
monastery	**Manastır**	mah**nahs**tır
monument	**Âbide**	**ah**beedeh
mosque	**Câmi**	**jaa**mee
museum	**Müze**	**mew**zeh
old town	**Eski şehir**	ehsk^{y}ee sheh**heer**
opera house	**Opera binası**	o**peh**rah beenahssı
palace	**Saray**	sahrah^{y}
park	**Park**	pahrk
parliament building	**Parlamento binası**	pahrlah**mehn**to bee**nah**ssı
planetarium	**Rasathane**	rahsaht**hah**neh
presidential palace	**Cumhurbaşkanlığı köşkü**	joom**hoor**bahshkahnlıı k^{y}urshkew
ruins	**Harabeler**	hahrahbehlehr
shopping area	**Alışveriş merkezi**	ahlıshvehreesh mehrk^{y}ehzee

square	**Meydan**	**meh^{y}**dahn
stadium	**Stadyum**	stahdyoom
statue	**Heykel**	heh^{y}kehl
stock exchange	**Borsa**	borsah
temple	**Tapınak**	tahpınahk
theatre	**Tiyatro**	tee**yah**tro
tomb	**Mezar**	mehzahr
tower	**Kule**	koo**leh**
town hall	**Belediye binası**	behlehdeeyeh beenahssı
university	**Üniversite**	ewneevehrseeteh
zoo	**Hayvanat bahçesi**	hah^{y}vah**naht** bahh-chehssee

Admission *Giriş*

Is ... open on Sundays?	**... pazar günleri açık mıdır?**	... pahzahr g^{y}ewnlehree ah**chık** mıdır
What are the opening hours?	**Hangi saatlerde açıktır?**	hahng^{y}ee sahahtlehrdeh ah**chık**tır
When does it close?	**Ne zaman kapanır?**	**neh** zahmahn kah**pah**nır
How much is the entrance fee?	**Giriş ücreti ne kadar?**	g^{y}eereesh ewjrehtee **neh** kahdahr
Is there any reduction for ...?	**... için indirim var mı?**	... ee**cheen** eendeereem vahr mı
children	**Çocuklar**	chojooklahr
the disabled	**Sakatlar**	sahkahtlahr
groups	**Gruplar**	grooplahr
pensioners	**Emekliler**	ehmehkleelehr
students	**Öğrenciler**	urrehnjeelehr
Do you have a guidebook (in English)?	**(İngilizce) rehber kitabınız var mı?**	(eeng^{y}ee**leez**jeh) rehhbehr k^{y}eetahbınız vahr mı
Can I buy a catalogue?	**Bir katalog satın alabilir miyim?**	beer kahtahlog sahtın ahlahbee**leer** meeyeem
Is it all right to take pictures?	**Fotoğraf çekilebilir mi?**	fotawrahf chehk^{y}eelehbee-leer mee

GİRİŞ SERBEST	ADMISSION FREE
FOTOĞRAF ÇEKMEK YASAKTIR	NO CAMERAS ALLOWED

Here are our tickets.	**İşte biletlerimiz.**	eesh**teh** bee**leht**lehree-meez

Who – What – When? *Kim – Ne – Ne zaman?*

What's that building?	**Bu ne binasıdır?**	boo **neh** beenahssıdır
Who was the ...?	**Bunun ... kimdir?**	boonoon ... k^{y}eemdeer
architect	**mimarı**	meemahrı
artist	**sanatçısı**	sah**naht**chıssı
painter	**ressamı**	rehssahmı
sculptor	**heykeltraşı**	heh^{y}kehltrahshı
Who built it?	**Kim inşa etti?**	k^{y}eem eenshah ehttee
Who painted that picture?	**Bu tabloyu kim yaptı?**	boo tahbloyoo k^{y}eem yahptı
When did he live?	**Ne zaman yaşadı?**	neh zahmahn yahshahdı
When was it built?	**Ne zaman inşa edildi?**	neh zahmahn eenshah ehdeeldee
Where's the house where ... lived?	**... yaşadığı ev nerededir?**	... yahshahdıı ehv **neh**rehdehdeer
We're interested in ...	**... ile ilgileniyoruz.**	... eeleh eelg^{y}eeleh-neeyorooz
antiques	**Antika eşya**	ahn**tee**kah ehshyah
archaeology	**Arkeoloji**	ahrk^{y}eholo**zhee**
art	**Sanat**	sahnaht
botany	**Botanik**	botah**neek**
coins	**Para ve madalya bilimi**	pahrah veh mah**dahl**yah beeleemee
economics	**Ekonomi**	ehkonomee
fine arts	**Güzel sanatlar**	g^{y}ewzehl sahnahtlahr
furniture	**Mobilya**	mo**beel**yah
geology	**Jeoloji**	zheholozhee
handicrafts	**El sanatları**	ehl sahnahtlahrı
history	**Tarih**	tahreeh
medicine	**Tıp**	tıp
music	**Müzik**	mew**zeek**
natural history	**Tabiat bilgisi**	tahbeeaht beelg^{y}eessee
ornithology	**Ornitoloji**	orneetolozhee
painting	**Resim**	reh**sseem**
politics	**Politika**	poleeteekah
pottery	**Çömlekcilik**	churmlehkjeeleek
religion	**Din**	deen
sculpture	**Heykeltraşlık**	heh^{y}k^{y}ehltrahshlık
zoology	**Zooloji**	zo-olozhee
Where's the ... department?	**... bölümü nerede?**	... burlewmew **neh**rehdeh

It's ...

amazing	**Şaşırtıcı.**	shahshırtıjı
awful	**Korkunç.**	kor**koonch**
beautiful	**Güzel.**	g^{y}ewzehl
gloomy	**Karanlık.**	kahrahnlık
impressive	**Etkileyici.**	ehtk^{y}eeleh^{y}eejee
interesting	**İlginç.**	eelg^{y}eench
magnificent	**Olağanüstü.**	olaa**ah**newstew
pretty	**Sevimli.**	sehveemlee
strange	**Tuhaf.**	too**hahf**
tremendous	**Heybetli.**	heh^{y}behtlee
ugly	**Çirkin.**	cheerk^{y}een

Religious services *İbadet*

Turkey is a Moslem country, and you'll certainly want to take the opportunity of visiting some of the nation's historic and impressive mosques.

There are a few rules that visitors should remember when visiting a mosque. You should take off your shoes at the entrance and go barefoot or put on a pair of oversized slippers. Women are not allowed to wander around during prayer time, but are required to stay discreetly at the back of the mosque.

Is there a ... near here?	**Yakınlarda bir ... var mıdır?**	yahkınlahrdah beer ... vahr mıdır
Catholic church	**katolik kilisesi**	kahto**leek** k^{y}eeleessehssee
Protestant church	**protestan kilisesi**	protehstahn k^{y}eelees-sehssee
mosque	**câmi**	jaa**mee**
synagogue	**sinagog**	seenahgog
What time is mass/the service?	**Ayin saat kaçta başlıyor?**	**ah**^{y}een sah**aht kahch**tah bahshlıyor
Where can I find a ... who speaks English?	**İngilizce bilen bir ... nerede bulabilirim?**	eeng^{y}ee**leez**jeh beelehn beer ... **neh**rehdeh boolahbeeleereem
priest/minister/ rabbi	**katolik rahip/ protestan rahip/ haham**	kahto**lleek rah**heep/ protehstahn **rah**heep/ hah**hahm**
I'd like to visit the church/mosque.	**Kiliseyi/Camiyi gezmek istiyorum.**	k^{y}eeleesseh^{y}ee/jah**mee**yee g^{y}ehzmehk eestee**yo**room

In the countryside *Şehir dısında*

Is there a scenic route to Izmir?	**İzmir'e güzel manzaralı bir yol var mı?**	**eez**meereh g^{Y}ewzehl mahnzahrahlı beer yol vahr mı
How far is it to Ankara?	**Ankara ne uzaklıkta?**	**ahn**kahrah neh oozahklık-tah
Can we get there on foot?	**Yürüyerek gidebilir miyiz?**	yewrew**yeh**rehk g^{Y}eedeh-beeleer meeyeez
How high is that mountain?	**Şu dağın yüksekliği ne kadardır?**	shoo **daa**ın yewksehkleeee **neh** kahdahrdır
What kind of ... is that?	**Bu ne çeşit bir ... dır?**	boo neh cheh**sheet** beer ... dır
animal/bird	**hayvan/kuş**	hah^{Y}**vahn**/koosh
flower/tree	**çiçek/ağaç**	chee**chehk**/**aa**ahch

Landmarks *Görüş*

bridge	**köprü**	k^{Y}urprew
cliff	**uçurum**	oochooroom
farm	**çiftlik**	cheeftleek
field	**tarla**	**tahr**lah
footpath	**yol**	yol
forest	**orman**	or**mahn**
garden	**bahçe**	bahhcheh
hill	**tepe**	teh**peh**
house	**ev**	ehv
lake	**göl**	g^{Y}url
meadow	**çayır**	chah^{Y}**ır**
mountain	**dağ**	daa
mountain pass	**geçit**	g^{Y}eh**cheet**
path	**patika**	pah**tee**kah
peak	**tepe**	teh**peh**
pond	**küçük göl**	k^{Y}ewchewk g^{Y}url
river	**nehir**	nehheer
road	**yol**	yol
sea	**deniz**	dehneez
spring	**kaynak**	kah^{Y}nahk
valley	**vâdi**	vaadee
village	**köy**	k^{Y}ur
vineyard	**bağ**	baa
wall	**sur**	soor
waterfall	**şelâle**	shehlaaleh
wood	**orman**	ormahn

ASKING THE WAY, see page 76

Relaxing

Your stay ought to include at least one visit to a nightclub with belly-dancing. Although every Turkish girl can do it, the best and most inventive performers are found at the top night spots – hence the most expensive. Enjoy some traditional folk dancing, like the Spoon Dance or Sword and Shield Dance of Bursa, and if you feel energetic, join in with the folk dancing at your local taverna.

Cinema (movies) – Theatre *Sinema Tiyatro*

What's on at the cinema tonight?	**Bu akşam sinemada ne oynuyor?**	boo **ahk**shahm seeneh-mahdah **neh oy**noo**yor**
What's playing at the ... Theatre?	**... tiyatrosunda ne oynuyor?**	... teeyahtrossoondah neh oynoo**yor**
What sort of play is it?	**Ne tür bir oyundur?**	neh tewr beer o**yoon**door
Who's it by?	**Kimin eseridir?**	k^y^eemeen ehssehreedeer
Can you recommend a ...?	**... tavsiye edebilir misiniz?**	... tahvseeyeh ehdeh-beeleer **mee**sseeneez
good film	**İyi bir film**	eeyee beer feelm
comedy	**Bir komedi**	beer **ko**mehdee
musical	**Bir müzikal**	beer mewzee**kahl**
Where's that new film directed by ... being shown?	**...(n)in yeni filmi nerede gösteriliyor?**	...(n)een yehnee feelmee nehrehdeh g^y^urstehree-leeyor
Who's in it?	**Kimler oynuyor?**	k^y^eemlehr **oy**noo**yor**
Who's playing the lead?	**Baş rolde kim oynuyor?**	bahsh **rol**deh k^y^eem **oy**noo**yor**
Who's the director?	**Rejisörü kim?**	rehzheesurrew k^y^eem
Which theatre is that new play by ... being performed at?	**... yeni oyunu hangi tiyatroda oynuyor?**	... yehnee oyoonoo hahng^y^ee teeyahtrodah **oy**noo**yor**

Is there a sound-and-light show on somewhere?	**Herhangi biryerde ses ve ışık gösterisi var mı?**	hehr**hahng**^{y}ee beer**yehr**deh sehss veh ıshık g^{y}urstehreessee vahr mı
What time does it begin?	**Saat kaçta başlıyor?**	sa**haht kahch**tah **bahsh**lıyor
Are there any seats for tonight?	**Bu akşam için yer var mı?**	boo **ahk**shahm ee**cheen** yehr vahr mı
How much are the tickets?	**Biletler ne kadar?**	beeleht**lehr neh** kahdahr
I'd like to reserve 2 seats for the show on Friday evening.	**Cuma akşamı için iki yer ayırtmak istiyorum.**	joo**mah ahk**shahmı ee**cheen** eek^{y}ee yehr ah^{y}ırtmahk eestee**yo**room
Can I have a ticket for the matinee on Tuesday?	**Salı günü ilk oyun için bir yer istiyorum?**	sah**lı** g^{y}ew**new** eelk o**yoon** ee**cheen** beer yehr eestee**yo**room
I'd like a seat in the stalls (orchestra).	**Salonda bir yer istiyorum.**	sah**lon**dah beer yehr eestee**yo**room
Not too far back.	**Çok arkada olmasın.**	chok **ahr**kahdah **ol**mahssın
Somewhere in the middle.	**Ortalarda bir yerde.**	ortah**lahr**dah beer yehrdeh
How much are the seats in the circle (mezzanine)?	**Balkondaki yerler ne kadar?**	bahlkondahk^{y}ee yehrlehr **neh** kahdahr
May I have a programme, please?	**Bir program verir misiniz?**	beer prograhm vehreer **mee**sseeneez
Where's the cloakroom?	**Vestiyer nerededir?**	vehsteeyehr **neh**rehdeh-deer

Özür dilerim, hepsi satıldı.	I'm sorry, we're sold out.
Sadece balkonda birkaç yer daha var.	There are only a few seats left in the circle (mezzanine).
Biletinizi görebilir miyim?	May I see your ticket?
Yeriniz burası.	This is your seat.

DAYS OF THE WEEK, see page 151

Opera – Ballet – Concert *Opera – Bale – Konser*

Can you recommend a(n) ...?	**... tavsiye edebilir misiniz?**	... tahvseeyeh ehdehbeeleer **mee**sseeneez
ballet	**Bale**	**bah**leh
concert	**Konser**	kon**sehr**
opera/operetta	**Opera/Operet**	ope**h**rah/opehreht
Where's the opera house/concert hall?	**Opera binası/Konser salonu nerededir?**	ope**h**rah bee**nah**ssı/kon**sehr** sahlonoo **neh**rehdehdeer
What's on at the opera tonight?	**Operada bu akşam ne var?**	ope**h**rahdah boo **ahk**shahm **neh** vahr
Who's singing/dancing?	**Kim şarkı söylüyor/Kim dans ediyor?**	k^{y}eem shahrkı surlew**yor**/k^{y}eem dahns ehdee**yor**
Which orchestra is playing?	**Hangi orkestra çalıyor?**	hahng^{y}ee ork^{y}ehstrah chahlı**yor**
What are they playing?	**Hangi eseri çalıyorlar?**	hahng^{y}ee ehssehree chahlı**yor**lahr
Who's the conductor/soloist?	**Orkestra şefi/Solist kimdir?**	ork**^{y}ehs**trah shehfee/so**leest k^{y}eem**deer

Nightclubs *Gece klüpleri*

Can you recommend a good nightclub?	**İyi bir gece klübü tavsiye edebilir misiniz?**	eeyee beer g^{y}ehjeh klewbew tahvseeyeh ehdehbee**leer mee**sseeneez
Is there a floor show?	**Atraksiyon var mı?**	ahtrahkseeyon vahr mı
I'd like to see some belly-dancing.	**Göbek dansı görmek isterim.**	g^{y}urbehk dahnsı g^{y}urrmehk eestehreem
What time does the show start?	**Şov saat kaçta başlıyor?**	shov sah**aht kahch**tah **bahsh**lıyor
Is evening dress required?	**Gece elbisesi mecburi midir?**	g^{y}ehjeh ehlbeessehssee mehjboo**ree** meedeer

Discos *Diskotekler*

Is there a discotheque in town?	**Şehirde diskotek var mı?**	shehheerdeh deeskotehk vahr mı
Would you like to dance?	**Dans eder misiniz?**	dahns ehdehr **mee**sseeneez

Sports *Sporlar*

With such an extensive coastline, swimming and boating are two sports that enjoy a lot of popularity. You'll be able to choose between fashionable beaches that are probably quite crowded and those that are untouched and empty. If you're a boating enthusiast then either hire your own boat or join an organised group tour. And if fishing is your sport, a fisherman can always be found to take you out for a day.

For the more sedentary there are a number of unusual spectator sports, including oil wrestling and camel wrestling. The former should be seen in Edirne in June, when the competitions are held. The spectacle of men wearing leather pants coated all over with oil trying to throw each other down is one not to be missed. Camel wrestling is a meeting of two moody males who snort, spit and spar together until one or other is declared the winner.

Is there a football (soccer) match anywhere this Saturday?	**Bir yerde futbol maçı var mı bu cumartesi?**	beer yehrdeh footbol mahchı vahr mı boo joo**mahr**tehssee
Which teams are playing?	**Hangi takımlar oynuyor?**	hahng^{y}ee tahkımlahr oynoo**yor**
Can you get me a ticket?	**Bana bir bilet alabilir misiniz?**	bahnah beer bee**leht** ahlahbeeleer **mee**sseeneez

basketball	**basketbol**	bahs**keht**bol
boxing	**boks**	boks
car racing	**araba yarışı**	ahrahbah yahrıshı
cycling	**bisiklete binmek**	beesseeklehteh **been**mehk
football (soccer)	**futbol**	**foot**bol
horse racing	**at yarışı**	aht yahrıshı
(horse-back) riding	**ata binmek**	ahtah beenmehk
mountaineering	**dağcılık**	daajılık
skiing	**kayak kaymak**	kah^{y}**ahk kah**^{y}mahk
swimming	**yüzmek**	yewz**mehk**
tennis	**tenis**	tehneess
volleyball	**voleybol**	vo**ley**^{y}bol
wrestling	**güreş**	g^{y}ewrehsh

I'd like to see a wrestling match.	**Bir güreş görmek istiyorum.**	beer g^{y}ewrehsh g^{y}urrmehk eesteе**yo**room
Is there any camel wrestling going on?	**Bir deve güreşi var mı?**	beer dehveh g^{y}ewrehshee vahr mı
What's the admission charge?	**Giriş ücreti ne kadar?**	g^{y}eereesh ewjrehtee **neh** kahdahr
Where's the nearest golf course?	**En yakın golf sahası nerededir?**	ehn yah**kın** golf sahhah**ssı** **neh**rehdehdeer
Where are the tennis courts?	**Tenis kortları nerededir?**	teh**neess kort**lahrı **neh**reh-dehdeer
What's the charge per ...?	**... ne kadardır?**	... **neh** kahdahrdır
day/round/hour	**Günlüğü/Maçı/Saatı**	g^{y}ewnlewew/mah**chı**/ sahah**tı**
Can I hire (rent) rackets?	**Raket kiralıyabilir miyim?**	rahk^{y}eht k^{y}eerahlıyah-bee**leer** meeyeem
Where's the race course (track)?	**Hipodrom nerededir?**	heepodrom **neh**rehdehdeer
Is there any good ... around here?	**Bu bölgede iyi bir ... var mı?**	boo burlg^{y}ehdeh eeyee beer ... vahr mı
fishing/hunting	**balık avlanır mı/ hayvan avlanır mı**	bah**lık** ahvlahnır mı/ hah^{y}**vahn** ahvlahnır mı
Do I need a permit?	**Avlama ruhsatına ihtiyacım var mı?**	**ahv**lahmah roohssahtınah eehtee**yah**jım vahr mı
Where can I get one?	**Nereden alabilirim?**	nehreh**dehn** ahlahbee-leereem
Can one swim in the lake/river?	**Gölde/Nehirde yüzülür mü?**	g^{y}url**deh**/nehheer**deh** yewzewlewr mew
Is there a swimming pool here?	**Burada bir yüzme havuzu var mı?**	**boo**rahdah beer yewzmeh hahvoozoo vahr mı
Is it open-air or indoor?	**Açık havada mı/ Kapalı havada mı?**	ah**chık** hahvahdah mı/ kahpahlı hahvahdah mı
Is it heated?	**Isıtma tertibatı var mıdır?**	ıssıtmah tehrteebahtı vahr mıdır
What's the temperature of the water?	**Suyun ısıgı kaç derecedir?**	sooyoon ıssıı kahch deh-rehjehdeer
Is there a sandy beach?	**Kumlu plaj var mı?**	koomloo plahzh vahr mı

On the beach *Plajda*

Is it safe to swim here?	**Burada yüzmek emniyetli midir?**	**boo**rahdah yewzmehk ehmneeyehtlee meedeer
Is there a lifeguard?	**Yüzme öğretmeni var mıdır?**	yewzmeh urrehtmehnee vahr mıdır
Is it safe for children?	**Çocuklar için emniyetli midir?**	chojooklahr ee**cheen** ehmneeyehtlee meedeer
The sea is very calm.	**Deniz çok sakin.**	dehneez chok sahkeen
There are some big waves.	**Büyük dalgalar var.**	bewyewk dahlgah**lahr** vahr
Are there any dangerous currents?	**Tehlikeli akıntılar var mıdır?**	tehhleek^{y}ehlee ahkıntılahr vahr mıdır
What time is high tide/low tide?	**Met/Cezir ne zamandır?**	meht/jehzeer **neh** zahmahndır
I'd like to hire a/an/some ...	**Bir ... kiralamak istiyorum.**	beer ... k^{y}eerahlah**mahk** eestee**yo**room
deck chair	**şezlong**	shehzlong
motor boat	**motorbot**	motorbot
rowing boat	**kayık**	kah^y**ık**
sailing boat	**yelkenli kayık**	yehlk^{y}ehnlee kah^y**ık**
sunshade (umbrella)	**güneş şemsiyesi**	g^{y}ewnehsh shehmseeyeh-ssee
water skis	**deniz kayağı**	dehneez kah^{y}aaı

ÖZEL PLAJ	PRIVATE BEACH
DENİZE GİRMEK YASAKTIR	NO BATHING

Winter sports *Kış sporları*

I'd like to ski.	**Kayak kaymak istiyorum.**	kah^y**ahk** kah^{y}mahk eestee**yo**room
I want to hire ...	**... kiralamak istiyorum.**	... k^{y}eerahlah**mahk** eestee**yo**room
poles	**Kayak sopası**	kah^y**ahk** sopahssı
ski boots	**Kayak ayakkabısı**	kah^y**ahk** ah^{y}ahkkahbıssı
skiing equipment	**Kayak takımı**	kah^y**ahk** tahkımı
skis	**Kayak**	kah^y**ahk**
Can I take skiing lessons?	**Kayak dersleri alabilir miyim?**	kah^y**ahk** dehrslehree ahlahbee**leer** meeyeem

Making friends

Introductions *Tanıştırmak*

May I introduce ...?	**Size ...i/ı tanıştırabilir miyim?**	seezeh ...ee/ı tahnıshtırahbeeleer meeyeem
John, this is ...	**John, bu ...'dir.**	John boo ...deer
My name is ...	**Adım ...'dir.**	ahdım ...deer
How do you do? (Pleased to meet you)	**Memnum oldum.**	mehmnoom **ol**doom
What's your name?	**Adınız ne?**	ahdınız neh
How are you?	**Nasılsınız?**	nah**ssıl**sınız
Fine, thanks. And you?	**İyiyim, teşekkür ederim. Siz nasılsınız?**	ee**yee**yeem tehsheh**kk^{y}ewr** ehdehreem. seez nah**ssıl**sınız

Follow-up *Daha iyi tanışmak*

How long have you been here?	**Ne zamandan beri buradasınız?**	**neh** zah**mahn**dahn behree boorahdahssınız
We've been here a week.	**Bir haftadır buradayız.**	**beer** hahftahdır boorahdah^{y}ız
Is this your first visit?	**Buraya ilk ziyaretiniz mi?**	boorah^{y}ah eelk zeeyahrehteeneez mee
No, we were here last year.	**Hayır, geçen yıl de buraya gelmiştik.**	hah^{y}ır g^{y}ehchehn yıl deh boorah^{y}ah g^{y}ehlmeeshteek
Are you enjoying your stay?	**Seyahatinizdan hoşlanıyor musunuz?**	seh^{y}ahhahteeneezdahn hoshlahnıyor **moo**ssoonooz
I like the landscape a lot.	**Çevreyi çok beğendim.**	chehvreh^{y}ee chok ba**yehn**deem
Do you travel a lot?	**Çok seyahat eder misiniz?**	chok seh^{y}ahhaht ehdehr **mee**sseeneez
Where do you come from?	**Nerelisiniz?**	**neh**rehleesseeneez
I'm from ...	**... denim/danım.**	... dehneem/dahnım
What nationality are you?	**Ne millettensiniz?**	**neh** meellehttehnseeneez

COUNTRIES, see page 146

I'm American.	**Amerikalıyım.**	ahmehree**kah**lıyım
I'm British.	**İngilizim.**	**eeng**ʸeeleezeem
I'm Canadian.	**Kanadalıyım.**	kah**nah**dahlıyım
I'm Irish.	**İrlandalıyım.**	eer**lahn**dahlıyım
Where are you staying?	**Nerede kalıyorsunuz?**	**neh**rehdeh kahlı**yor**soonooz
Are you on your own?	**Tek başınıza mısınız?**	tehk bahshınızah **mı**ssınız
I'm with my ...	**... beraberim.**	... beh**rah**behreem
wife/husband	**Karımla/Kocamla**	kahrımlah/kojahmlah
family	**Ailemle**	aheelehmleh
children	**Çocuklarımla**	chojooklahrımlah
friend	**Arkadaşımla**	ahrkahdahshımlah

father/mother	**baba/anne**	bahbah/**ahn**neh
son/daughter	**oğul/kız**	**a**wool/kız
brother/sister	**erkek kardeş/kız kardeş**	ehrkʸehk kahrdehsh/kız kahrdehsh
uncle/aunt	**amca, dayı*/hala, teyze****	ahmjah dahʸı/hahlah **teh**ʸzeh
nephew/niece	**erkek yeğen/kız yeğen**	ehrkʸehk yayehn/kız yayehn

Are you married/single?	**Evli misiniz/Bekâr mısınız?**	ehvlee **mee**sseeneez/behkaar **mı**ssınız
Do you have any children?	**Çocuğunuz var mı?**	chojoooonooz vahr mı
What do you think of the country?	**Memleket hakkında ne düşünüyorsunuz?**	mehmlehkʸeht hahkkındah **neh** dewshewnew**yor**soonooz
What do you do?	**Mesleğiniz nedir?**	mehslayeeneez **neh**deer
I'm a student.	**Öğrenciyim.**	urrehnjeeyeem
What are you studying?	**Ne okuyorsunuz?**	**neh** okoo**yor**soonooz
I'm here on a business trip.	**İş seyahatindeyim.**	eesh sehʸahhahteen-dehʸeem
Do you play cards/chess?	**Kağıt/Satranç oynar mısınız?**	kaaıt/sahtrahnch oy**nahr** **mı**ssınız

* Father's/mother's brother; ** father's/mother's sister.

The weather *Hava*

What a lovely day!	**Ne nefis bir gün!**	**neh** nehfeess beer g^{y}ewn
What awful weather!	**Ne korkunç bir hava!**	neh kor**koonch** beer hahvah
Isn't it cold/ hot today?	**Bugün ne soğuk/ sıcak!**	boogewn neh sawook/ sıjahk
Is it usually as warm as this?	**Her zaman böyle sıcak olur mu?**	hehr zahmahn burleh sıjahk o**loor** moo
Do you think it's going to ... tomorrow?	**Sizce yarın hava ... olur?**	seezjeh yahrın hahvah ... o**loor**
be a nice day	**güzel mi**	g^{y}ewzehl mee
rain	**yağmurlu mu**	yaamoorloo moo
snow	**karlı mı**	kahrlı mı
What is the weather forecast?	**Hava raporunda ne dediler?**	hahvah rahpo**roon**dah **neh** dehdeelehr

cloud	**bulut**	booloot
fog	**sis**	seess
frost	**don**	don
ice	**buz**	booz
lightning	**şimşek**	sheemshehk
moon	**ay**	ah^{y}
rain	**yağmur**	**yaa**moor
sky	**gök**	g^{y}urk
snow	**kar**	kahr
star	**yıldız**	yıldız
sun	**güneş**	g^{y}ewnehsh
thunder	**gök gürültüsü**	g^{y}urk g^{y}ewrewltewssew
thunderstorm	**fırtına**	fırtınah
wind	**rüzgâr**	rewz**gaar**

Invitations *Davet*

Would you like to have dinner with us on ...?	**... günü bizimle akşam yemeği yemek ister misiniz?**	... g^{y}ewnew bee**zeem**leh ahkshahm yehmayee yeh**mehk** eestehr **mee**sseeneez
May I invite you to lunch?	**Sizi öğle yemeğine davet edebilir miyim?**	seezee urleh yehmayeeneh dahveht ehdehbee**leer** meeyeem

DAYS OF THE WEEK, see page 151

Can you come round for a drink this evening?	**Bu akşam bir içki içmeye gelebilir misiniz?**	boo ahkshahm beer eechk^{y}ee eechmeh^{y}eh g^{y}ehlehbee**leer** **mee**sseeneez
There's a party. Are you coming?	**Bir parti var. Siz de geliyor musunuz?**	beer **pahr**tee vahr. seez deh g^{y}ehlee**yor** **moo**ssoonooz
That's very kind of you.	**Çok naziksiniz.**	**chok** nahzeekseeneez
Great. I'd love to come.	**Fevkalâde. Büyük bir zevkle gelirim.**	fehvkahlaadeh. bewyewk beer zehvkleh g^{y}ehleereem
What time shall we come?	**Saat kaçta gelelim?**	sahaht kahchtah g^{y}ehlehleem
May I bring a friend?	**Bir arkadaş getirebilir miyim?**	beer **ahr**kahdahsh g^{y}ehteerehbeeleer meeyeem
I'm afraid we have to leave now.	**Maalesef gitmemiz gerekiyor.**	mah**ah**lehssehf g^{y}eetmehmeez g^{y}ehrehk^{y}ee**yor**
Next time you must come to visit us.	**Gelecek sefere de biz sizi bekleriz.**	g^{y}ehlehjehk sehfehreh deh beez seezee **behk**lehreez

Dating *Buluşma*

Do you mind if I smoke?	**Sigara içmem sizi rahatsız eder mi?**	see**gah**rah eech**mehm** seezee rahhahtsız ehdehr mee
Would you like a cigarette?	**Sigara ister misiniz?**	see**gah**rah ees**tehr** **mee**sseeneez
Do you have a light, please?	**Acaba ateşiniz var mı?**	ah**jah**bah ahtehsheeneez vahr mı
Why are you laughing?	**Neden gülüyorsunuz?**	nehdehn g^{y}ewlew**yor**soonooz
Is my Turkish that bad?	**Türkçem o kadar kötü mü?**	tewrkchehm o kahdahr k^{y}urtew mew
Do you mind if I sit here?	**Buraya oturabilir miyim?**	boorah^{y}ah otoorahbee**leer** meeyeem
Can I get you a drink?	**Size bir içki getirebilir miyim?**	seezeh beer eechk^{y}ee g^{y}ehteerehbee**leer** meeyeem
Are you waiting for someone?	**Birisini mi bekliyorsunuz?**	beereesseenee mee behklee**yor**soonooz

Are you free this evening?	**Bu akşam serbest misiniz?**	boo **ahk**shahm sehrbehst **mee**sseeneez
Would you like to go out with me tonight?	**Bu akşam benimle çıkar mısınız?**	boo **ahk**shahm behneem-leh chı**kahr mı**ssınız
Would you like to go dancing?	**Dansa gitmek ister misiniz?**	**dahn**sah g^{y}eet**mehk** eestehr **mee**sseeneez
I know a good discotheque.	**İyi bir diskotek biliyorum.**	eeyee beer deeskotehk beelee**yo**room
Shall we go to the cinema (movies)?	**Sinemaya gidelim mi?**	seenehmah^{y}ah g^{y}eedeh-**leem** mee
Would you like to go for a drive?	**Arabayla gezmek ister misiniz?**	ahrah**bah**^{y}lah g^{y}ehzmehk eester **mee**sseeneez
Where shall we meet?	**Nerede buluşalım?**	**neh**rehdeh boolooshahlım
I'll pick you up at your hotel.	**Sizi otelinizden alırım.**	see**zee** otehleeneezdehn ahlırım
I'll call for you at 8.	**Sizi saat 8'de ararım.**	see**zee** sah**aht** 8 deh ahrahrım
May I take you home?	**Sizi evinize götürebilir miyim?**	see**zee** ehveeneezeh g^{y}urtewrehbee**leer** meeyeem
Can I see you again tomorrow?	**Sizi yarın tekrar görebilir miyim?**	see**zee yah**rın tehkrahr g^{y}urehbee**leer** meeyeem
What's your telephone number?	**Telefon numaranız kaç?**	tehleh**fon** noomahrahnız kahch

and you might answer:

I'd love to, thank you.	**Elbette, teşekkür ederim.**	ehlbehtteh tehshehk**kk^{y}ewr** ehdehreem
Thank you, but I'm busy.	**Teşekkür ederim ama meşgulüm.**	tehshehk**kk^{y}ewr** ehdehreem ahmah mehsh**goo**lewm
Leave me alone, please!	**Rahat bırakın, lütfen!**	rah**haht** bırahkın **lewt**fehn
Thank you, it's been a wonderful evening.	**Teşekkür ederim, fevkalâde bir akşam geçirdim.**	tehshehk**kk^{y}ewr** ehdehreem fehvkah**laa**deh beer **ahk**-shahm g^{y}ehcheerdeem
I've enjoyed myself.	**Çok hoşlandım.**	chok hosh**lahn**dım

Shopping Guide

This shopping guide is designed to help you find what you want with ease, accuracy and speed. It features:

1. A list of all major shops, stores and services (p. 98).
2. Some general expressions required when shopping to allow you to be specific and selective (p. 100).
3. Full details of the shops and services most likely to concern you. Here you'll find advice, alphabetical lists of items and conversion charts listed under the headings below.

LAUNDRY, see page 29/HAIRDRESSER'S, see page 30

Shops, stores and services *Dükkânlar, mağazalar ve hizmet*

Shops normally open from 9 or 9.30 a.m. to 7 p.m., Monday to Saturday. On the coast, some establishments are closed during the afternoon in the summer, but this doesn't apply to enterprises dealing with tourists. Often, small shops in tourist areas will stay open later, as well as opening on Sundays.

The bustling bazaars will be the most fascinating places on the tourist's shopping spree. There especially you'll have to be ready to haggle for many items, though much merchandise now has a set price, some bazaars are immense labyrinths where you'll find everything from shoe laces to gold earrings, from potatoes to fine Bursa silk.

Where's the nearest ...?	**En yakın ... nerededir?**	ehn yah**kın** ... **neh**rehdehdeer
antique shop	**antikacı dükkânı**	**ahn**teekahjı dewkkaanı
art gallery	**sanat galerisi**	sah**naht** gahlehree**ssee**
baker's	**fırın**	fırın
bank	**banka**	**bahn**kah
barber's	**berber**	behrbehr
beauty salon	**güzellik salonu**	g^{y}ewzeh**lleek** sahlo**noo**
bookshop	**kitabevi**	k^{y}ee**tahb**ehvee
butcher's	**kasap dükkânı**	kah**sahp** dewkkaanı
cake shop	**pastane**	pahs**tah**neh
camera shop	**fotoğrafçı dükkânı**	fotawrahfchı dewkkaanı
carpet seller's	**halıcı**	hahlıjı
chemist's	**eczane**	ehj**zah**neh
dairy	**mandıra**	**mahn**dırah
delicatessen	**şarküteri**	shahrk^{y}ewtehree
dentist	**dişçi**	deesh**chee**
department store	**büyük mağaza**	bewyewk **maa**ahzah
dressmaker's	**kadın terzisi**	kahdın tehrzeessee
drugstore	**eczane**	ehj**zah**neh
dry cleaner's	**kuru temizleyici**	kooroo tehmeezleh^y**ee**jee
electrical goods shop	**elektrikçi dükkânı**	ehlehktreek**chee** dewkkaanı
fishmonger's	**balıkçı dükkânı**	bah**lık**chı dewkkaanı
florist's	**çiçekçi dükkânı**	cheechehk**chee** dewkkaanı
furrier's	**kürkçü dükkânı**	k^{y}ewrkchew dewkkaanı
gas station	**benzin istasyonu**	behnzeen eestahsyonoo
gift shop	**hediye dükkânı**	hehdeeyeh dewkkaanı
greengrocer's	**manav**	mah**nahv**
grocer's	**bakkal dükkânı**	bahkkahl dewkkaanı

hairdresser's (ladies/men)	**kuaför/berber**	kooahfurr/behrbehr
hardware store	**nalbur**	**nahl**boor
hospital	**hastane**	hahstahneh
ironmonger's	**nalbur**	**nahl**boor
jeweller's	**kuyumcu**	kooyoom**joo**
laundry	**çamaşırhane**	chahmahshır**hah**neh
library	**kütüphane**	k^{y}ewtewp**hah**neh
market	**pazar**	pah**zahr**
newsagent's	**gazeteci**	gahzehtehjee
newsstand	**bayii**	bah^{y}eeee
optician	**gözlükçü**	g^{y}urzlewkchew
pastry shop	**pastane**	pahs**tah**neh
petrol station	**benzin istasyonu**	behnzeen eestahsyonoo
photographer	**fotoğrafçı**	fotawrahfchı
police station	**karakol**	kahrah**kol**
post office	**postane**	postahneh
second-hand shop	**eskici dükkânı**	ehsk^{y}eejee dewkkaanı
shoemaker's (repairs)	**kunduracı**	**koon**doorahjı
shoe shop	**ayakkabı mağazası**	ah^{y}ahkkahbı maaahzahssi
shopping centre	**alışveriş merkezi**	ahlıshvehreesh mehrk^{y}ehzee
souvenir shop	**hâtıra eşyası satan dükkân**	haatırah ehshyahssı sah-tahn dewkkaan
sporting goods shop	**spor mağazası**	spor **maa**ahzahssı
stationer's	**kirtasiye dükkânı**	k^{y}eertahsseeyeh dewkkaa-nı
supermarket	**süpermarket**	sew**pehr**mahrk^{y}eht
sweet shop	**şekerci dükkânı**	shehk^{y}ehrjee dewkkaanı
tailor's	**erkek terzisi**	ehrk^{y}ehk **tehr**zeessee
tea room	**pastane**	pahstahneh
telegraph office	**postane**	postahneh
tobacconist's	**tütün satıcısı**	tew**tewn** sahtıjıssı
toy shop	**oyuncakçı dükkânı**	o**yoon**jahkchı dewkkaanı
travel agency	**seyahat acentası**	seh^{y}ahhaht ah**jehn**tahssı
vegetable store	**manav**	mahnahv
veterinarian	**veteriner**	vehtehree**nehr**
watchmaker's	**saatçi**	sahahtchee
wine merchant	**şarap tüccarı**	shahrahp tewjjahrı

GİRİŞ	ENTRANCE
ÇIKIŞ	EXIT
İMDAT ÇIKIŞI	EMERGENCY EXIT

General expressions *Genel tabirler*

Where? *Nerede?*

Where's there a good ...?	**Nerede iyi bir ... var?**	**neh**rehdeh eeyee beer ... vahr
Where can I find a ...?	**Nerede ... bulabilirim?**	**neh**rehdeh ... boolahbeelee**reem**
Where's the main shopping area?	**Asıl alış veriş merkezi neredir?**	ahssıl ahlısh vehreesh mehrk^{y}ehzee **neh**rehdehdeer
Is it far from here?	**Buradan uzak mı?**	boorahdahn oo**zahk** mı
How do I get there?	**Oraya nasıl gidebilirim?**	**o**rah^{y}ah nah**ssıl** g^{y}eedehbeeleereem

İNDİRİMLİ SATIŞLAR SALE

Service *Hizmet*

Can you help me?	**Bana yardım edebilir misiniz?**	bahnah **yahr**dım ehdehbeeleer **mee**sseeneez
I'm just looking.	**Sadece bakıyorum.**	**sah**dehjeh bahkı**yo**room
Do you sell ...?	**... satıyor musunuz?**	... sah**tı**yor **moo**ssoonooz
I'd like to buy ...	**... satın almak istiyorum.**	... sahtın ahlmahk eestee**yo**room
Do you have any ...?	**... var mı?**	... vahr mı
Where's the ... department?	**... bölümü nerede?**	... burlewmew **neh**rehdeh
Where is the lift (elevator)/escalator?	**Asansör/Yürüyen merdiven nerede?**	ahssahn**surr**/yewrewyehn mehrdeevehn **neh**rehdeh

That one *Onu*

Can you show me ...?	**... gösterebilir misiniz?**	... g^{y}urstehrehbee**leer** **mee**sseeneez
this/that	**Bunu/Şunu**	boo**noo**/schoo**noo**
the one in the window/in the display case	**Vitrindeki/Camekânın içindekini**	veetreendehkee/jahmehkaanın eecheendehk^{y}eenee

Defining the article *Eşyanın tanımı*

I'd like a ... one.	**... bir tane istiyorum.**	... beer **tah**neh eestee**yo**room
big	**Büyük**	bew**yewk**
cheap	**Ucuz**	oo**jooz**
dark	**koyu renk**	koyoo rehnk
good	**İyi**	eeyee
heavy	**Ağır**	aaır
large	**Büyük**	bew**yewk**
light (weight)	**Hafif**	hah**feef**
light (colour)	**Açık**	ahchık
oval	**Oval**	oh**vahl**
rectangular	**Dikdörtgen**	deekdurrtg^{y}ehn
round	**Yuvarlak**	yoovahrlahk
small	**Küçük**	k^{y}ew**chewk**
square	**Kare**	**kah**reh
sturdy	**Sağlam**	saalahm
I don't want anything too expensive.	**Çok pahalı birşey istemiyorum.**	chok pahhahlı beersheh^y ees**teh**meeyoroom

Preference *Tercih*

Can you show me some others?	**Daha başkalarını gösterebilir misiniz?**	dah**hah** bahshkahlahrını g^{y}urstehrehbeeleer **mee**sseeneez
Don't you have anything ...?	**... birşey yok mu?**	... **beer**sheh^y **yok** moo
cheaper/better	**Daha ucuz/Daha iyi**	dah**hah** oo**jooz**/dah**hah** eeyee
larger/smaller	**Daha büyük/Daha küçük**	dah**hah** bew**yewk**/dah**hah** k^{y}ew**chewk**

How much *Ne kadar?*

How much is this?	**Bu ne kadar?**	boo **neh** kahdahr
How much are they?	**Bu ne kadar?**	boo **neh** kahdahr
I don't understand.	**Anlamıyorum.**	ahn**lah**mıyoroom
Please write it down.	**Lütfen yazar mısınız.**	**lewt**fehn yah**zahr** **mı**ssınız
I don't want to spend more than ... lira.	**... liradan fazla harcamak istemiyorum.**	... leerahdahn fahzlah hahrjahmahk ees**teh**meeyoroom

COLOURS, see page 113

Decision *Karar*

It's not quite what I want.	**Tam olarak istediğim değil.**	tahm olahrahk eestehdeeeem da**yeel**
No, I don't like it.	**Hayır, bunu beğenmedim.**	**hah**^{y}ır boonoo ba**yehn**mehdeem
I'll take it.	**Bunu alacağım.**	boo**noo** ahlahjaaım

Ordering *Ismarlamak*

Can you order it for me?	**Bunu benim için ısmarlar mısınız?**	boo**noo** behneem eecheen ısmahrlahr **mı**ssınız
How long will it take?	**Ne kadar zaman sürer?**	**neh** kahdahr zahmahn sewrehr

Delivery *Teslim*

I'll take it with me.	**Kendim götürürüm.**	k^{y}ehndeem g^{y}urtewrewrewm
Deliver it to the ... Hotel.	**... Oteli'ne teslim edin.**	... otehleeneh tehsleem ehdeen
Please send it to this address.	**Lütfen şu adrese gönderin.**	**lewt**fehn shoo ahdrehsseh g^{y}urndehreen
Will I have any difficulty with the customs?	**Gümrükte herhangi bir zorlukla karşılaşabilir miyim?**	g^{y}ewmrewkteh hehr**hahn**g^{y}ee beer zorlooklah kahrshılahshahbee**leer** meeyeem

Paying *Ödemek*

How much is it?	**Bu ne kadardır?**	boo **neh** kahdahrdır
Can I pay by traveller's cheque?	**Traveller's çeki ile ödeyebilir miyim?**	'traveller's' chehk^{y}ee eeleh urdeh^{y}ehbee**leer** meeyeem
Do you accept dollars/pounds?	**Dolar/Sterlin kabul eder misiniz?**	dolahr/stehrleen kahbool eh**der mee**sseeneez
Can I get the VAT (sales tax) back?	**KDV'yi geri alabilir miyim?**	kahdehvehyee g^{y}ehree ahlahbee**leer** meeyeem
I think there's a mistake in the bill.	**Sanıyorum hesabınızda hata var.**	sahnıyoroom hehssahbınızdah hah**tah** vahr

Anything else? *Başka?*

No, thanks, that's all.	**Yok, mersi, yeter.**	yok mehrsee yeh**tehr**
Yes. I'd like ...	**Evet, ... istiyorum.**	**eh**veht ... eestee**yo**room
Can you show me ...?	**... gösterebilir misiniz?**	... g^{y}urstehrehbee**leer mee**sseeneez
May I have a bag, please?	**Çanta verir misiniz, lütfen?**	chahntah vehreer **mee**sseeneez **lewt**fehn
Could you wrap it up for me, please?	**Benim için sarabilir misiniz, lütfen?**	behneem eecheen sahrahbee**leer mee**sseeneez **lewt**fehn
May I have a receipt?	**Makbuz alabilir miyim?**	mahkbooz ahlahbee**leer** meeyeem

Dissatisfied? *Memnun olmayan*

Can you exchange this, please?	**Bunu değiştirebilir misiniz, lütfen?**	boonoo dayeeshteerehbeeleer **mee**sseeneez **lewt**fehn
I want to return this.	**Şunu geri vermek istiyorum.**	shoonoo g^{y}ehree vehrmehk eestee**yo**room
I'd like a refund.	**Parayı geri almak istiyorum.**	pahrah^{y}ı g^{y}ehree **ahl**mahk eestee**yo**room
Here's the receipt.	**İşte makbuz.**	eesh**teh** mahkbooz

Size yardım edebilir miyim?	Can I help you?
Ne ... istersiniz?	What ... would you like?
renk/biçin **kalite/miktar**	colour/shape quality/quantity
Ne yazık ki bizde yok.	I'm sorry, we don't have any.
Maalesef kalmadı.	We're out of stock.
Onu sizin için ısmarlayalım mı?	Shall we order it for you?
Kendiniz mi götürürsünüz yoksa gönderelim mi?	Will you take it with you or shall we send it?
Daha başka birşey var mı?	Anything else?

Bookshop – Stationer's *Kitabevi – Kırtasiye*

In Turkey, bookshops and stationers' are usually separate shops. Newspapers and magazines are sold at newsstands.

Where's the nearest ...?	**En yakın ... nerededir?**	ehn yah**kın** ... **neh**rehdehdeer
bookshop	**kitabevi**	k^{y}ee**tah**behvee
stationer's	**kırtasiye mağazası**	kır**tah**sseeyeh **maa**ahzahssı
newsstand	**bayii**	**bah**^{y}eeee
Where can I buy an English-language newspaper?	**Nereden bir İngilizce gazete satın alabilirim?**	**neh**rehdehn beer eeng^{y}**ee**leezjeh gahzehteh sahtın ahlahbeelee**reem**
Can you recommend a good bookshop?	**İyi bir kitabevi tavsiye edebilir misiniz?**	eeyee beer k^{y}eetahbehvee tahvseeyeh ehdehbee**leer** **mee**sseeneez
Where's the guidebook section?	**Rehber kitapları nerededir?**	rehh**behr** k^{y}ee**tahp**lahrı **neh**rehdehdeer
Where do you keep the English books?	**İngilizce kitaplar nerede?**	eeng^{y}**ee**leezjeh k^{y}eetahplahr **neh**rehdeh
Do you have any of ...'s books in English?	**...'in ingilizce kitabı var mı?**	...een eeng^{y}ee**leez**jeh k^{y}eetah**bı** vahr mı
Do you have second-hand books?	**Kullanılmış kitabınız var mı?**	koollahnıl**mısh** k^{y}eetahbınız vahr mı
I want to buy a/an/some ...	**... istiyorum.**	... eesteey**o**room
address book	**Bir adres defteri**	beer ahdrehss **dehf**tehree
adhesive tape	**seloteyp**	sehloteh^{y}p
ball-point pen	**Bir tükenmez kalem**	beer tewkehnmehz kah**lehm**
book	**Bir kitap**	beer k^{y}ee**tahp**
calendar	**Takvim**	tahkveem
carbon paper	**Karbon kâğıdı**	kahr**bon** kaaıdı
crayons	**Mum boya**	moom boyah
dictionary	**Bir sözlük**	beer surzlewk
Turkish-English	**Türkçe-İngilizce**	tewrkcheh-eeng^{y}ee**leez**jeh
pocket	**Cep sözlüğü**	jehp surzlewew
drawing pins	**Raptiye**	rahpteeyeh
envelopes	**Birkaç mektup zarfı**	beer**kahch** mehktoop **zah**rfı
eraser	**Bir silgi**	beer seelg^{y}ee

exercise book	**Bir defter**	beer dehftehr
felt-tip pen	**Keçe kalem**	kʸeh**cheh** kah**lehm**
fountain pen	**Bir dolmakalem**	beer dol**mah**kahlehm
glue	**Zamk**	zahmk
grammar book	**Bir gramer kitabı**	beer grah**mehr** kʸeetahbı
guidebook	**Rehber kitabı**	rehhbehr kʸeetah**bı**
ink	**Mürekkep**	mewreh**kkehp**
black/red/blue	**siyah/kırmızı/mavi**	seeyah/kırmızı/mah**vee**
(adhesive) labels	**(Yapışkan) Etiket**	(yahpıshkahn) ehtee**kʸeht**
magazine	**Bir dergi**	beer dehrgʸee
map	**Bir harita**	beer hah**ree**tah
street map	**Bir şehir planı**	beer sheh**heer** plahnı
road map of ...	**Bir karayolları haritası ...**	beer kahrahʸollahrı hahreetahssı
mechanical pencil	**Mekanik kurşun kalem**	mehkahneek koorshoon kahlehm
newspaper	**Bir ... gazetesi**	beer ... gahzehtehssee
American/English	**Amerikan/İngiliz**	ahmehree**kahn**/ eeng**ʸee**leez
notebook	**Bir not defteri**	beer not **dehf**tehree
note paper	**Mektup kâğıdı**	mehktoop kaaıdı
paintbox	**Bir boya kutusu**	beer boyah kootoossoo
paper	**Kâğıt**	kaa**ıt**
paperback	**Bir cep kitabı**	beer jehp kʸeetahbı
paperclips	**Ataş**	ahtahsh
paper napkins	**Kağıt peçete**	kaaıt pehchehteh
paste	**Yapıştırıcı**	yahpıshtırıjı
pen	**Kalem**	kahlehm
pencil	**Bir kurşun kalem**	beer koor**shoon** kahlehm
pencil sharpener	**Bir kalemtıraş**	beer kahlehmtırahsh
playing cards	**Oyun kâğıdı**	o**yoon** kaaıdı
pocket calculator	**Hesap makinesi**	hehssahp mahkʸeenehssee
postcard	**Bir kartpostal**	beer kahrtpostahl
propelling pencil	**Mekanik kurşun kalem**	mehkahneek koor**shoon** kahlehm
refill (for a pen)	**Yedek kalem içi**	yehdehk kahlehm eechee
rubber	**Bir silgi**	beer seelgʸee
ruler	**Bir cetvel**	beer jehtvehl
staples	**Tel raptiye**	tehl rahpteeyeh
string	**Sicim**	see**jeem**
thumbtacks	**Raptiye**	rahpteeyeh
tissue paper	**İpek kâğıdı**	eepehk kaaıdı
tracing paper	**Kopya kâğıdı**	kopyah kaaıdı
travel guide	**Rehber kitabı**	rehhbehr kʸeetahbı
typewriter ribbon	**Bir daktilo şeridi**	beer dahk**tee**lo shehreedee
typing paper	**Daktilo kâğıdı**	dahk**tee**lo kaaıdı
writing pad	**Bir bloknot**	beer bloknot

Camping equipment *Kamp malzemesi*

I'd like a/an/ some ...	**... istiyorum.**	... eestee**yo**room
axe	**Balta**	bahltah
backpack	**Sırt çantası**	sırt **chahn**tahssı
blanket	**Battaniye**	bahtahneeyeh
bottle-opener	**Şişe açacağı**	shee**sheh** ahchahjaaı
bucket	**Kova**	ko**vah**
butane gas	**Bütangaz**	bew**tahn**gahz
campbed	**Kamp yatağı**	kahmp yahtaaı
can opener	**Konserve açacağı**	kon**sehr**veh ahchahjaaı
candles	**Mum**	moom
(folding) chair	**(Portatif) İskemle**	(portahteef) ees**k^{y}ehm**leh
charcoal	**Odun kömürü**	**o**doon k^{y}urmewrew
clothes pegs	**Çamaşır mandalı**	chahmahshır mahndahlı
compass	**Pusula**	poo**ssoo**lah
cool box	**Soğutma çantası**	sawootmah **chahn**tahssı
corkscrew	**Tirbuşon**	teerbooshon
crockery	**Tabak-çanak**	tahbahk-chahnahk
cutlery	**Çatal-bıçak takımı**	chahtahl-bıchahk tahkımı
deck chair	**Şezlong**	shehzlong
first-aid kit	**İlk yardım kutusu**	eelk yahrdım kootoossoo
fishing tackle	**Olta**	**ol**tah
flashlight	**Cep feneri**	jehp fehnehree
food box	**Yiyecek kutusu**	yeeyehjehk kootoossoo
frying pan	**Tava**	tahvah
groundsheet	**Çadır zemini**	chahdır zehmeenee
hammer	**Çekiç**	chehk^{y}eech
hammock	**Hamak**	hah**mahk**
ice pack	**Soğutma torbası**	sawootmah torbahssı
kerosene	**Gazyağı**	**gahz**yaaı
kettle	**Çaydanlık**	chah^{y}dahnlık
lamp	**Lamba**	**lahm**bah
lantern	**Fener**	fehnehr
mallet	**Çekiç**	chehk^{y}eech
map	**Harita**	hahreetah
matches	**Kibrit**	k^{y}eebreet
mattress	**Hava yatağı**	hahvah yahtaaı
methylated spirits	**İspirto**	ees**peer**to
mosquito net	**Cibinlik**	jeebeenleek
pail	**Kova**	kovah
paper napkins	**Kağıt peçete**	kaaıt pehchehteh
paraffin	**Gazyağı**	gahzyaaı
penknife	**Çakı**	chahkı
picnic basket	**Piknik sepeti**	peekneek sehpehtee

CAMPING, see page 32

pillow	**Yastık**	yahstık
plastic bag	**Plastik torba**	plahsteek torbah
rope	**Halat**	hahlaht
rucksack	**Sırt çantası**	sırt chahntahssı
saucepan	**Tencere**	**tehn**jehreh
scissors	**Makas**	mahkahss
screwdriver	**Tornavida**	tornah**vee**dah
sleeping bag	**Uyku tulumu**	ooykoo tooloomoo
(folding) table	**(Portatif) Masa**	(portahteef) mahssah
tent	**Çadır**	chahdır
tent pegs	**Çadır kazıkları**	chahdır kah**zık**lahrı
tent pole	**Çadır direği**	chahdır deerayee
tinfoil	**Alüminyum kâğıdı**	alewmeenyoom kaaıdı
tin opener	**Konserve açacağı**	kon**sehr**veh ahchahjaaı
tool kit	**Âlet çantası**	aaleht chahntahssı
torch	**Cep feneri**	**jehp** fehnehree
vacuum flask	**Termos**	tehrmos
washing-up liquid	**Bulaşık deterjanı**	boolahshık dehtehr**zhah**nı
washing powder	**Çamaşır tozu**	chahmahshır tozoo
water carrier	**Su bidonu**	soo beedonoo
water flask	**Matara**	mah**tah**rah
wood alcohol	**İspirto**	ees**peer**to

Crockery *Tabak – çanak*

cups	**fincanlar**	feenjahnlahr
mugs	**bardaklar**	bahrdahklahr
plates	**tabaklar**	tahbahklahr
saucers	**fincan tabakları**	feen**jahn** tahbahklahrı
tumblers	**bardaklar**	bahrdahklahr

Cutlery *Çatal – bıçak*

forks	**çatallar**	chahtahllahr
knives	**bıçaklar**	bıchahklahr
spoons	**kaşıklar**	kahshıklahr
teaspoons	**çay kaşıkları**	chah^{y} kahshıklahrı
(made of) plastic	**plastikten**	plahsteektehn
(made of) stainless steel	**paslanmaz çelik**	pahslahnmahz chehleek

Chemist's (drugstore) *Eczane*

Chemist's identified by the sign *Eczane* or *Eczanesi*, are open from 8 a.m. to 8 p.m. The address of an all-night chemist's will be in the window. Some drugs (even common ones, like certain types of headache tablets) are occasionally in short supply, so take along with you any drugs that you use on a regular basis. To find out which chemist's is on duty, dial 011.

For perfume and cosmetics, you must go to a *parfümeri*.

This section has been divided into two parts:

1. Pharmaceutical–medicine, first-aid etc ...
2. Toiletry–toilet articles, cosmetics

General *Genel*

Where's the nearest (all-night) chemist's?	**En yakın (nöbetçi) eczane nerededir?**	ehn yah**kın** (nurbehtchee) ehj**zah**neh **neh**rehdehdeer
What time does the chemist's open/close?	**Eczane saat kaçta açılır/kapanır?**	ehj**zah**neh sah**aht kahch**-tah ahchı**lır**/kahpah**nır**

1 – Pharmaceutical *İlaçlar*

I'd like something for ...	**... için birşey istiyorum.**	... eecheen beer**sheh**^{y} eestee**yo**room
a cold/a cough	**Nezle/Öksürük**	nehzleh/urksewrewk
hay fever	**Saman nezlesi**	sah**mahn** nehzlehssee
insect bites	**Böcek sokması**	burjehk sokmahssı
sunburn	**Güneş yanığı**	g^{y}ewnehsh yahnııı
travel sickness	**Yol tutması**	yol tootmahssı
an upset stomach	**Mide bozulması**	**mee**deh bo**zool**mahssı
Can you prepare this prescription for me?	**Şu reçeteyi benim için hazırlar mısınız?**	shoo rehchehteh^{y}ee behneem eecheen hahzır-**lahr** mıssınız
Can I get it without a prescription?	**Reçetesiz alabilir miyim?**	rehchehtehsseez ahlah-bee**leer** meeyeem
Shall I wait?	**Beklemem gerekir mi?**	behklehmehm g^{y}ehreh-**k^{y}eer** mee

DOCTOR, see page 137

Can I have a/an/some ...?	**... alabilir miyim?**	... ahlahbee**leer** meeyeem
analgesic	**Ağrı kesici**	aarı k^y^ehsseejee
antiseptic cream	**Yara merhemi**	yahrah mehrhehmee
aspirin	**Aspirin**	ahspeereen
bandage	**Sargı**	sahrgı
elastic bandage	**Esnek sargı**	ehsnehk sahrgı
Band-Aids	**Plaster**	plahstehr
chlorine tablets	**Klor tabletleri**	klor tahblehtlehree
condoms	**Prezervatif**	prehzehrvahteef
contraceptives	**Doğum kontrol ilacı**	da**woom** kontrol eelahjı
corn plasters	**Nasır için plaster**	nahssır eecheen plahstehr
cotton wool (absorbent cotton)	**Pamuk**	pahmook
cough drops	**Boğaz pastili**	bawahz pahsteelee
disinfectant	**Dezenfektan**	dehzehnfehktahn
ear drops	**Kulak damlası**	koolahk **dahm**lahssı
Elastoplast	**Plaster**	plahstehr
eye drops	**Göz damlası**	g^y^urz **dahm**lahssı
first-aid kit	**İlkyardım çantası**	eelkyahrdım chahntahssı
gauze	**Gazlı bez**	gahzlı behz
insect repellent	**Böceklerden korunmak için ilaç**	burjehklehrdehn koroonmahk eecheen eelahch
iodine	**Tentürdiyod**	tehntewrdeeyod
iron tablets	**Demir hapı**	dehmeer hahpı
laxative	**Müshil**	mewssheel
mouthwash	**Gargara**	gahrgahrah
nose drops	**Burun damlası**	booroon **dahm**lahssı
quinine tablets	**Kinin hapı**	k^y^eeneen hahpı
sanitary towels (napkins)	**Adet bezi**	ahdeht behzee
sleeping pills	**Uyku ilacı**	ooykoo eelahjı
suppositories	**Fitil**	feeteel
... tablets	**... tablet**	... tahbleht
tampons	**Tampon**	tahmpon
thermometer	**Derece**	dehrehjeh
throat lozenges	**Boğaz pastili**	bawahz pahsteelee
tissues	**Kağıt mendil**	kaaıt mehndeel
tranquillizers	**Sakinleştirici**	sahk^y^eenlehshteereejee
vitamin pills	**Vitamin**	veetahmeen

ZEHİR	POISON
İÇİLMEZ	FOR EXTERNAL USE ONLY

2 – Toiletry *Güzellik malzemesi*

I'd like a/an/ some ...	**... istiyorum.**	... eestee**yo**room
after-shave lotion	**Tıraş losyonu**	tırahsh los**yo**noo
astringent lotion	**Yüz losyonu**	yewz losyonoo
bath salts	**Banyo tuzu**	**bahn**yo toozoo
blusher (rouge)	**Allık**	**ah**llık
body lotion	**Vücut losyonu**	vewjoot los**yo**noo
bubble bath	**Banyo köpüğü**	**bahn**yo k^{y}urpewew
cream	**Krem**	krehm
for dry/normal/ greasy skin	**kuru/normal/ yağlı cilt için**	kooroo/normahl/ yaalı jeelt eecheen
cleansing cream	**Temizleme kremi**	tehmeezlehmeh krehmee
foundation cream	**Fondöten kremi**	fondurtehn krehmee
moisturizing cream	**Nemlendirici krem**	nehmlehndeereejee krehm
night cream	**Gece kremi**	g^{y}ehjeh krehmee
deodorant	**Deodorant**	dehodorahnt
emery board	**Manikür takımı**	mahneek^{y}ewr tahkımı
eyebrow pencil	**Kaş kalemi**	kahsh kahlehmee
eyeliner	**Göz kalemi**	g^{y}urz kahlehmee
eye shadow	**Far**	fahr
face flannel	**Makyaj havlusu**	mahkyahzh hahvloossoo
face powder	**Pudra**	**poo**drah
hand cream	**El kremi**	ehl krehmee
lipsalve	**Dudak kremi**	doodahk krehmee
lipstick	**Ruj**	roozh
make-up remover pads	**Makyaj pamuğu**	mahkyahzh pahmoooo
mascara	**Rimel**	reemehl
nail brush	**Tırnak fırçası**	tırnahk fırchahssı
nail clippers	**Tırnak makası**	tırnahk mahkahssı
nail file	**Madeni tırnak törpüsü**	mahdehnee tırnahk **turr**pewssew
nail polish	**Tırnak cilâsı**	tırnahk jeelaassı
nail polish remover	**Aseton**	ahssehton
nail scissors	**Tırnak makası**	tırnahk mahkahssı
oil	**Yağ**	yaa
perfume	**Parfüm**	pahrfewm
powder	**Pudra**	**poo**drah
razor	**Tıraş makinesi**	tırahsh mahk^{y}ee**neh**ssee
razor blades	**Tıraş bıçağı**	tırahsh bıchaaı
rouge	**Allık**	**ah**llık
safety pins	**Çengelli iğne**	chehng^{y}ehllee eeneh
shaving brush	**Tıraş fırçası**	tırahsh fırchahssı

shaving cream	**Tıraş kremi**	tırahsh krehmee
soap	**Sabun**	sahboon
sponge	**Sünger**	sewng^{y}ehr
sun-tan cream	**Güneş kremi**	g^{y}ewnehsh krehmee
sun-tan oil	**Güneş yağı**	g^{y}ewnehsh yaaı
talcum powder	**Talk pudrası**	tahlk poodrahssı
tissues	**Kâğıt mendil**	kaaıt mehndeel
toilet paper	**Tuvalet kâğıdı**	toovahleht kaaıdı
toilet water	**Kolonya**	ko**lon**yah
toothbrush	**Diş fırçası**	deesh fırchahssı
toothpaste	**Diş macunu**	deesh mahjoonoo
tweezers	**Cımbız**	jımbız

For your hair *Saçınız için*

bobby pins	**pens**	pehnss
colour shampoo	**nüans verici boya**	newahns vehreejee boyah
comb	**tarak**	tahrahk
curlers	**bigudi**	bee**goo**dee
dry shampoo	**kuru şampuan**	kooroo shahmpooahn
dye	**saç boyası**	sahch boyahssı
hairbrush	**saç fırçası**	sahch fırchahssı
hair gel	**jöle**	**zhur**leh
hairgrips	**pens**	pehns
hair lotion	**saç losyonu**	sahch los**yo**noo
hairpins	**firkete**	feerk^{y}ehteh
hair slide	**saç tokası**	sahch tokahssı
hair spray	**spreyi**	spreh^{y}ee
setting lotion	**saç sertleştirici**	sahch sehrtlehshtee-reejee
shampoo	**şampuan**	shahmpooahn
for dry/greasy (oily) hair	**kuru/yağlı saç için**	**koo**roo/**yaa**lı sahch eecheen
tint	**nüans verici boya**	newahns vehreejee boyah
wig	**peruk**	pehrook

For the baby *Bebek için*

baby food	**bebek maması**	behbehk mahmahssı
bib	**önlük**	urnlewk
dummy (pacifier)	**emzik**	ehmzeek
feeding bottle	**biberon**	beebehron
nappies (diapers)	**kundak**	koondahk
plastic pants	**plastik çocuk donu**	plahsteek chojook donoo
powder	**talk pudrası**	tahlk poodrahssı

Clothing *Giyim*

If you want to buy something specific, prepare yourself in advance. Look at the list of clothing on page 116. Get some idea of the colour, material and size you want. They're all listed on the next few pages.

General *Genel*

I'd like ...	**... istiyorum.**	... eesteeyoroom
I want ... for a (10-year-old) boy/girl.	**Bir erkek çocuğu/kız çocuğu (10 yaşında) için ... istiyorum.**	beer ehrk^{y}ehk chojoooo/ kız chojoooo (10 yahshın-dah) eecheen ... eesteeyoroom
I'd like something like this.	**Bu çeşit birşey istiyorum.**	boo chehsheet beersheh^y eesteeyoroom
I like the one in the window.	**Vitrindekini beğendim.**	veetreendehk^{y}eenee bayehndeem
How much is that per metre?	**Metresi ne kadar?**	mehtrehssee **neh** kahdahr

1 centimetre (cm.)	= 0.39 in.	1 inch	= 2.54 cm.
1 metre (m.)	= 39.37 in.	1 foot	= 30.5 cm.
10 metres	= 32.81 ft.	1 yard	= 0.91 m.

Colour *Renk*

I'd like something in ...	**... birşey istiyorum.**	... beer**sheh^y** eesteeyoroom
I'd like a darker/ lighter shade.	**Daha koyu/Daha açık tonda birşey istiyorum.**	dah**hah** koyoo/dah**hah** ahchık tondah beer**sheh^y** eesteeyoroom
I'd like something to match this.	**Buna uygun birşey istiyorum.**	boonah ooygoon beer-**sheh^y** eesteeyoroom
I don't like the colour.	**Rengini beğenmedim.**	rehng^{y}eenee bayehnmeh-deem

beige	**bejrengi**	**behzh**rehng^{y}ee
black	**siyah**	seeyahh
blue	**mavi**	mahvee
brown	**kahverengi**	kahhvehrehng^{y}ee
golden	**dore**	doreh
green	**yeşil**	yehsheel
grey	**gri**	gree
mauve	**leylak rengi**	leh^{y}lahk rehng^{y}ee
orange	**portakal rengi**	portah**kahl** rehng^{y}ee
pink	**pembe**	**peh**mbeh
purple	**mor**	mor
red	**kırmızı**	kırmızı
scarlet	**kızıl**	kızıl
silver	**gümüş rengi**	g^{y}ewmewsh rehng^{y}ee
turquoise	**türkuvaz**	tewrkoovahz
white	**beyaz**	beh^{y}ahz
yellow	**sarı**	sahrı
light ...	**açık**	ahchık
dark ...	**koyu**	koyoo

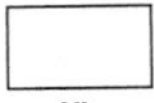

düz
(dewz)

çizgili
(cheez**g^{y}ee**lee)

noktalı
(nok**tah**lı)

kareli
(kah**reh**lee)

desenli
(dehssehnlee)

Fabric *Kumaş*

Do you have anything in ...?	**... kumaşından birşey var mı?**	... koomahshındahn beer**sheh^{y}** vahr mı
Is that ...?	**Bu ...?**	boo
handmade	**el işi mi**	ehl eeshee mee
imported	**ithal malı mı**	eethahl mahlı mı
made here	**yerli mi**	yehrlee mee
I'd like something finer.	**Daha ince birşey istiyorum.**	dah**hah** eenjeh beer**sheh^{y}** eesteeyoroom
Do you have anything of better quality?	**Daha iyi kaliteli birşeyiniz var mı?**	dahhah eeyee kahleetehlee beer**sheh^{y}**eeneez vahr mı
What's it made of?	**Neden yapılmıştır?**	nehdehn yahpılmıshtır

cambric	**patiska**	pahteeskah
camel-hair	**devetüyü**	dehvehtewyew
chiffon	**şifon**	sheefon
corduroy	**fitilli kadife**	feeteellee kahdeefeh
cotton	**pamuklu**	pahmookloo
crepe	**krep**	krehp
denim	**blucin kumaşı**	bloojeen koomahshı
felt	**keçe**	k^y^ehcheh
flannel	**flânel**	flaanehl
gabardine	**gabardin**	gahbahrdeen
lace	**dantel**	**dahn**tehl
leather	**deri**	dehree
linen	**keten**	k^y^ehtehn
poplin	**poplin**	popleen
satin	**saten**	sahtehn
silk	**ipek**	eepehk
suede	**süet**	seweht
towelling	**havlu kumaş**	hahvloo koomahsh
velvet	**kadife**	kahdeefeh
velveteen	**ince fitilli kadife**	eenjeh feeteellee kahdeefeh
wool	**yün**	yewn
worsted	**kamgarn**	kahmgahrn

Is it ...?

pure cotton	**Saf pamuklu mudur?**	sahf pahmookloo moodoor
pure wool	**Saf yünlü müdür?**	sahf yewnlew mewdewr
synthetic	**Sentetik midir?**	sehntehteek meedeer
crease (wrinkle) resistant	**Buruşmaz mı?**	boorooshmahz mı
Is it hand washable/ machine washable?	**El ile mi yıkanır/ Makine ile mi yıkanır?**	ehl eeleh mee yıkahnır/mahk^y^eeneh eeleh mee yıkahnır

Size *Beden*

I take size 38.	**38 beden giyiyorum.**	38 behdehn g^y^ee**yee**yoroom
Could you measure me?	**Ölçülerimi alır mısınız?**	urlchewlehreemee ah**lır** **mıs**sınız
I don't know the Turkish sizes.	**Türkiye'deki bedenleri bilmiyorum.**	tewrk^y^eeyehdehk^y^ee behdehnlehree **beel**meeyoroom

Sizes can vary somewhat from one manufacturer to another, so be sure to try on shoes and clothing before you buy.

Women *Kadın*

Dresses/Suits						
American	8	10	12	14	16	18
British	10	12	14	16	18	20
Turkish	36	38	40	42	44	46

Stockings						
American / British	8	8½	9	9½	10	10½
Continental	0	1	2	3	4	5

Shoes				
American	5½	6½	7½	8½
British	4	5	6	7
Continental	37	38	39	40

Men *Erkek*

Suits/Overcoats						
American / British	36	38	40	42	44	46
Turkish	46	48	50	52	54	56

Shirts				
American / British	15	16	17	18
Turkish	38	41	43	45

Shoes									
American / British	5	6	7	8	8½	9	9½	10	11
Continental	38	39	41	42	43	43	44	45	46

A good fit? *Uydu mu?*

Can I try it on?	**Bunu deneyebilir miyim?**	boo**noo** dehneh^{y}ehbee**leer** meeyeem
Where's the fitting room?	**Giyinme kabini nerededir?**	g^{y}eeyeenmeh kahbeenee **neh**rehdehdeer
Is there a mirror?	**Ayna var mı?**	ah^{y}nah vahr mı
It fits very well.	**Çok iyi uydu.**	chok eeyee **ooy**doo
It doesn't fit.	**Uymadı.**	**ooy**mahdı

NUMBERS, see page 147

It's too ...	**Çok ...**	chok
short/long	**kısa/uzun**	kıssah/oozoon
tight/loose	**dar/bol**	dahr/bol
How long will it take to alter?	**Düzeltmesi ne kadar zaman sürer?**	dew**zehlt**mehssee **neh** kahdahr zahmahn sewrehr

Clothes and accessories *Elbiseler ve aksesuarlar*

I'd like a/an/some ...	**... istiyorum.**	... eestee**yo**room
anorak	**Anorak**	ahnorahk
bathing cap	**Bone**	**bo**neh
bathing suit	**Mayo**	mah^{y}o
bathrobe	**Sabahlık**	sahbahhlık
blouse	**Bulüz**	boolewz
bow tie	**Papyon**	pahpyon
bra	**Sütyen**	sewtyehn
braces	**Pantalon askısı**	pahntahlon ahskıssı
cap	**Kasket**	kahsk^{y}eht
cardigan	**Hırka**	hırkah
coat (woman's/man's)	**Manto/Palto**	**mahn**to/**pahl**to
dress	**Elbise**	ehlbeesseh
dressing gown	**Sabahlık**	sahbahhlık
evening dress (woman's)	**Gece elbisesi**	g^{y}ehjeh ehlbee**ssehs**see
girdle	**Korse**	korseh
gloves	**Eldiven**	ehldeevehn
handbag	**El çantası**	**ehl** chahntahssı
handkerchief	**Mendil**	mehndeel
hat	**Şapka**	shahpkah
jacket	**Ceket**	jehk^{y}eht
jeans	**Blucin**	bloojeen
jersey	**Kazak**	kahzahk
jumper (Br.)	**Kazak**	kahzahk
kneesocks	**Uzun çorap**	oozoon chorahp
nightdress	**Gecelik**	g^{y}ehjehleek
overalls	**Tulum**	tooloom
pair of ...	**Bir çift ...**	beer cheeft
panties	**Külot**	kewlot
pants (Am.)	**Pantalon**	pahntahlon
panty girdle	**Korse**	korseh
panty hose	**Külotlu çorap**	k^{y}ewlotloo chorahp
parka	**Anorak**	ahnorahk

pullover	**Kazak**	kahzahk
polo neck (turtle-neck)	**Dik yakalı**	**deek** yahkahlı
round-neck	**Yuvarlak yakalı**	yoovahr**lahk** yahkahlı
V-neck	**V-yakalı**	**vee**yahkahlı
with long/short sleeves	**Uzun/Kısa kollu**	oozoon/kıssah kolloo
sleeveless	**Kolsuz**	kolsooz
pyjamas	**Pijama**	pee**zhah**mah
raincoat	**Yağmurluk**	yaamoorlook
scarf	**Atkı**	ahtkı
shirt	**Gömlek**	g^{y}urmlehk
shorts	**Şort**	short
skirt	**Etek**	ehtehk
slip	**İç eteklik**	eech ehtehkleek
socks	**Erkek çorabı**	ehrk^{y}ehk chorahbı
sports jacket	**Spor ceket**	spor jehk^{y}eht
stockings	**Çorap**	chorahp
suit (man's)	**Erkek elbisesi**	ehrk^{y}ehk ehlbeessehssee
suit (woman's)	**Tayyör**	tah^{y}yurr
suspenders (Am.)	**Pantalon askısı**	pahntahlon ahskıssı
sweater	**Kazak**	kahzahk
sweatshirt	**Koton kazak**	koton kahzahk
swimming trunks	**Erkek mayosu**	erk^{y}ehk mah^{y}ossoo
swimsuit	**Mayo**	mah^{y}o
T-shirt	**Tişort**	teeshort
tie	**Kravat**	krahvaht
tights	**Külotlu çorap**	kewlotloo chorahp
tracksuit	**Eşofman**	ehshofmahn
trousers	**Pantalon**	pahntahlon
umbrella	**Şemsiye**	shehmseeyeh
underpants	**Don**	don
undershirt	**Fanilâ**	fah**nee**laa
vest (Am.)	**Yelek**	yehlehk
vest (Br.)	**Fanilâ**	fah**nee**laa
waistcoat	**Yelek**	yehlehk

belt	**kemer**	k^{y}ehmehr
buckle	**toka**	**to**kah
button	**düğme**	**dew**meh
collar	**yaka**	yahkah
pocket	**cep**	jehp
press stud (snap fastener)	**çıtçıt**	chıtchıt
zip (zipper)	**fermuar**	fehrmooahr

Shoes *Ayakkabı*

I'd like a pair of ...	**Bir çift ... istiyorum.**	beer cheeft ... eesteeyoroom
boots	**çizme**	cheezmeh
plimsolls (sneakers)	**tenis ayakkabısı**	tehneess ah^{y}ahkkahbıssı
sandals	**sandalet**	sahndahleht
shoes	**ayakkabı**	ah^{y}ahkkahbı
flat	**düz**	dewz
with a heel	**ökçeli**	urkchehlee
with leather soles	**kösele tabanlı**	k^{y}ursehleh tah**bahn**lı
with rubber soles	**kauçuk tabanlı**	kahoochook tah**bahn**lı
slippers	**terlik**	tehrleek
These are too ...	**Çok ...**	chok
narrow/wide	**dar/bol**	dahr/bol
big/small	**büyük/küçük**	bewyewk/k^{y}ewchewk
Do you have a larger/smaller size?	**Daha büyük/Daha küçük numarası yok mu?**	dah**hah** bewyewk/dah**hah** k^{y}ewchewk noomahrahssı yok moo
Do you have the same in black?	**Aynısının siyahı var mı?**	ah^{y}nıssının seeyahhı **vahr** mı
cloth	**kumaş**	koomahsh
leather	**deri**	dehree
rubber	**kauçuk**	kahoochook
suede	**süet**	seweht
Is it real leather?	**Bu gerçek deri midir?**	boo g^{y}ehrchehk dehree meedeer
I need some shoe polish/shoelaces.	**Ayakkabı boyası/bağı lâzım.**	ah^{y}ahkkahbı boyahssı/baaı laazım

Shoes worn out? Here's the key to getting them fixed again:

Can you repair these shoes?	**Bu ayakkabıları tamir edebilir misiniz?**	boo ah^{y}ahkkahbılahrı **tah**meer ehdehbee**leer** **mee**sseeneez
Can you stitch this?	**Bunu dikebilir misiniz?**	boo**noo** deek^{y}ehbee**leer** **mee**sseeneez
I'd like new soles and heels.	**Yeni taban ve ökçe istiyorum.**	yehnee tahbahn veh urkcheh eestee**yo**room
When will they be ready?	**Ne zaman hazır olur?**	**neh** zahmahn hahzır oloor

COLOURS, see page 113

Electrical appliances *Elektrik aletleri*

You will find both 110- and 220-volt, 50 cycles A.C., so check before you plug in.

What's the voltage?	**Voltaj nedir?**	voltahzh **neh**deer
Do you have a battery for this?	**Bunun için bir piliniz var mı?**	boonoon eecheen beer peeleeneez **vahr** mı
This is broken. Can you repair it?	**Bu bozuk. Tamir edebilir misiniz?**	boo bo**zook. tah**meer ehdehbee**leer mee**sseeneez
Can you show me how it works?	**Bunun nasıl çalıştığını bana gösterir misiniz?**	boonoon nahssıl chahlıshtıını bahnah g^{y}urstehr**eer mee**sseeneez
I'd like (to hire) a video cassette.	**Bir video kaset (kiralamak) istiyorum.**	beer vee**deh**o kahsseht (k^{y}eerahlahmahk) eestee**yo**room
I'd like a/an/some ...	**... istiyorum.**	... eestee**yo**room
adaptor	**Adaptör**	ahdahpturr
amplifier	**Amplifikatör**	ahmpleefeekahturr
bulb	**Ampul**	ahmpool
clock-radio	**Uyandıran radyo**	ooyahndırahn rahdyo
electric toothbrush	**Elektrikli diş fırçası**	ehlehktreeklee deesh **fır**chahssı
extension lead (cord)	**Uzatma kordonu**	oozahtmah kordonoo
hair dryer	**Saç kurutma makinesi**	sahch koorootmah mahk^{y}eenehssee
headphones	**Kulaklık**	koolahklık
(travelling) iron	**(Yolculuk için küçük) Ütü**	(yoljoolook eecheen k^{y}ewchewk) ewtew
kettle	**Elektrikli çaydanlık**	ehlehktreeklee chah^{y}dahnlık
lamp	**Lamba**	**lahm**bah
plug	**Fiş**	feesh
portable ...	**Portatif ...**	portahteef
radio	**Radyo**	**rah**dyo
car radio	**Otomobil radyosu**	otomobeel **rahd**yossoo
record player	**Pikap**	peekahp
shaver	**Tıraş makinesi**	tırahsh mahk^{y}eenehssee
speakers	**Hoparlör**	hopahrlurr
(cassette) recorder	**Teyp**	teh^{y}p
(colour) television	**(Renkli) Televizyon**	(rehnklee) tehlehveezyon
transformer	**Transformatör**	trahnsformahturr
video-recorder	**Video**	vee**deh**o

Grocer's *Bakkal dükkânı*

I'd like some bread, please.	**Ekmek istiyorum.**	ehk**mehk** eesteeyoroom
What sort of cheese do you have?	**Ne tür peyniriniz var?**	neh tewr peh^{y}neereeneez vahr
A piece of ...	**Bir parça ...**	beer **pahr**chah
that one	**bundan**	boondahn
the one on the shelf	**raftakinden**	rahftahk^{y}eendehn
I'll have one of those, please.	**Şunlardan bir tane istiyorum, lütfen.**	shoonlahrdahn beer **tah**neh eesteeyoroom **lewt**fehn
May I help myself?	**Kendim alabilir miyim?**	k^{y}ehndeem ahlahbee**leer** meeyeem
I'd like ...	**... istiyorum.**	... eestee**yo**room
a kilo of apples	**Bir kilo elma**	beer k^{y}eelo ehlmah
half a kilo of tomatoes	**Yarım kilo domates**	yahrım k^{y}eelo domahtehss
100 grams of butter	**100 gram tereyağ**	100 grahm teh**reh**^{y}aa
a litre of milk	**1 litre süt**	1 leetreh sewt
half a dozen eggs	**6 tane yumurta**	6 tahneh yoomoortah
4 slices of salami	**4 dilim salam**	4 deeleem sahlahm
a packet of tea	**Bir paket çay**	beer pahk^{y}eht chah^{y}
a jar of jam	**Bir kavanoz reçel**	beer kahvahnoz rehchehl
a tin (can) of peaches	**Bir kutu şeftali**	beer kootoo shehftahlee
a tube of mustard	**Bir tüp hardal**	beer tewp hahrdahl
a box of chocolates	**Bir kutu çukulata**	beer kootoo chookoo**lah**tah

1 kilogram or kilo (kg.) = 1000 grams (g.)

100 g. = 3.5 oz.	½ kg. = 1.1 lb.
200 g. = 7.0 oz.	1 kg. = 2.2 lb.

1 oz. = 28.35 g.
1 lb. = 453.60 g.

1 litre (l.) = 0.88 imp. qt. or 1.06 U.S. qt.

1 imp. qt. = 1.14 l.	1 U.S. qt. = 0.95 l.
1 imp. gal. = 4.55 l.	1 U.S. gal. = 3.8 l.

FOOD, see also page 64

Jeweller's – Watchmaker's *Kuyumcu – Saatçi*

Could I see that, please?	**Şunu görebilir miyim, lütfen?**	**shoo**noo g^{y}urrehbee**leer** meeyeem lewtfehn
Do you have anything in gold?	**Altından birşeyiniz var mı?**	ahltın**dahn beer**sheh^{y}eeneez vahr mı
How many carats is this?	**Bu kaç kırat?**	boo kahch kıraht
Is this real silver?	**Bu gerçek gümüş müdür?**	**boo** g^{y}ehr**chehk** g^{y}ewmewsh mewdewr
Can you repair this watch?	**Bu saati tamir edebilir misiniz?**	**boo** sahahtee tahmeer ehdehbee**leer mee**sseeneez
The ... is broken.	**... kırılmış.**	... kırılmısh
glass/spring strap/winder	**Camı/Yayı** **Kayışı/Pimi**	jahmı/yah^{y}ı kah^{y}ıshı/peemee
I'd like this watch cleaned.	**Bu saati temizletmek istiyorum.**	**boo** sahahtee tehmeezleht**mehk** eesteey**o**room
When will it be ready?	**Ne zaman hazır olur?**	**neh** zahmahn hahzır oloor
I'd like a/an/some ...	**... istiyorum.**	... eestee**yo**room
alarm clock	**Çalar saat**	chahlahr sahaht
battery	**Pil**	peel
bracelet	**Bilezik**	beelehzeek
brooch	**Broş**	brosh
chain	**Zincir**	zeenjeer
cigarette case	**Sigara tabakası**	see**gah**rah tahbahkahssı
cigarette lighter	**Çakmak**	chahkmahk
clip	**İğne**	eeneh
clock	**Saat**	sahaht
cross	**Haç**	hahch
cuff links	**Kol düğmesi**	**kol** dewmehssee
cutlery	**Çatal-bıçak takımı**	chahtahl–bıchahk tahkımı
earrings	**Küpe**	kewpeh
gem	**Değerli taş**	day**ehr**lee tahsh
jewel box	**Mücevher kutusu**	mewjehvhehr kootoossoo
music box	**Müzik kutusu**	mewzeek kootoossoo
necklace	**Kolye**	kolyeh
pendant	**Pandantif**	pahndahnteef
pin	**İğne**	eeneh
pocket watch	**Cep saati**	jehp sahahtee

powder compact	**Pudriyer**	poodreeyehr
ring	**Yüzük**	yewzewk
engagement ring	**Nişan yüzüğü**	nee**shahn** yewzewew
signet ring	**Mühürlü yüzük**	mewhewrlew yewzewk
wedding ring	**Alyans**	ahlyahns
rosary	**Tespih**	tehspeeh
silverware	**Gümüş çatal-bıçak-kaşık**	g^{y}ewmewsh chahtahl-bıchahk-kahshık
tie clip/pin	**Kravat iğnesi**	krahvaht **ee**nehssee
watch	**saat**	sahaht
automatic	**Otomatik**	otomahteek
digital	**Dijital**	deezheetahl
quartz	**Kuars**	kooahrs
with a second hand	**Saniye göstergeli**	**sah**neeyeh g^{y}urstehr-g^{y}ehlee
waterproof	**Su geçirmez**	soo g^{y}ehcheermehz
watchstrap	**Kol saati kayışı**	kol sahahtee kah^{y}ıshı
wristwatch	**Kol saati**	kol sahahtee

amber	**kehribar**	k^{y}ehreebahr
amethyst	**ametist**	ahmehteest
chromium	**krom**	krom
copper	**bakır**	bahkır
coral	**mercan**	mehrjahn
crystal	**kristal**	kreestahl
cut glass	**kesme cam**	k^{y}ehs**meh** jahm
diamond	**elmas**	ehlmahss
emerald	**zümrüt**	zewmrewt
enamel	**mineli**	**mee**nehlee
gold	**altın**	ahltın
gold plated	**altın kaplama**	ahltın kahplahmah
ivory	**fildişi**	**feel**deeshee
jade	**yeşim**	yehsheem
onyx	**oniks**	**o**neeks
pearl	**inci**	eenjee
pewter	**kalay**	kahlah^y
platinum	**platin**	plahteen
ruby	**yâkut**	yaakoot
sapphire	**safir**	sahfeer
silver	**gümüş**	g^{y}ewmewsh
silver plated	**gümüş kaplama**	g^{y}ewmewsh kahplah-mah
stainless steel	**paslanmaz çelik**	pahslahnmahz chehleek
topaz	**topaz**	topahz
turquoise	**firuze**	feeroozeh

Optician *Gözlükçü*

I've broken my glasses.	**Gözlüğüm kırıldı.**	g^{y}urzlewewm kırıl**dı**
Can you repair them for me?	**Tamir edebilir misiniz?**	tahmeer ehdehbee**leer** **mee**sseeneez
When will they be ready?	**Ne zaman hazır olur?**	**neh** zahmahn hahzır oloor
Can you change the lenses?	**Camları değiştirebilir misiniz?**	jahmlahrı dayeeshteereh-bee**leer** **mee**sseeneez
I'd like tinted lenses.	**Renkli cam istiyorum.**	rehnk**lee** jahm eestee**yo**room
The frame is broken.	**Çerçeve kırıldı.**	chehrchehveh kırıl**dı**
I'd like a spectacle case.	**Bir gözlük kılıfı istiyorum.**	beer g^{y}urz**lewk** kılıfı eestee**yo**room
I'd like to have my eyesight checked.	**Gözlerimi kontrol ettirmek istiyorum.**	g^{y}urzlehreemee **kon**trol eht-teer**mehk** eestee**yo**room
I'm short-sighted/long-sighted.	**Ben miyopum/hipermetropum.**	behn meeyo**poom**/heepehrmehtro**poom**
I'd like some contact lenses.	**Kontakt lens istiyorum.**	kon**tahkt** lehns eestee**yo**room
I've lost one of my contact lenses.	**Kontakt lenslerimden birini kaybettim.**	kon**tahkt** lehnslehreem-dehn **bee**reenee kah^{y}beh**tteem**
Could you give me another one?	**Bir yedek lens verebilir misiniz?**	beer yeh**dehk** lehns veh-rehbee**leer** **mee**sseeneez
I have hard/soft lenses.	**Sert/Yumuşak lenslerim var.**	**sehrt**/yoomoo**shahk** lehnslehreem **vahr**
Do you have any contact-lens fluid?	**Kontakt lens sıvısı var mı?**	kon**tahkt** lehns sıvıssı **vahr** mı
I'd like to buy a pair of sunglasses.	**Güneş gözlüğü satın almak istiyorum.**	g^{y}ew**nehsh** g^{y}urzlewew sahtın ahlmahk eestee-**yo**room
May I look in a mirror?	**Aynada kendime bakabilir miyim?**	ah^{y}nahdah k^{y}ehndeemeh bahkahbee**leer** meeyeem
I'd like to buy a pair of binoculars.	**Dürbün satın almak istiyorum.**	dewrbewn sahtın ahlmahk eestee**yo**room
How much do I owe you?	**Borcum ne kadar?**	borjoom **neh** kahdahr

Photography *Fotoğraf*

I'd like a(n) ... camera.	**... bir fotoğraf makinesi istiyorum.**	... beer fotawrahf mahk^y^eenehssee eesteeyoroom
automatic	**Otomatik**	otomahteek
inexpensive	**Pahalı olmayan**	pahhahlı olmah^y^ahn
simple	**Basit**	bahsseet
Can you show me some cine (movie)/ video cameras, please.	**Lütfen bana film/ video kameralarını gösterin.**	lewtfehn bahnah feelm/veedeho kahmehrahlahrını g^y^urstehreen
I'd like to have some passport photos taken.	**Vesikalık fotoğraf çektirmek istiyorum.**	vehsseekahlık fotawrahf chehkteermehk eesteeyoroom

Film *Filmler*

I'd like a film for this camera.	**Bu fotoğraf makinesı için film istiyorum.**	boo fotawrahf mahk^y^eenehssı eecheen feelm eesteeyoroom
black and white	**siyah-beyaz film**	seeyahbeh^y^ahz feelm
colour	**renkli film**	rehnklee feelm
colour negative	**renkli fotoğraf filmi**	rehnklee fotawrahf feelmee
colour slide	**renkli slayd filmi**	rehnklee slah^y^d feelmee
cartridge	**kaset**	kahsseht
disc film	**disk film**	deesk feelm
roll film	**makara film**	mahkahrah feelm
video cassette	**video kaset**	veedeho kahsseht
24/36 exposures	**24/36 pozluk**	24/36 pozlook
this size	**bu büyüklükte**	boo bewyewklewkteh
artificial light type	**suni ışık filmi**	soonee ıshık feelmee
daylight type	**gün ışığı filmi**	g^y^ewn ıshııı feelmee
fast (high-speed)	**yüksek hızlı film**	yewksehk hızlı feelm
fine grain	**ince grenli**	eenjeh grenhnlee

Processing *Banyo etmek*

How much do you charge for processing?	**Banyo için ne kadar ücret alıyorsunuz?**	bahnyo eecheen neh kahdahr ewjreht ahlıyorsoonooz

I'd like ... prints of each negative.	**Her negatiften ... kopya basılmasını istiyorum.**	hehr nehgahteeftehn ... kopyah bahssılmahssını eesteeyoroom
with a mat finish	**mat baskı**	maht bahskı
with a glossy finish	**parlak baskı**	pahrlahk bahskı
Will you enlarge this, please?	**Bunu büyültebilir misiniz, lütfen?**	boonoo bewyewltehbeeleer meesseeneez lewtfehn
When will the photos be ready?	**Fotoğraflar ne zaman hazır olur?**	fotawrahflahr **neh** zahmahn hahzır oloor

Accessories and repairs *Aksesuar ve tamir*

I'd like a/an/some ...	**... istiyorum.**	... eesteeyoroom
battery	**Pil**	peel
cable release	**Deklanşör**	dehklahnshurr
camera case	**Fotoğraf çantası**	fotawrahf **chahn**tahssı
filter	**Filtre**	feeltreh
for black and white	**Siyah-beyaz**	seeyahhbeh^{y}ahz
for colour	**Renkli**	rehnklee
flash cube	**Flaş kübü**	flahsh kewbew
flash gun	**Flaş**	flahsh
lens	**Objektif**	obzhehkteef
telephoto lens	**Teleobjektif**	**teh**lehobzhehkteef
wide-angle lens	**Geniş açılı objektif**	g^{y}ehneesh ahchılı obzhehkteef
lens cap	**Objektif kapağı**	obzhehkteef kahpaaı
Can you repair this camera?	**Bu fotoğraf makinesini tamir edebilir misiniz?**	boo fotawrahf mahk^{y}eeneh-sseenee tahmeer ehdehbeeleer meesseeneez
The film is jammed.	**Film sıkıştı.**	feelm sıkıshtı
There's something wrong with the ...	**... arızalı.**	...**ah**rızahlı
exposure counter	**Poz sayar**	poz sah^{y}ahr
film winder	**Film sarıcı**	feelm sahrıjı
flash attachment	**Flaş**	flahsh
lens	**Objektif**	obzhehkteef
light meter	**Pozometre**	pozo**meh**treh
rangefinder	**Telemetre**	tehleh**meh**treh
shutter	**Obtüratör**	obtewrahturr

NUMBERS, see page 147

Tobacconist's *Tekel bayii*

Turkish tobacco is widely exported and blended to produce well-known cigarettes at home and abroad. Foreign cigarettes are heavily taxed and therefore very expensive.

A packet of cigarettes, please.	**Bir paket sigara, lütfen.**	beer pah**k^{y}eht** see**gah**rah **lewt**fehn
Do you have any American/English cigarettes?	**Amerikan/İngiliz sigarası var mı?**	ahmehreekahn/een**g^{y}ee**leez seegahrahssı **vahr** mı
I'd like a carton.	**Bir karton istiyorum.**	**beer** kahrton eestee**yo**room
Give me a/some ..., please.	**... verin, lütfen.**	... veh**reen lewt**fehn
candy	**Akide şekeri**	ah**k^{y}ee**deh shehk^{y}ehree
chewing gum	**Çiklet**	cheekleht
chocolate	**Çukolata**	chookolahtah
cigarette case	**Bir sigara tabakası**	beer seegahrah tahbahkahssı
cigarette holder	**Bir sigara ağızlığı**	beer seegahrah aaızlıı
cigarettes	**Sigara**	seegahrah
filter-tipped/ without filter	**Filtreli/ Filtresiz**	feeltrehlee/ feeltrehsseez
light/dark tobacco	**Açık/Koyu tütün**	ahchık/koyoo tewtewn
mild/strong	**Hafif/Sert**	hahfeef/sehrt
menthol	**Mentollü**	mehntollew
king-size	**Uzun**	oozoon
cigars	**Birkaç puro**	beerkahch pooro
lighter	**Bir çakmak**	**beer** chahkmahk
lighter fluid/gas	**benzinli/gazlı**	behnzeenlee/gahzlı
matches	**Kibrit**	k^{y}eebreet
pipe	**Bir pipo**	**beer** peepo
pipe cleaners	**Pipo temizleyen**	pee**po** tehmeezleh^{y}ehn
pipe tobacco	**Pipo tütünü**	pee**po** tewtewnew
pipe tool	**Pipo takımı**	pee**po** tahkımı
postcard	**Kartpostal**	**kahrt**postahl
snuff	**Enfiye**	ehnfeeyeh
stamps	**Posta pulu**	**pos**tah pooloo
sweets	**Akide şekeri**	ahk^{y}eedeh shehk^{y}ehree

BÜFE
KIOSK

Miscellaneous *Çeşitli*

Souvenirs *Hatıra*

Bazaars, markets and shops all over Turkey are full of exciting things to buy. Many of the goods make their way to Istanbul but some are better and cheaper in their own areas. Fixed prices are becoming more common but when you do bargain, bargain with firmness. And if you're offered tea or coffee during the process, accept it as a perfectly sincere gesture.

backgammon	**tavla**	**tahv**lah
carpet	**halı**	hahlı
ceramic tiles/ plates	**seramik döşeme/ tabak**	sehrahmeek durshehmeh/ tahbahk
copperware	**bakır eşya**	bahkır ehshyah
crystal	**kristal**	kreestahl
embroidery	**el işi**	**ehl** eeshee
hubble-bubble pipe	**nargile**	nahr**g^y^ee**leh
icon	**ikon**	eekon
leather/suede goods	**deri süet**	dehree seweht
meerschaum pipe	**lületaşı pipo**	lewlehtahshı peepo
prayer mat	**namaz seccâdesi**	nahmahz sehjjaadehssee
samovar	**semaver**	sehmahvehr
spices	**baharatlar**	bahhahrahtlahr
towel	**havlu**	hahvloo
Telkâri silverware	**Telkâri gümüş eşya**	tehlkaaree g^y^ewmewsh ehshyah
Turkish delight	**lokum**	lokoom
worry beads	**tespih**	tehspeeh

Records-Cassettes *Plak-Kaset*

Do you have any records by ...?	**... '(n)in plâğı var mı?**	... (n)een plaaı vahr mı
I'd like a ...	**... istiyorum.**	... eestee**yo**room
(blank) cassette	**Bir (boş) kaset**	beer (bosh) kahsseht
video cassette	**Bir video-kaset**	beer vee**de**ho-kahsseht
compact disc	**Bir kompakt disk**	beer kompahkt deesk

L.P. (33 rpm)	**LP (33 lük)**	ehlpee (33 lewk)
Single (45 rpm)	**45 lik**	45 leek

Can I listen to this record?	**Bu plâğı dinleyebilir miyim?**	**boo** plaaı deenleh^{y}eh-bee**leer** meeyeem
chamber music	**oda müziği**	odah mewzeeee
classical music	**klasik müzik**	**klah**sseek mewzeek
folk music	**halk müziği**	**hahlk** mewzeeee
instrumental music	**enstrümantal müzik**	ehnstrew**mahn**tahl mewzeek
jazz	**caz**	jahz
light music	**hafif müzik**	hah**feef** mewzeek
orchestral music	**orkestra müziği**	ork^{y}**ehs**trah mewzeeee
pop music	**pop müzik**	**pop** mewzeek

Toys *Oyuncaklar*

I'd like a toy/ game ...	**... bir oyuncak/ oyun istiyorum.**	... beer oyoon**jahk**/oyoon eesteey**o**room
for a boy	**Bir erkek çocuk için**	beer ehr**k^{y}ehk** chojook eecheen
for a 5-year-old girl	**5 yaşında bir kız çocuk için**	**5** yahshındah beer **kız** chojook eecheen
(beach) ball	**top (deniz topu)**	top (deh**neez** topoo)
bucket and spade (pail and shovel)	**kova ve kürek**	kovah veh k^{y}ewrehk
buildings blocks (bricks)	**inşaat kutusu**	een**shahaht** kootoossoo
card game	**iskambil oyunu**	eeskahm**beel** oyoonoo
chess set	**satranç takımı**	sah**trahnch** tahkımı
doll	**oyuncak bebek**	oyoon**jahk** behbehk
electronic game	**elektronik oyun**	ehlehktro**neek** oyoon
flippers	**palet**	pahleht
puzzle	**puzzle**	**poozz**leh
roller skates	**tekerlekli paten**	tehk^{y}ehrlehklee pahtehn
snorkel	**şnorkel**	**shnork**^{y}ehl
stuffed animal	**bezden oyuncak hayvan**	behzdehn oyoon**jahk** hah^{y}vahn
toy car	**oyuncak otomobil**	oyoon**jahk** otomobeel

Your money: banks-currency

Banks are open from 8.30 or 9 a.m. to 5 or 5.30 p.m., Monday to Friday, with an hour's lunch break between midday and 1.30 p.m. Currency can usually be exchanged up to 4 p.m. After hours, money can be exchanged at major hotels. Remember to take your passport for identification, and keep the exchange slips.

Eurocheques can be changed at central offices and large branches of major banks. Credit cards are accepted by hotels and establishments used to dealing with visitors. Traveller's cheques can be changed at banks and large hotels. When cashing traveller's cheques in a three-star or higher rated hotel you may find that a small commission is charged. Otherwise the rate should be the same as at the Turkish Central Bank.

At larger banks there's sure to be someone who speaks English. At most tourist resorts, if there isn't a bank, you'll find small currency exchange offices.

Currency *Para*

The monetary unit is the Turkish pound, *lira* (abbreviated TL).

Coins: 50, 100, 500, 1000TL.
Banknotes: 1,000, 5,000, 10,000, 20,000 and 50,000TL.

General *Genel*

Where's the nearest bank?	**En yakın banka nerededir?**	**ehn** yahkın **b**ahnkah neh-rehdehdeer
Where's the nearest currency exchange office?	**En yakın kambiyo bürosu nerededir?**	**ehn** yahkın **kam**beeyo bewrossoo **neh**rehdehdeer

KAMBİYO
CURRENCY EXCHANGE OFFICE

What time does the bank open/close?	**Bankalar saat kaçta açılır/kapanır?**	**bahn**kahlahr sahaht kahchtach ahchı**lır**/ kahpah**nır**

At the bank *Bankada*

I'd like to change some dollars/ pounds.	**Birkaç dolar/sterlin çevirmek istiyorum.**	**beer**kahch dolahr/ stehrleen chehveer**mehk** eestee**yo**room
I'd like to cash a traveller's cheque.	**Traveller's çek bozdurmak istiyorum.**	'traveller's' chehk bozdoor**mahk** eestee**yo**room
What's the exchange rate?	**Kambiyo kuru nedir?**	**kahm**beeyo kooroo **neh**deer
How much commission do you charge?	**Ne kadar komisyon alıyorsunuz?**	**neh** kahdahr komeesyon ahlı**yor**soonooz
Can you telex my bank in London?	**Londra'daki bankama telex çekebilir misiniz?**	londrah dahk^{y}ee **bahn**kahmah **teh**lehx chehk^{y}ehbeeleer **mee**sseeneez
I have a/an/some ...	**... var.**	... **vahr**
credit card	**Kredi kartım**	**kreh**dee kahrtım
Eurocheques	**Öroçekim**	**ur**rochehk^{y}eem
I'm expecting some money from New York. Has it arrived?	**New York'dan para bekliyorum. Geldi mi acaba?**	new york dahn pahrah behklee**yo**room. g^{y}ehl**dee** mee ahjahbah
Please give me ... notes (bills) and some small change.	**Lütfen ... liralık ve gerisini bozuk para verin.**	**lewt**fehn ... leerahlık veh g^{y}ehreesseenee bozook pahrah vehreen
Give me ... large notes and the rest in small notes.	**... liralık bütün para ve gerisini bozuk para verir misiniz.**	... leerahlık bewtewn pahrah veh g^{y}ehreesseenee bozook pahrah vehreer meesseeneez

Deposits – Withdrawals *Yatırmak – Çekmek*

I'd like to ...	**... istiyorum.**	... eestee**yo**room
open an account	**Bir hesap açtırmak**	**beer** hehssahp ahchtır**mahk**
withdraw ... lira	**... lira çekmek**	... leerah chehk**mehk**
How much do I have in my account?	**Hesabımda ne kadar para var?**	hehssahbımdah **neh** kahdahr pahrah vahr

NUMBERS, see page 147

I'd like to pay this into my account.	**Bunu hesabıma yatırmak istiyorum.**	**boo**noo hehssahbımah yahtır**mahk** eestee**yo**room

Business terms *İş terimleri*

My name is ...	**Adım ... dir.**	ahdım ... deer
Here's my card.	**Kartımı vereyim.**	kahrtımı vehreh^{y}eem
I have an appointment with ...	**... ile randevum var.**	... eeleh rahndehvoom **vahr**
Can you give me an estimate of the cost?	**Bana bir fiyat tahmini verebilir misiniz?**	bahnah **beer** feeyaht tahhmeenee vehrehbee**leer** **mee**sseeneez
What's the rate of inflation?	**Enflasyon oranı yüzde kaç?**	ehnflahsyon orahnı yewzdeh kahch
Can you provide me with an interpreter/a secretary?	**Bana bir tercüman/sekreter bulabilir misiniz?**	bahnah beer tehrjewmahn/**seh**krehtehr boolahbee**leer** **mee**sseeneez
Where can I make photocopies?	**Nerede fotokopi çekebilirim?**	**neh**rehdeh fotokopee chehk^{y}ehbeelee**reem**

amount	**miktar**	**meek**tahr
balance	**bilanço**	bee**lahn**cho
capital	**sermaye**	**sehr**mah^{y}eh
cheque	**çek**	**chehk**
contract	**sözleşme**	surz**lehsh**meh
discount	**tenzilat**	tehnzee**laht**
expenses	**masraflar**	mahsrahflahr
export	**ihraç**	eeh**rahch**
import	**ithal**	eet**hahl**
interest	**faiz**	**fah**eez
investment	**yatırım**	**yah**tırım
invoice	**fatura**	**fah**toorah
loss	**kayıp**	kah^{y}ıp
mortgage	**ipotek**	ee**po**tehk
payment	**ödeme**	urdehmeh
percentage	**yüzde**	**yewz**deh
price	**fiyat**	fee**yaht**
profit	**kâr**	**kaar**
purchase	**satın alma**	sahtın ahlmah
sale	**satış**	sah**tısh**
share	**hisse senedi**	**hees**seh sehnehdee
value	**değer**	day**ehr**

At the post office

Post offices can be identified by the letters PTT in black on a yellow background. City post offices, and those in many towns, are open 24 hours a day, weekends included, for telephoning and sometimes for sending telegrams and changing money. For other services they may open until 8 p.m. Smaller offices are open Monday to Saturday until 5 or 6 p.m. only, and may close for lunch.

Street post boxes are yellow. The words *yurt dışı* (yoort dıshı) mean 'abroad', *yurt içi* (yoort eechee) 'inland', and *şehir içi* (shehheer eechee) 'local'.

It is advisable to send all foreign mail by air.

Where's the nearest post office?	**En yakın postane nerededir?**	**ehn** yahkın **pos**tahneh **neh**rehdehdeer
What time does the post office open/close?	**Postane saat kaçta açılır/kapanır?**	**pos**tahneh sahaht kahch**tah** achılır/kahpah**nır**
A stamp for this letter/postcard, please.	**Bu mektup/kartpostal için pul, lütfen.**	**boo** mehktoop/kahrtpostahl eecheen pool **lewt**fehn
A ...-lira stamp, please.	**... liralık posta pulu lütfen.**	... leerahlık **pos**tah pooloo **lewt**fehn
What's the postage for a letter to London?	**Londra'ya mektup kaça gider?**	londrahyah mehktoop **kah**chah **g^{y}ee**dehr
What's the postage for a postcard to Los Angeles?	**Los Angeles'e kartpostal kaça gider?**	los angeles'eh kahrtpostahl **kah**chah **g^{y}ee**dehr
Where's the letter box (mailbox)?	**Posta kutusu nerede acaba?**	**pos**tah kootoossoo **neh**rehdeh ahjahbah
I'd like to send this parcel.	**Bu paketi göndermek istiyorum.**	boo pahk^{y}ehtee g^{y}urndehr**mehk** eestee**yo**room

Do I need to fill in a customs declaration form?	**Gümrük beyanname-si doldurmam lâzım mı?**	g^{y}ewmrewk beh^{y}ahnnah-mehssee doldoormahm **laa**zım mı
I want to send this (by) ...	**Bunu ... göndermek istiyorum.**	**boo**noo ... g^{y}urndehr**mehk** eesteey**o**room
airmail	**uçak ile**	oo**chahk** eeleh
express (special delivery)	**ekspres**	**ehks**prehss
registered mail	**taahhütlü**	tahah**hhewt**lew
At which counter can I cash an international money order?	**Yurt dışından gelen havaleyi hangi gişede bozdurabilirim?**	yoort dı**shın**dahn g^{y}ehlehn hahvahleh^{y}ee **hahn**g^{y}ee g^{y}eeshehdeh bozdoorahbeelee**reem**
Where's the poste restante (general delivery)?	**Postrestant nerededir?**	**post**rehstahnt **neh**rehdeh-deer
Is there any post (mail) for me?	**Benim için posta var mı?**	behneem eecheen postah vahr mı
My name is ...	**Adım ...**	ah**dım**

POSTA PULU	STAMPS
PAKET	PARCELS
HAVALE	MONEY ORDERS

Telegrams – Telex *Telgraf – Telex*

Telegrams to foreign countries can be sent normal or urgent (*acele*); there is also a lightning service (*yıldırım*) for destinations within Turkey.

I'd like to send a telegram/telex.	**Bir telgraf/telex çekmek istiyorum.**	beer **tehl**grahf/**teh**lehx chehk**mehk** eesteey**o**room
May I have a form, please?	**Bir form alabilir miyim, lütfen?**	beer **form** ahlahbee**leer** meeyeem **lewt**fehn
How much is it per word?	**Kelimesi kaçadır?**	k^{y}ehleemehssee kah**chah**-dır
How long will a cable to Boston take?	**Boston'a bir telgraf ne kadar zamanda gider?**	bostonah beer **tehl**grahf **neh** kahdahr zahmahndah g^{y}**ee**dehr

Telephoning *Telefon etmek*

Tokens for public telephones are sold at post offices and sometimes by dealers outside. There are three sizes: large, medium and small. The first two are suitable for long distance and international calls, the third for phoning locally.

Where's the telephone?	**Telefon neresidir?**	**teh**lehfon **neh**rehdehdeer
I'd like a ... telephone token.	**... telefon jetonu istiyorum.**	... **teh**lehfon zhehtonoo eesteе**yo**room
small	**Küçük**	k^{y}ewchewk
medium	**Normal**	normahl
large	**Büyük**	bewyewk
Where's the nearest telephone booth?	**En yakın telefon kulübesi neresidir?**	**ehn** yahkın **teh**lehfon koolewbehssee **neh**rehdehdeer
May I use your phone?	**Telefonunuzu kullanabilir miyim?**	**teh**lehfonoonoozoo koollahnahbee**leer** meeyeem
Do you have a telephone directory for Ankara?	**Ankara telefon rehberi var mı?**	ahnkahrah **teh**lehfon rehhbehree **vahr** mı
I'd like to telephone to England.	**İngiltereye telefon etmek istiyorum.**	eeng^{y}eeltehreh^{y}eh **teh**lehfon ehtmehk eestee**yo**room
What's the dialling (area) code for ...?	**... telefon kodu nedir?**	... **teh**lehfon kodoo **neh**deer
How do I get the international operator?	**Yurt dışına telefon etmek için hangi numarayı çevirmem gerek?**	yoort dıshınah **teh**lehfon ehtmehk eecheen **hahn**g^{y}ee **noo**mahrah^{y}ı chehveermehm **g^{y}eh**rehk

Operator *Santral memuru*

Do you speak English?	**İngilizce biliyor musunuz?**	eeng^{y}eeleezjeh beelee**yor** moossoonooz
I'd like Istanbul 323 45 67.	**İstanbul 323 45 67 istiyorum.**	eestahnbool 323 45 67 eestee**yo**room
Can you get me this number?	**Bu numarayı bağlar mısınız?**	boo **noo**mahrah^{y}ı baalahr mıssınız

NUMBERS, see page 147

I'd like to place a personal (person-to-person) call.	**İhbarlı aramak istiyorum.**	eeh**bahr**lı ahrah**mahk** eesteeyoroom
I'd like to reverse the charges (call collect).	**Ödemeli aramak istiyorum.**	urdehmehlee ahrah**mahk** eesteeyoroom
Will you tell me the cost of the call afterwards?	**Görüşmeden sonra fiyatı söyler misiniz?**	g^{y}urrewshmehdehn sonrah feeyahtı surlehr **mee**sseeneez

Telephone alphabet *Kodlama listesi*

A	**Adana**	ahdahnah	N	**Nazilli**	nahzeellee
B	**Balıkesir**	bahlıkehsseer	O	**Ordu**	ordoo
C	**Ceyhan**	jeh^{y}hahn	Ö	**Ödemiş**	urdehmeesh
Ç	**Çorum**	choroom	P	**Pazar**	pahzahr
D	**Diyarbakır**	deeyahrbakır	Q	**Quebek**	kvehbehk
E	**Edirne**	ehdeerneh	R	**Rize**	reezeh
F	**Fatsa**	fahtsah	S	**Samsun**	sahmsoon
G	**Giresun**	g^{y}eerehssoon	T	**Trabzon**	trahbzon
H	**Hatay**	hahtah^{y}	U	**Urfa**	oorfah
I	**Irmak**	ırmahk	Ü	**Ünye**	ewnyeh
İ	**İstanbul**	eestahnbool	V	**Van**	vahn
J	**Jandarma**	zhahndahrmah	W	**dubl v**	doobl v
K	**Kastamonu**	kahstahmonoo	X	**iks**	eeks
L	**Lüleburgaz**	lewlehboorgahz	Y	**Yozgat**	yozgaht
M	**Manisa**	mahneessah	Z	**Zonguldak**	zongooldahk

Speaking *Konuşmak*

Hello, this is ... speaking.	**Alo, ben ...**	ahlo behn
I'd like to speak to ...	**... ile konuşmak istiyorum.**	... eeleh konooshmahk eesteeyoroom
Is that ...?	**... misiniz.**	... **mee**sseeneez
Speak louder/more slowly, please.	**Daha yüksek/Daha yavaş konuşun, lütfen.**	**dah**hah yewksehk/**dah**hah yahvahsh konooshoon **lewt**fehn

Not there *Yok*

When will he/she be back?	**Ne zaman geri döner?**	**neh** zahmahn g^{y}ehree dur**nehr**

Will you tell him/her I called?	**Aradığımı söyler misiniz?**	ahrahdıımı sur**lehr** **mee**sseeneez
My name is ...	**Adım ...**	ah**dım**
Would you ask him/her to call me?	**Beni aramasını söyler misiniz?**	behnee ahrahmahssını sur-**lehr** **mee**sseeneez
Would you take a message, please?	**Bir mesaj alır mısınız, lütfen?**	beer mehsahzh ah**lır** mıssınız **lewt**fehn

Bad luck *Aksilikler*

Would you try again later, please?	**Biraz sonra tekrar dener misiniz, lütfen?**	beerahz sonrah tehkrahr dehnehr meesseeneez lewtfehn
Operator, you gave me the wrong number.	**Yanlış numara vermişsiniz.**	yahnlısh **noo**mahrah vehrmeeshseeneez

Charges *Ücret*

What was the cost of that call?	**Bu görüşmenin fiyatı ne kadar?**	**boo** g^{y}urrewshmehneen feeyahtı **neh** kahdahr
I want to pay for the call.	**Bu görüşmenin ücretini ödemek istiyorum.**	**boo** g^{y}urrewshmehneen ewjrehteenee urdeh**mehk** eestee**yo**room

Sizi biri telefonla aradı.	There's a telephone call for you.
Hangi numarayı arıyorsunuz?	What number are you calling?
Hatlar meşgul.	The line's engaged.
Cevap vermiyor.	There's no answer.
Yanlış numarayı çevirdiniz.	You've got the wrong number.
Telefon bozuk.	The phone is out of order.
Bir dakika, lütfen.	Just a moment.
Bekleyin, lütfen.	Hold on, please.
Şu anda dışarıda.	He's/She's out at the moment.

Doctor

Most large hotels have doctors on call, many of whom speak a language other than Turkish. Medical standards are high but queues are long at public hospitals, so it would be quicker to contact a private hospital in an emergency. In Ankara, Istanbul and Izmir, there are American hospitals.

General *Genel*

Can you get me a doctor?	**Bana bir doktor çağırır mısınız?**	bahnah beer **dok**tor chaaırır **mı**ssınız
Is there a doctor here?	**Burada doktor var mı?**	**boo**rahdah **dok**tor **vahr** mı
I need a doctor, quickly.	**Çabuk bir doktor lâzım.**	**chah**book beer **dok**tor laazım
Where can I find a doctor who speaks English?	**İngilizce bilen bir doktor nerede bulabilirim?**	eeng^{y}ee**leez**jeh beelehn beer **dok**tor **neh**rehdeh boolahbeelee**reem**
Where's the surgery (doctor's office)?	**Muayenehane neredir?**	mooah^{y}ehnehhahneh **neh**rehdehdeer
What are the surgery (office) hours?	**Muayene saatleri ne zamandır?**	mooah^{y}ehneh sahahtlehree **neh** zahmahndır
Could the doctor come to see me here?	**Doktor beni görmeye buraya gelebilir mi?**	**dok**tor behnee g^{y}urmeh^{y}eh **boo**rah^{y}ah g^{y}ehlehbee**leer** mee
What time can the doctor come?	**Doktor saat kaçta gelebilir?**	**dok**tor sahaht **kahch**tah g^{y}ehlehbee**leer**
Can you recommend a/an ...?	**Bana bir ... tavsiye edebilir misiniz?**	bahnah beer ... tahvseeyeh ehdehbee**leer** **mee**sseeneez
general practitioner	**dahiliyeci**	dahheeleeyehjee
children's doctor	**çocuk doktoru**	cho**jook** doktoroo
eye specialist	**göz doktoru**	**g^{y}urz** doktoroo
gynaecologist	**jinekolog**	zheenehkolog
Can I have an appointment ...?	**... randevu verebilir misiniz?**	... rahndehvoo vehrehbee**leer** **mee**sseeneez
tomorrow	**Yarın için**	**yah**rın eecheen
as soon as possible	**Bir an önce**	**beer** ahn urnjeh

CHEMIST'S, see page 108

Parts of the body *Vücut uzuvları*

appendix	**apandis**	ahpahndeess
arm	**kol**	kol
back	**sırt**	sırt
bladder	**idrar torbası**	eed**rahr** torbahssı
bone	**kemik**	k^{y}ehmeek
bowel	**barsak**	bahrsahk
breast	**meme**	mehmeh
chest	**göğüs**	g^{y}urewss
ear	**kulak**	koolahk
eye(s)	**göz(ler)**	g^{y}urz(lehr)
face	**yüz**	yewz
finger	**parmak**	pahrmahk
foot	**ayak**	ah^{y}ahk
genitals	**cinsel organlar**	jeen**sehl** orgahnlahr
hand	**el**	ehl
head	**baş**	bahsh
heart	**kalp**	kahlp
jaw	**çene**	chehneh
joint	**eklem**	ehklehm
kidney	**böbrek**	burbrehk
knee	**diz**	deez
leg	**bacak**	bahjahk
ligament	**bağ**	baa
lip	**dudak**	doodahk
liver	**karaciğer**	kah**rah**jeeehr
lung	**akciğer**	**ahk**jeeehr
mouth	**ağız**	aaız
muscle	**adele**	ahdehleh
neck	**boyun**	boyoon
nerve	**sinir**	seeneer
nervous system	**sinir sistemi**	see**neer** seestehmee
nose	**burun**	booroon
rib	**kaburga kemiği**	kah**boor**gah k^{y}ehmeeee
shoulder	**omuz**	omooz
skin	**cilt**	jeelt
spine	**belkemiği**	**behl**k^{y}ehmeeee
stomach	**mide**	meedeh
tendon	**kiriş**	k^{y}eereesh
thigh	**but**	boot
throat	**boğaz**	bawahz
thumb	**başparmak**	**bahsh**pahrmahk
toe	**ayakparmağı**	ah^{y}**ahk**pahrmaaı
tongue	**dil**	deel
tonsils	**bademcikler**	bah**dehm**jeeklehr
vein	**damar**	dahmahr

Accident – Injury *Kaza – Yara*

There's been an accident.	**Bir kaza oldu.**	beer kahzah oldoo
My child has had a fall.	**Çocuğum düştü.**	chojoo**oom** dewshtew
He/She has hurt his/her head.	**Başından yaralandı.***	bahshın**dahn** yahrahlahndı
He's/She's unconscious.	**Bayıldı.**	bah^{Y}**ıl**dı
He's/She's bleeding heavily.	**Kanaması var.**	kahnahmahssı **vahr**
He's/She's (seriously) injured.	**(Ağır) Yaralı.**	(aa**ır**) yahrahlı
His/Her arm is broken.	**Kolu kırık.**	koloo kırık
His/Her ankle is swollen.	**Ayak bileği şiş.**	ah^{Y}**ahk** beelayee sheesh
I've been stung.	**Sokuldum.**	sokooldoom
I've got something in my eye.	**Gözümde birşey var.**	g^{Y}urzewmdeh **beer**sheh^{Y} **vahr**
I've got a/an ...	**... var.**	... vahr
boil	**Çıban**	chı**bahn**
bruise	**Çürük**	chewrewk
graze	**Sıyrık**	sıyrık
lump	**Yumru**	yoomroo
rash	**İsilik**	eesseeleek
wound	**Yara**	yahrah
I've got a blister/an insect bite.	**Su topladı/Böcek soktu.**	soo toplahdı/bur**jehk** soktoo
I've ... my hand.	**Elimi ...**	ehleemee
burned	**yaktım**	yahktım
cut	**kestim**	kehsteem
I can't move my ...	**... hareket ettiremiyorum.**	... hahrehk^{Y}eht ehttee**reh**meeyoroom
It hurts.	**Acıyor.**	ahjı**yor**

* Personal pronouns are not normally used, and the verb ending remains the same for both *he* and *she*.

Nereniz acıyor?	Where does it hurt?
Ne zamandan beri bu ağrı var?	How long have you had this pain?
Ne tür ağrıdır?	What kind of pain is it?
hafif/sancılı/nabız gibi atan devamlı/zaman zaman beliren	dull/sharp/throbbing constant/on and off
Kırık/Burkuk Çıkık/Yırtık.	It's broken/It's sprained It's dislocated/It's torn.
Röntgen çekilmesi gerekiyor.	I want you to have an X-ray taken.
Alçıya koymam gerekecek.	I'll have to put it in plaster.
Mikrop kapmış.	It's infected.
Tetanoza karşı aşılandınız mı?	Have you been vaccinated against tetanus?
Size bir iğne yapacağım.	I'll give you an injection.
Size bir ağrı kesici veriyorum.	I'll give you a painkiller.

Illness *Hastalık*

I'm not feeling well.	**Kendimi pek iyi hissetmiyorum.**	k^{y}ehndeemee **pehk** eeyee hee**sseht**meeyoroom
I'm ill.	**Hastayım.**	**hahs**tah^{y}ım
I feel ...		
dizzy	**Başım dönüyor.**	bah**shım** durnewyor
nauseous	**Bulantım var.**	boolahntım vahr
shivery	**Titriyorum.**	teetree**yo**room
I've got a fever.	**Ateşim var.**	ahteh**sheem vahr**
My temperature is 38 degrees.	**Derecem 38°.**	dehrehjehm 38°
I've been vomiting.	**Kustum.**	koos**toom**
I'm constipated.	**Kabızım.**	kahbızım
I've got diarrhoea.	**Barsaklarım bozuk.**	bahrsahklahrım bozook
My ... hurt(s).	**... acıyor.**	... ahjı**yor**

I've got (a/an) ...	**... var.**	... vahr
asthma	**Astımım**	ahstı**mım**
indigestion	**Hazımsızlık**	hahzımsız**lık**
palpitations	**Çarpıntım**	chahrpın**tım**
rheumatism	**Romatizmam**	romahteez**mahm**
ulcer	**Ülserim**	ewlsehreem
I've got (a/an) ...		
backache	**Belim ağrıyor.**	behleem aarı**yor**
cough	**Öksürüyorum.**	urksewrew**yo**room
cramp	**Kramp girdi.**	**krahmp** g^{y}eerdee
earache	**Kulağım ağrıyor.**	koolaaım aarı**yor**
headache	**Başım ağrıyor.**	bah**shım** aarı**yor**
nosebleed	**Burnum kanıyor.**	boor**noom** kahnı**yor**
sore throat	**Boğazım ağrıyor.**	bawah**zım** aarı**yor**
stomach ache	**Midem ağrıyor.**	mee**dehm** aarı**yor**
sunstroke	**Güneş çarptı.**	g^{y}ew**nehsh** chahrptı
stiff neck	**Boynum tutuldu.**	boy**noom** tootooldoo
I have difficulties breathing.	**Nefes zorluğu çekiyorum.**	nehfehss zorloooo chehkee**yo**room
I have a pain in my chest.	**Göğsümde bir ağrı var.**	g^{y}urssewmdeh beer aarı vahr
I had a heart attack ... years ago.	**... yıl evvel kalp krizi geçirdim.**	... yıl ehvvehl **kahlp** kreezee g^{y}ehcheerdeem
My blood pressure is too high/too low.	**Tansiyonum çok yüksek/çok düşük.**	tahnseeyonoom **chok** yewksehk/**chok** dewshewk
I'm allergic to ...	**... e/a allerjim var.**	... eh/ah ahllehr**zheem** vahr
I'm diabetic.	**Şeker hastasıyım.**	sheh**k^{y}ehr** hahstahssı**yım**

Women's section — *Kadın bölümü*

I've got period pains.	**Aybaşı ağrılarım var.**	ah^{y}bah**shı** aarılah**rım** vahr
I have a vaginal infection.	**Dölyolum mikrop kapmış.**	durlyoloom meekrop kahpmısh
I'm on the pill.	**Doğum kontrol hapı alıyorum.**	dawoom kon**trol** hahpı ahlı**yo**room
I haven't had a period for 2 months.	**İki aydır aybaşı olmadım.**	eek^{y}ee ah^{y}dır ah^{y}bahshı **ol**mahdım
I'm (3 months) pregnant.	**(3 aylık) Hamileyim.**	(3 ah^{y}lık) hahmeeleh^{y}eem

Ne kadar zamandan beri kendinizi böyle hissediyorsunuz?	How long have you been feeling like this?
Bu ilk kez mi oluyor?	Is this the first time you've had this?
Ataşinizi/Tansiyonunuzu ölçeceğim.	I'll take your temperature/blood pressure.
Kolunuzu sıvayın, lütfen.	Roll up your sleeve, please.
Lütfen (belinize kadar) soyunun.	Please undress (down to the waist).
Oraya uzanın, lütfen.	Please lie down over there.
Ağzınızı açın.	Open your mouth.
Derin nefes alın.	Breathe deeply.
Neresi acıyor?	Where does it hurt?
... olmuşsunuz.	You've got (a/an) ...
Apandisit	appendicitis
Gastrit	gastritis
Grip	flu
... iltihabı	inflammation of ...
Kızamık	measles
Sarılık	jaundice
Sistit	cystitis
Zatürree	pneumonia
Zehirlenmişsiniz/Zührevi bir hastalığa yakalanmışsınız.	You've got food poisoning/venereal disease.
Bulaşıcıdır/Bulaşıcı değildir.	It's contagious/It's not contagious.
Size bir iğne yapacağım.	I'll give you an injection.
Kan/Abdest/İdrar numunesi istiyorum.	I'd like a specimen of your blood/stools/urine.
... gün yatakta kalmanız gerekiyor.	You must stay in bed for ... days.
Bir uzmana gitmeniz gerekiyor.	I want you to see a specialist.
Genel sağlık kontrolu için hastaneye gitmeniz gerekiyor.	I want you to go to the hospital for a general check-up.

Prescription – Treatment *Reçete – Tedavi*

This is my usual medicine.	**Herzaman bu ilacı alırım.**	**hehr**zahmahn **boo** eelahjı ahlırım
Can you give me a prescription for this?	**Bunun için bir reçete verebilir misiniz?**	**boo**noon eecheen beer rehchehteh vehrehbee**leer mee**sseeneez
Can you prescribe a/an/some ...?	**... için reçete yazabilir misiniz?**	... eecheen rehchehteh yahzahbee**leer mee**-sseeneez
antidepressant	**Depresyona karşı ilaç**	dehprehsyo**nah** kahrshı eelahch
painkiller	**Ağrı kesici**	aarı k^{Y}ehseejee
sleeping pills	**Uyku ilacı**	ooy**koo** eelahjı
tranquillizer	**Sakinleştirici**	sahk^{Y}eenlehshteereejee
I'm allergic to antibiotics/penicillin.	**Antibiotiğe/Penisiline allerjim var.**	ahnteebee**o**teeeh/pehnee**ssee**leeneh **ahl**-lehrzheem vahr
I don't want anything too strong.	**Çok sert birşey istemiyorum.**	**chok** sehrt beersheh^{Y} ees**teh**mee**yo**room
How many times a day should I take it?	**Bundan günde kaç kez almalıyım?**	**boon**dahn g^{Y}ewndeh **kahch** k^{Y}ehz ahlmahlıyım
Must I swallow them whole?	**Bunları bütün olarak mı yutacağım?**	**boon**lahrı bew**tewn** olah-rahk mı yootahjaaım

Nasıl bir tedavi görüyorsunuz?	What treatment are you having?
Hangi ilaçları alıyorsunuz?	What medicine are you taking?
İğneyle mi yoksa ağız yolu ile mı?	By injection or orally?
Bu ilaçtan ... 2 çay kaşığı alın.	Take 2 teaspoons of this medicine ...
... saat'te bir	every ... hours
günde ... kez	... times a day
yemeklerden önce/sonra	before/after each meal
sabah/gece	in the morning/at night
ağrı olursa	if there is any pain
... gün için	for ... days

CHEMIST'S, see page 108

Fee *Ücret*

How much do I owe you?	**Borcum ne kadar?**	borjoom **neh** kahdahr
May I have a receipt for my health insurance?	**Sağlık sigortam için makbuz verir misiniz?**	saa**lık** seegortahm eecheen mahkbooz veh**reer mee**sseeneez
Can I have a medical certificate?	**Bana bir sağlık raporu verir misiniz?**	bahnah beer saa**lık** rahporoo veh**reer mee**sseeneez
Would you fill in this health insurance form, please?	**Bu sağlık sigortası formunu doldurur musunuz, lütfen?**	boo saa**lık** seegortahssı formoonoo doldoo**roor moo**ssoonooz **lewt**fehn

Hospital *Hastane*

Please notify my family.	**Lütfen aileme bildirin.**	**lewt**fehn aheelehmeh beeldeereen
What are the visiting hours?	**Ziyaret saatleri nedir?**	zeeyah**reht** sahahtlehree **neh**deer
When can I get up?	**Ne zaman kalkabilirim?**	**neh** zahmahn kahlkahbeelee**reem**
When is the doctor coming?	**Doktor ne zaman gelecek?**	**dok**tor **neh** zahmahn g^{y}ehlehjehk
I'm in pain.	**Ağrı içindeyim.**	aarı eecheendeh^{y}eem
I can't eat.	**Yemek yiyemiyorum.**	yehmehk yee**yeh**mee**yo**room
I can't sleep.	**Uyuyamıyorum.**	ooyoo**yah**mı**yo**room
Where is the bell?	**Zil nerede?**	zeel **neh**rehdeh

nurse	**hastabakıcı**	hahstahbahkıjı
patient	**hasta**	hahstah
anaesthetic	**anestezi**	ahnehs**teh**zee
blood transfusion	**kan nakli**	kahn nahklee
injection	**iğne**	eeneh
operation	**ameliyat**	ahmehleeyaht
bed	**yatak**	yahtahk
bedpan	**oturak**	otoorahk
thermometer	**derece**	dehrehjeh

Dentist *Dişçi*

Can you recommend a good dentist?	**İyi bir dişçi tavsiye edebilir misiniz?**	ee**yee** beer deeshchee tahvseeyeh ehdehbee**leer mee**sseeneez
Can I make an (urgent) appointment to see Dr. ...?	**Doktor ... den (acele) randevu alabilir miyim?**	**dok**tor ... dehn (ahjehleh) rahndehvoo ahlahbee**leer** meeyeem
Couldn't you make it earlier?	**Daha erken olamaz mi?**	**dah**hah ehrk^{y}ehn o**lah**-mahz mee
I have a broken tooth.	**Dişim kırık.**	dee**sheem** kırık
I have a toothache.	**Dişim ağrıyor.**	dee**sheem** aarı**yor**
I have an abscess.	**Dişimde abse var.**	deesheemdeh ahbseh vahr
This tooth hurts.	**Bu dişim acıyor.**	boo dee**sheem** ahjı**yor**
at the top	**üstteki**	ewstteh**k^{y}ee**
at the bottom	**aşağıdaki**	ahshaaıdah**k^{y}ee**
at the front	**ön taraftaki**	urn tahrahftah**k^{y}ee**
at the back	**arkadaki**	ahrkahdah**k^{y}ee**
Can you fix it temporarily?	**Şimdilik tamir edebilir misiniz?**	sheemdeeleek tahmeer ehdehbee**leer mee**-sseeneez
I don't want it taken out.	**Çekilmesini istemiyorum.**	chehk^{y}eelmehsseenee ees**teh**mee**yo**room
Could you give me an anaesthetic?	**Anestezi verebilir misiniz?**	ahnehs**teh**zee veh-rehbee**leer mee**sseeneez
I've lost a filling.	**Dolgumu kayb ettim.**	dolgoomoo kah^{y}b ehtteem
The gum is ...	**Diş etlerim ...**	**deesh** ehtlehreem
very sore	**çok ağrıyor**	chok aarı**yor**
bleeding	**kanıyor**	kahnı**yor**
I've broken this denture.	**Takma dişlerim kırıldı.**	tahk**mah** deeshlehreem kırıldı
Can you repair this denture?	**Takma dişlerimi tamir edebilir misiniz?**	tahk**mah** deeshlehreemee tahmeer ehdehbee**leer mee**sseeneez
When will it be ready?	**Ne zaman hazır olur?**	**neh** zahmahn hahzır oloor

Reference section

Where do you come from? *Nerelisiniz?*

Africa	**Afrika**	**ahf**reekah
Asia	**Asya**	**ahs**yah
Australia	**Avustralya**	ahvoos**trahl**yah
Europe	**Avrupa**	**ahv**roopah
North America	**Kuzey Amerika**	koo**zeh**^{y} ahmehreekah
South America	**Güney Amerika**	g^{y}ew**neh**^{y} ahmehreekah
Algeria	**Cezayir**	jeh**zah**^{y}eer
Armenia	**Ermenistan**	ehrmehneestahn
Bulgaria	**Bulgaristan**	bool**gah**reestahn
Canada	**Kanada**	**kah**nahdah
China	**Çin**	cheen
Cyprus	**Kıbrıs**	**kı**brıs
Denmark	**Danimarka**	dahnee**mahr**kah
England	**İngiltere**	eeng^{y}eel**teh**reh
France	**Fransa**	**frahn**sah
Georgia	**Gürcüstan**	g^{y}ewrjewstahn
Germany	**Almanya**	ahl**mahn**yah
Great Britain	**Büyük Britanya**	bew**yewk** breetahnyah
Greece	**Yunanistan**	yoo**nah**neestahn
Hungary	**Macaristan**	mahjahreestahn
India	**Hindistan**	**heen**deestahn
Iraq	**Irak**	ırahk
Iran	**İran**	**ee**rahn
Ireland	**İrlanda**	eer**lahn**dah
Italy	**İtalya**	ee**tahl**yah
Japan	**Japonya**	zhah**pon**yah
Luxembourg	**Lüksemburg**	**lewk**sehmboorg
Netherlands	**Hollanda**	**ho**llahndah
New Zealand	**Yeni Zelanda**	yeh**nee** zeh**lahn**dah
Poland	**Polonya**	po**lon**yah
Russia	**Rusya**	**roos**yah
Scotland	**İskoçya**	ees**koch**vah
Spain	**İspanya**	**ees**pahnyah
Sweden	**İsveç**	**ees**vehch
Switzerland	**İsviçre**	ees**veech**reh
Syria	**Suriye**	**soo**reeyeh
Turkey	**Türkiye**	**tewr**keeyeh
United States	**Amerika Birleşik Devletleri**	ahmehreekah beerleh**sheek** dehvlehtlehree
Wales	**Galler Ülkesi**	gah**llehr** ewlk^{y}**eh**ssee

Numbers *Sayılar*

0	**sıfir**	sıfir
1	**bir**	beer
2	**iki**	**eek^{y}ee**
3	**üç**	ewch
4	**dört**	durrt
5	**beş**	behsh
6	**altı**	ahltı
7	**yedi**	yeh**dee**
8	**sekiz**	seh**k^{y}eez**
9	**dokuz**	do**kooz**
10	**on**	on
11	**on bir**	on beer
12	**on iki**	on **eek^{y}ee**
13	**on üç**	on ewch
14	**on dört**	on durrt
15	**on beş**	on behsh
16	**on altı**	on ahltı
17	**on yedi**	on yeh**dee**
18	**on sekiz**	on seh**k^{y}eez**
19	**on dokuz**	on do**kooz**
20	**yirmi**	yeer**mee**
21	**yirmi bir**	yeer**mee** beer
22	**yirmi iki**	yeer**mee** **eek^{y}ee**
23	**yirmi üç**	yeer**mee** ewch
24	**yirmi dört**	yeer**mee** durrt
25	**yirmi beş**	yeer**mee** behsh
26	**yirmi altı**	yeer**mee** ahltı
27	**yirmi yedi**	yeer**mee** yeh**dee**
28	**yirmi sekiz**	yeer**mee** seh**k^{y}eez**
29	**yirmi dokuz**	yeer**mee** do**kooz**
30	**otuz**	**otooz**
31	**otuz bir**	**otooz** beer
32	**otuz iki**	**otooz** **eek^{y}ee**
33	**otuz üç**	**otooz** ewch
40	**kırk**	kırk
41	**kırk bir**	kırk beer
42	**kırk iki**	kırk **eek^{y}ee**
43	**kırk üç**	kırk ewch
50	**elli**	ehl**lee**
51	**elli bir**	ehl**lee** beer
52	**elli iki**	ehl**lee** **eek^{y}ee**
53	**elli üç**	ehl**lee** ewch
60	**altmış**	ahlt**mısh**
61	**altmış bir**	ahlt**mısh** beer
62	**altmış iki**	ahlt**mısh** **eek^{y}ee**

63	**altmış üç**	ahlt**mısh** ewch
70	**yetmiş**	yeht**meesh**
71	**yetmiş bir**	yeht**meesh** beer
72	**yetmiş iki**	yeht**meesh** eek^{y}**ee**
73	**yetmiş üç**	yeht**meesh** ewch
80	**seksen**	sehk**sehn**
81	**seksen bir**	sehk**sehn** beer
82	**seksen iki**	sehk**sehn** eek^{y}**ee**
83	**seksen üç**	sehk**sehn** ewch
90	**doksan**	dok**sahn**
91	**doksan bir**	dok**sahn** beer
92	**doksan iki**	dok**sahn** eek^{y}**ee**
93	**doksan üç**	dok**sahn** ewch
100	**yüz**	yewz
101	**yüz bir**	yewz beer
102	**yüz iki**	yewz eek^{y}**ee**
110	**yüz on**	yewz on
120	**yüz yirmi**	yewz yeer**mee**
130	**yüz otuz**	yewz o**tooz**
140	**yüz kırk**	yewz kırk
150	**yüz elli**	yewz ehl**lee**
160	**yüz altmış**	yewz ahlt**mısh**
170	**yüz yetmiş**	yewz yeht**meesh**
180	**yüz seksen**	yewz sehk**sehn**
190	**yüz doksan**	yewz dok**sahn**
200	**iki yüz**	eek^{y}**ee** yewz
300	**üç yüz**	ewch yewz
400	**dört yüz**	durrt yewz
500	**beş yüz**	behsh yewz
600	**altı yüz**	ahltı yewz
700	**yedi yüz**	yeh**dee** yewz
800	**sekiz yüz**	seh**k^{y}eez** yewz
900	**dokuz yüz**	do**kooz** yewz
1000	**bin**	been
1100	**bin yüz**	been yewz
1200	**bin iki yüz**	been eek^{y}**ee** yewz
2000	**iki bin**	eek^{y}**ee** been
5000	**beş bin**	behsh been
10,000	**on bin**	on been
50,000	**elli bin**	ehl**lee** been
100,000	**yüz bin**	yewz been
1,000,000	**bir milyon**	beer meel**yon**
1,000,000,000	**bir milyar**	beer meel**yahr**

first	**ilk**	eelk
second	**ikinci**	eek^y**een**jee
third	**üçüncü**	ew**chewn**jew
fourth	**dördüncü**	**dur**dewnjew
fifth	**beşinci**	beh**sheen**jee
sixth	**altıncı**	**ahl**tınjı
seventh	**yedinci**	yeh**deen**jee
eighth	**sekizinci**	**seh**k^{y}eezeenjee
ninth	**dokuzuncu**	**do**koozoonjoo
tenth	**onuncu**	**o**noonjoo
once/twice	**bir kez/iki kez**	**beer** k^{y}ehz/eek^y**ee** k^{y}ehz
three times	**üç kez**	**ewch** k^{y}ehz
a half/half (adj.)	**yarım**	yah**rım**
half a ...	**yarım ... den**	yah**rım** ... dehn
half of ...	**yarı (sı)**	**yah**rı (sı)
a quarter/one third	**dörtte bir/üçte bir**	**durr**tteh beer/**ewch**teh beer
a pair of	**çift**	cheeft
a dozen	**düzine**	dewzeeneh
one per cent	**yüzde bir**	yewz**deh** beer
3.4%	**yüzde 3,4**	yewz**deh** ewch weerg^{y}ewl durrt
1981	**bin dokuz yüz seksen bir**	been do**kooz** yewz sehk**sehn** beer
1992	**bin dokuz yüz doksan iki**	been do**kooz** yewz dok**sahn** eek^{y}ee
2003	**iki bin üç**	eek^y**ee** been ewch

Year and age *Yıl ve yaş*

year	**yıl**	yıl
leap year	**artık yıl**	ahr**tık** yıl
decade	**on yıl**	**on** yıl
century	**yüzyıl**	**yewz**yıl
this year	**bu yıl**	**boo** yıl
last year	**geçen yıl**	g^{y}eh**chehn** yıl
next year	**gelecek yıl**	g^{y}ehleh**jehk** yıl
each year	**her yıl**	**hehr** yıl
2 years ago	**iki yıl önce**	eek^y**ee** yıl urnjeh
in one year	**bir yıl içinde**	**beer** yıl eecheendeh
the 16th century	**16'ncı yüzyıl**	on ahltinjı yewzyıl
in the 20th century	**20'nci yüzyılda**	yeermeenjee yewzyıldah

How old are you?	**Kaç yaşındasınız?**	**kahch** yahshındahssınız
I'm 30 years old.	**Otuz yaşındayım.**	ot**ooz** yahshındah^{y}ım
He/She was born in 1980.	**O 1980 yılında doğdu.**	o been do**kooz** yewz sehk**sehn** yılındah dawdoo
What is his/her age?	**Yaşı kaç?**	yahshı kahch
Children under 16 are not admitted.	**16 yaşından küçük çocukların girmesi yasaktır.**	16 yahshındahn k^{y}ewchewk chojooklah**rın** g^{y}eermehssee yah**sahk**tır

Seasons *Mevsimler*

spring/summer	**ilkbahar/yaz**	**eelk**bahhahr/yahz
autumn/winter	**sonbahar/kış**	**son**bahhahr/kısh
in spring	**ilkbaharda**	**eelk**bahhahrdah
during the summer	**yaz boyunca**	yahz boyoonjah
in autumn	**sonbaharda**	**son**bahhahrdah
during the winter	**kış boyunca**	kısh boyoonjah
high season	**mevsim içi**	mehv**seem** eechee
low season	**mevsim dışı**	mehv**seem** dıshı

Months *Aylar*

January	**Ocak**	ojahk
February	**Şubat**	shoobaht
March	**Mart**	mahrt
April	**Nisan**	neessahn
May	**Mayıs**	mah^{y}ıss
June	**Haziran**	hahzeerahn
July	**Temmuz**	tehmmooz
August	**Ağustos**	aaoostos
September	**Eylül**	eh^{y}lewl
October	**Ekim**	ehk^{y}eem
November	**Kasım**	kahssım
December	**Aralık**	ahrahlık
in September	**Eylülde**	eh^{y}lewldeh
since October	**Ekim'den beri**	ehk^{y}eem**dehn** behree
the beginning of January	**Ocak başı**	**ojahk** bahshı
the middle of February	**Şubat ortası**	shoo**baht** ortahssı
the end of March	**Mart sonu**	**mahrt** sonoo

Days and Date *Gün ve tarih*

What day is it today? **Bugün günlerden ne?** boog^{y}ewn g^{y}ewnlehr**dehn** neh

Sunday	**Pazar**	pah**zahr**
Monday	**Pazartesi**	pah**zahr**tehssee
Tuesday	**Salı**	sahlı
Wednesday	**Çarşamba**	chahrshahm**bah**
Thursday	**Perşembe**	pehrshehm**beh**
Friday	**Cuma**	**joo**mah
Saturday	**Cumartesi**	**joo**mahrtehssee

It's ...

July 1	**Bir Temmuz.**	beer **teh**mmooz
March 10	**On Mart.**	on mahrt
in the morning	**sabahları**	sah**bahh**lahrı
during the day	**gündüzleri**	**g^{y}ewn**dewzlehree
in the afternoon	**öğleden sonraları**	urleh**dehn** sonrahlahrı
in the evening	**akşamları**	ahk**shahm**lahrı
at night	**geceleri**	g^{y}eh**jeh**lehree
the day before yesterday	**önceki gün**	urnjehk^{y}ee g^{y}ewn
yesterday	**dün**	dewn
today	**bugün**	**boo**g^{y}ewn
tomorrow	**yarın**	yahrın
the day after tomorrow	**öbürgün**	ur**bewr**g^{y}ewn
the day before	**evvelki gün**	ehvvehlk^{y}ee g^{y}ewn
the next day	**önümüzdeki gün**	urnewmewzdehk^{y}ee g^{y}ewn
two days ago	**iki gün evvel**	**eek^{y}ee** g^{y}ewn ehvvehl
in three days' time	**üç gün içinde**	**ewch** g^{y}ewn ee**cheen**deh
last week	**geçen hafta**	g^{y}eh**chehn** **hahf**tah
next week	**gelecek hafta**	g^{y}ehleh**jehk** **hahf**tah
for a fortnight (two weeks)	**iki haftalık**	**eek^{y}ee** hahftahlık
birthday	**doğum günü**	daw**oom** g^{y}ewnew
day	**gün**	g^{y}ewn
day off	**tatil günü**	tah**teel** g^{y}ewnew
holiday	**izin**	ee**zeen**
holidays	**tatil**	tah**teel**
vacation	**tatil**	tah**teel**
week	**hafta**	**hahf**tah
weekday	**hafta içi**	hahftah eechee
weekend	**hafta sonu**	hahf**tah** sonoo
working day	**iş günü**	**eesh** g^{y}ewnew

Public holidays *Millî bayramlar*

The following are the holidays when banks, schools, offices and shops are closed.

January 1	**Yılbaşı**	New Year's Day
April 23	**23 Nisan Çocuk Bayramı**	National Independence and Children's Day
May 19	**Gençlik ve Spor Bayramı**	Youth and Sports Day
August 30	**Zafer Bayramı**	Victory Day
October 29	**Cumhuriyet Bayramı**	Republic Day

Apart from these civic celebrations, there are two important Muslim holy periods which are based on the lunar calendar. The first follows the four weeks daylight fasting and prayer of Ramadan (*Ramazan*) and is called *Şeker Bayramı* (Sugar Holy Days), lasting three to five days. Two months and ten days later comes the four-to-five day *Kurban Bayramı* festival.

Greetings and wishes *Selâm ve kutlama*

Merry Christmas!	**Neşeli Noeller!**	**neh**shehlee noehllehr
Happy New Year!	**Yeni yılınız kutlu olsun!**	yehnee yılınız koot**loo** ol**soon**
Happy Easter!	**Paskalya'nız kutlu olsun!**	pahs**kahl**yahnız koot**loo** ol**soon**
Happy birthday!	**Doğum günün kutlu olsun!**	daw**oom** g^y^ewnewn koot**loo** ol**soon**
Best wishes!	**İyi dileklerimle!**	ee**yee** deelehklehreemleh
Congratulations!	**Candan kutlarım!**	jahndahn kootlahrım
Good luck/ All the best!	**Bol şanslar!**	bol shahnslahr
Have a good trip!	**İyi yolculuklar!**	ee**yee** yoljoolook**lahr**
Have a good holiday!	**İyi tatiller!**	ee**yee** tahtee**llehr**
My regards to ...	**...'e selâmlar.**	...eh sehlaamlahr

What time is it? *Saat kaç?*

Excuse me. Can you tell me the time?	**Affedersiniz, saatin kaç olduğunu söyleyebilir misiniz?**	**ah**ffehdehrsseeneez sah-ahteen kahch oldoooonoo surleh^{y}ehbee**leer** **mee**sseeneez
It's ...		
five past one	**Biri beş geçiyor***	beer**ee** behsh g^{y}ehcheey**or**
ten past two	**İkiyi on geçiyor**	eek^{y}ee**yee** on g^{y}ehcheey**or**
a quarter past three	**Üçü çeyrek geçiyor**	ew**chew** cheh^{y}rehk g^{y}ehcheey**or**
twenty past four	**Dördü yirmi geçiyor**	durr**dew** yeermee g^{y}ehcheey**or**
twenty-five past five	**Dördü yirmibeş geçiyor**	durr**dew** yeermeebehsh g^{y}ehcheey**or**
half past six	**Altı buçuk**	ahltı boochook
twenty-five to seven	**Yediye yirmibeş var**	yehdee**yeh** yeermeebehsh vahr
twenty to eight	**Sekize yirmi var**	sehk^{y}ee**zeh** yeermee vahr
a quarter to nine	**Dokuza çeyrek var**	dokoo**zah** cheh^{y}rehk vahr
ten to ten	**Ona on var**	o**nah** on vahr
five to eleven	**Onbire beş var**	onbee**reh** behsh vahr
twelve o'clock (noon/midnight)	**Oniki (öğle/ gece yarısı)**	oneek^{y}ee (urleh/g^{y}eh**jeh** yahrıssı)
in the morning	**sabahları**	sahbahhlahrı
in the afternoon	**öğleden sonra**	urlehdehn sonrah
in the evening	**akşamları**	ahkshahmlahrı
The train leaves at ...	**Tren saat ... de hareket ediyor.**	trehn sahaht ... deh hahrehk^{y}eht ehdee**yor**
13.04 (1.04 p.m.)	**on üç sıfır dört**	on ewch sıfır durt
0.40. (0.40 a.m.)	**sıfır kırk**	sıfır kırk
in five minutes	**beş dakika içinde**	**behsh** dahk^{y}eekah eecheendeh
in a quarter of an hour	**çeyrek saat içinde**	cheh^{y}rehk sahaht eecheendeh
half an hour ago	**yarım saat önce**	yah**rım** sahaht urnjeh
about two hours	**yaklaşık iki saat**	yahklahshık **eek^{y}ee** sahaht
more than 10 minutes	**on dakikadan fazla**	**on** dahk^{y}eekahdahn fahzlah
The clock is fast/slow.	**Saat ileri gidiyor/ geri kalıyor.**	sahaht eelehree g^{y}eedee**yor** g^{y}ehree kahlı**yor**

* In daily conversation time is expressed as shown here. However, official time uses a 24 hour clock which means that after noon, hours are counted from 13 to 24.

Common abbreviations *Kısaltmalar*

A.A.	**Anadolu Ajansı**	a Turkish press agency
A.B.D.	**Amerika Birleşik Devletleri**	U.S.A.
Apt.	**apartman**	apartment
As.	**Askerî/asistan**	military/assistant
As. Iz.	**Askerî Inzibat**	military police
B.	**Bay**	Mr.
bkz.	**bakınız**	see
B.M.	**Birleşmiş Milletler**	United Nations
Bn.	**Bayan**	Mrs., Miss
Cad.	**cadde**	avenue
D.D.Y.	**Devlet Deniz Yolları**	Turkish National Shipping Lines
Doç.	**doçent**	professor
Gnl.	**general**	general
İ.E.T.T.	**İstanbul Elektrik Tramvay Tünel**	Istanbul Municipal Transport
İst.	**İstanbul**	Istanbul
Krs	**kuruş**	kurus (1 lira = 100 kuruş)
Mah.	**Mahallesi**	borough, quarter of the city
M.Ö.	**Milâttan önce**	B.C.
M.S.	**Milâttan Sonra**	A.D.
msl.	**meselâ**	e.g.
No., Nr.	**numara**	number
P.K.	**posta kutusu**	post office box
P.T.T.	**Posta Telegraf Telefon**	Post, telegraph and telephone office
s.	**sayfa**	page
Sok.	**sokak**	street
S.S.C.B.	**Sovyet Sosjalist Cumhuriyetler Birliği**	U.S.S.R.
T.B.M.M.	**Türkiye Büyük Millet Meclisi**	Parliament of Turkey
T.C.	**Türkiye Cumhuriyeti**	Republic of Turkey
T.C.D.D.Y.	**Türkiye Cumhuriyeti Devlet Demir Yolları**	Turkish State Railways
T.L.	**Türk Lirası**	Turkish Lira
T.T.O.K.	**Türk Turing Otomobil Kurumu**	Turkish Touring Club
Tel.	**telefon**	telephone
T.H.Y.	**Türk Hava Yolları**	Turkish Airlines
T.R.T.	**Türkiye Radyo ve Televizyonu**	Turkish Radio and Television Company

Signs and notices *Levhalar ve uyarılar*

You're sure to encounter some of these signs or notices on your trip:

Açık	Open
Asansör	Lift (elevator)
Bayanlar	Ladies
Baylar	Gentlemen
Bisiklet yolu	Cycle path
Boş	Vacant
Boş yer yok/Boş oda yok	No vacancy/No rooms
Çekiniz	Pull
Çevirmen	Translator
Çıkış	Exit
Danışma	Information
Dikkat	Caution
Dikkat, köpek var!	Beware of the dog
Dokunmayınız	Do not touch
Dolu/Doludur	Sold out
Giriş	Entrance
Giriş ücreti	Entrance fee
Girmek yasaktır	No entrance/No admission
Hepsi satıldı	Sold out (stock)
İçmek yasaktır	Non potable water
İçme suyu	Drinking water
İmdat çıkışı	Emergency exit
İşi olmayanların girmesi kesinlikle yasaktır	Entrance for authorised personnel only
İtiniz	Push
Kapalı	Closed
Kapıyı çalmadan giriniz	Enter without knocking
Kasa	Cash desk
Kiralık	To let/For hire (rent)
Lütfen zili çalınız	Please ring
Meşgûl	Occupied
Ölüm tehlikesi	Danger of death
Özel	Private
Rezerve	Reserved
Satılık	For sale
Sıcak	Hot
Sigara içmek yasaktır	Smoking forbidden
Soğuk	Cold
Tehlike	Danger
Tasfiye satışı	End of season sale
... yasaktır	... forbidden
Yer kalmamıştır	Sold out

Emergency *Tehlikeli durum*

By the time the emergency is upon you it's too late to turn to this page for the appropriate expression. So have a look at this list beforehand and, if you want to be on the safe side, learn the expressions in capitals.

Call the police	**Polis çağırın**	poleess chaaırın
Consulate	**Konsolosluk**	konsoloslook
DANGER	**TEHLİKE**	tehhleek^{y}eh
Embassy	**Büyükelçilik**	bewyewk^{y}ehlcheeleek
FIRE	**YANGIN**	yahngın
Gas	**Gaz**	gahz
Get a doctor	**Doktor çağırın**	**dok**tor chaaırın
Go away	**Gidiniz**	g^{y}eedeeneez
HELP	**İMDAT**	**eem**daht
Get help quickly	**Çabuk yardım isteyin**	**chah**book yahrdım ees-teh^{y}een
I'm ill	**Hastayım**	hahstah^{y}ım
I'm lost	**Kayboldum**	**kah^{y}**boldoom
Leave me alone	**Beni rahat bırakın**	behnee rah**haht** bırahkın
LOOK OUT	**DİKKAT**	**deek**kaht
Poison	**Zehir**	zehheer
POLICE	**POLİS**	poleess
Stop that man/woman	**Şu erkeyi/kadını durdurun**	**shoo** ehrkeh^{y}ee/kahdını doordooroon
STOP THIEF	**HIRSIZI YAKALAYIN**	hırsızı yahkahlah^{y}**ın**

Lost! *Bulanan seyler*

Where's the ...?	**... nerededir?**	... **neh**rehdehdeer
lost property (lost and found) office	**Kayıp eşya bürosu**	kah^{y}**ıp** ehshyah bewrossoo
police station	**Karakol**	kahrahkol
I want to report a theft.	**Bir hırsızlık olayını ihbar etmek istiyorum.**	beer hırsızlık olah^{y}ını eehbahr eht**mehk** eestee**yo**room
My ... has been stolen.	**... um/im/am çalındı.**	... oom/eem/ahm chahlındı
I've lost my ...	**... kaybettim.**	... **kah^{y}**behtteem
handbag	**El çantamı**	**ehl** chahntahmı
money	**Paramı**	pahrahmı
passport	**Pasaportumu**	pahssahportoomoo
wallet	**Para cüzdanımı**	pahrah jewzdahnımı

CAR ACCIDENTS, see page 79

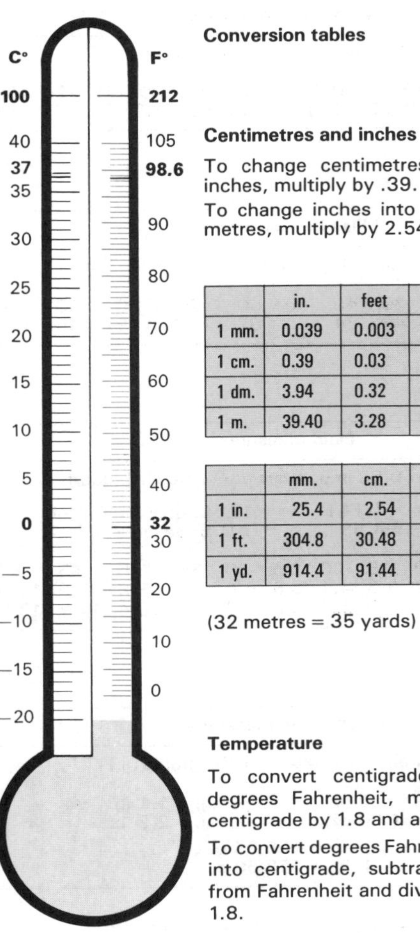

Conversion tables

Centimetres and inches

To change centimetres into inches, multiply by .39.

To change inches into centimetres, multiply by 2.54.

	in.	feet	yards
1 mm.	0.039	0.003	0.001
1 cm.	0.39	0.03	0.01
1 dm.	3.94	0.32	0.10
1 m.	39.40	3.28	1.09

	mm.	cm.	m.
1 in.	25.4	2.54	0.025
1 ft.	304.8	30.48	0.305
1 yd.	914.4	91.44	0.914

(32 metres = 35 yards)

Temperature

To convert centigrade into degrees Fahrenheit, multiply centigrade by 1.8 and add 32.

To convert degrees Fahrenheit into centigrade, subtract 32 from Fahrenheit and divide by 1.8.

Kilometres into miles

1 kilometre (km.) = 0.62 miles

km.	10	20	30	40	50	60	70	80	90	100	110	120	130
miles	6	12	19	25	31	37	44	50	56	62	68	75	81

Miles into kilometres

1 mile = 1.609 kilometres (km.)

miles	10	20	30	40	50	60	70	80	90	100
km.	16	32	48	64	80	97	113	129	145	161

Fluid measures

1 litre (l.) = 0.88 imp. quart or = 1.06 U.S. quart

1 imp. quart = 1.14 l.
1 imp. gallon = 4.55 l.

1 U.S. quart = 0.95 l.
1 U.S. gallon = 3.8 l.

litres	5	10	15	20	25	30	35	40	45	50
imp. gal.	1.1	2.2	3.3	4.4	5.5	6.6	7.7	8.8	9.9	11.0
U.S. gal.	1.3	2.6	3.9	5.2	6.5	7.8	9.1	10.4	11.7	13.0

Weights and measures

1 kilogram or kilo (kg.) = 1000 grams (g.)

100 g. = 3.5 oz.
200 g. = 7.0 oz.

½ kg. = 1.1 lb.
1 kg. = 2.2 lb.

1 oz. = 28.35 g.
1 lb. = 453.60 g.

CLOTHING SIZES, see page 115/YARDS AND INCHES, see page 112

A very basic grammar

Even though it now uses the Roman alphabet, the Turkish language still remains somewhat exotic, being completely different from our own language and, indeed, from any other European language. Its proven relations are a mere handful of central Asian dialects and Mongolian, though some experts believe it to be a member of a far-flung family of languages possibly including Finnish and Hungarian.

It's impossible to cover Turkish grammar completely in only a few pages so only its salient features will be dealt with here.

Two essential characteristics of Turkish, which pervade every aspect of the language, are its use of suffixes and its vocal harmony. We'll begin with these.

Suffixes

Where English uses separate words such as prepositions, possessive adjectives and verbs, Turkish expresses the sense by means of suffixes, i.e. endings added to the root word.

Some incredibly long words can be built up this way. An example with which the Turks themselves like to startle foreigners is this:

Avrupalılaştırılamıyanlardanmısınız?
Are you one of those who can't be Europeanized?

However, you'll be able to get by without having to master such dinosaur-like constructions!

Vocal harmony

In any one word you can only use vowels from one of two distinct groups. The choice is set by the first vowel in the word.

Vowel group 1	Vowel group 2
a, ı, o, u	**e, i, ü, ö**

ad name
adı his name

köy village
köyü his village

As an exercise, look back at our dinosaur word given under *suffixes* and you'll find that, since the first vowel is **a**, *all* the subsequent vowels are also taken from Group 1. Foreign words often constitute exceptions to this rule.

Closely related to vocal harmony is a sort of consonantal change that operates in Turkish. The terminal consonant often changes when a suffix is added to the root word.

mutfak kitchen — direct object: **mutfağı**

The rules for determining exactly which vowel from one of the two groups is inserted and which new consonant replaces the original terminal consonant are very complicated. A bit of astute detective work will sometimes be required before you realize that, for instance, the standard plural ending for nouns **-ler** can also come out as **-lar**, **lör**, etc.

Nouns

As in English, the Turkish noun has no gender. However, there is no definite article (*the*) either.

The plural is formed by adding **-ler** to the singular (subject to the rules of vocal harmony).

çiçek	flower	**çiçekler**	flowers
araba	car	**arabalar**	cars

The English indefinite article (*a, an*) is expressed in Turkish by **bir**.

polis the policeman **bir polis** a policeman

Turkish nouns have six cases, differentiated by suffixes. They are as follows: absolute (roughly the same as our subject), accusative (direct object), possessive (also used for noun complement), dative (indirect object), locative (indicating where something is) and ablative (indicating movement away from a person or a thing). The suffixes are subject to the rules of vocal harmony and consonantal change.

	Singular		Plural
Absolute	**köy**	the village	**köyler**
Accusative	**köyü**	(I see) the village	**köyleri**
Possessive	**köyün**	of the village	**köylerin**
Dative	**köye**	(I gave) to the village	**köylere**
Locative	**köyde**	in the village	**köylerde**
Ablative	**köyden**	from the village	**köylerden**

Adjectives

The adjective precedes the noun and doesn't change.

uzun yol the long road **uzun yollar** the long roads

Pronouns

	I	you	he/she/it	we	you	they
Absolute	**ben**	**sen**	**o**	**biz**	**siz**	**onlar**
Accusative	**beni**	**seni**	**onu**	**bizi**	**sizi**	**onları**
Possessive	**benim**	**senin**	**onum**	**bizim**	**sizin**	**onların**
Dative	**bana**	**sana**	**ona**	**bize**	**size**	**onlara**
Locative	**bende**	**sende**	**onda**	**bizde**	**sizde**	**onlarda**
Ablative	**benden**	**senden**	**ondan**	**bizden**	**sizden**	**onlardan**

The subject (absolute) pronoun is not generally used in a sentence since the verb ending is enough to indicate the person.

Possessive adjectives

The English possessive adjectives (*my*, *your*, etc.) are expressed in Turkish by suffixes (which again follow the rules of vocal harmony and consonantal change):

After a consonant				After a vowel			
my	**-im**	our	**-imiz**	my	**-m**	our	**-miz**
your	**-in**	your	**-iniz**	your	**-n**	your	**-niz**
his/her/its	**-i**	their	**-leri**	his/her/its	**-si**	their	**-leri**

köyüm my village **köyü** his village

Note that in this example the **-üm** and **-ü** endings are variants of the basic **-im** and **-i** endings, due to the rules of vocal harmony.

Postpositions

A certain number of English prepositions are expressed in Turkish by postpositions (that is, words placed *after* the noun).

kardeș brother **kardeși gibi** like a brother

Verbs

In Turkish the future, present and past tenses overlap to a certain extent, and the examples given below can in most cases be used to cover all these three tenses.

We're giving just two simple verbs here, *to be* and *to take*.

The verb *to be* merely takes the form of a suffix.

I am	**-im**	we are	**-iz**
you are	**-sin**	you are	**-siniz**
he/she/it is	**(-dir/-tir)**	they are	**(-dir/-tir)ler**

Evde-y-im. I'm at home. (the **y** goes in to avoid the contact of two vowels)

The verb *to take:*

Infinitive: **almak** root element: **al** (+ **ı** to avoid the contact between two consonants)

I'm taking	**alı-yor-um**	we're taking	**alı-yor-uz**
you're taking	**alı-yor-sun**	you're taking	**alı-yor-sunuz**
he's taking	**alı-yor**	they're taking	**alı-yor-lar**

-yor indicates present tense. **-um**, **-sum**, etc., are harmony-modified versions of the verb *to be.*

Negative form

A verb is turned into the negative by inserting **-me** immediately after the root element of the verb.

beklemek to wait
bekli-yor-um I'm waiting **bekle-mi-yor-um** I'm not waiting

Questions

The interrogative particle **mi** turns the immediately preceding word into a question.

Türksünüz. You are Turkish.
Türk müsünüz? * Are you Turkish?

* **mi** becomes **mü** due to vocal harmony.

The verb [illegible]

Negative form

[illegible]

Questions

[illegible]

Dictionary
and alphabetical index

English—Turkish

appliance alet 119
appointment randevu 30, 131, 137, 145
apricot kayısı 53
April Nisan 150
archaeology arkeoloji 83
architect mimar 83
area code telefon kodu 134
arm kol 138, 139
arrival varış 65
arrive, to varmak 65, 66, 68; gelmek 68, 130
art sanat 83
art gallery sanat galerisi 81, 98
artichoke enginar 40, 49
artificial suni 124
artificial sweetener sakarin 37
artist sanatçı 83
ashtray küllük 27, 36
Asia Asya 146
ask, to sormak 136; *(for)* istemek 25; *(order)* ısmarlamak 61
asparagus kuşkonmaz 49
aspirin aspirin 109
asthma astım 141
astringent lotion yüz losyonu 110
at -da/de 15
at least en azından 24
at once hemen 31
aubergine patlıcan 42, 49
August Ağustos 150
aunt (*father's sister*) hala 93; (*mother's sister*) teyze 93
Australia Avustralya 146
Austria Avusturya 146
automatic otomatik 20, 122, 124
autumn sonbahar 150
awful korkunç 84, 94

B
baby bebek 24, 111
baby food bebek maması 111
babysitter çocuk bakıcısı 27
back sırt 138
backache bel ağrısı 141
backpack sırt çantası 106
bad kötü 14, 95
bag çanta 17, 18, 103
baggage bagaj 18, 26, 31, 71
baggage cart bagaj arabası 18, 71
baggage check bagaj deposu 71
baked fırında 45, 46, 51
baker's fırın 98
balance *(account)* bilanço 131
balcony balkon 23
ball *(inflated)* top 128
ballet bale 88
ball-point pen tükenmez kalem 104
banana muz 53, 64
bandage sargı 109
Band-Aid plaster 109
bangle bilezik 121
bangs kâkül 30
bank *(finance)* banka 98, 129, 130
bar bar 67
barber's berber 30, 98
basketball basketbol 89
bath *(hotel)* banyo 23, 25, 27
bathing cap bone 116
bathing suit mayo 116
bathrobe sabahlık 116
bath salts banyo tuzu 110
bath towel banyo havlusu 27
battery pil 121, 125; *(car)* akü 75, 78
bazaar çarşı 81
beach plaj 90, 91
beach ball deniz topu 128
bean fasulye 49
beard sakal 31
beautiful güzel 14, 84
beauty salon güzellik salonu 30, 98
bed yatak 24, 142, 144
bed and breakfast yatak ve kahvaltı 24
bedpan oturak 144
beef sığır 46
beer bira 57, 64
beet(root) pancar 42, 49
before önce 15, 29, 143, 151
begin, to başlamak 87
beginning baş 150
behind arkada 15, 77
beige bejrengi 113
bell *(electric)* zil 144
bellboy belboy 26
belly-dancing göbek dansı 88
below altında 15
belt kemer 117
bend *(road)* viraj 79
berth kuşet 69, 70, 71
better daha iyi 14, 25, 101
between arasında 15
bicycle bisiklet 74
big büyük 14, 101, 118
bigger daha büyük 25
bill hesap 28, 31, 62, 102
billion *(Am.)* milyar 148

binoculars dürbün 123
bird kuş 85
birthday doğum günü 151, 152
biscuit *(Br.)* bisküvi 64
bitter acı 61
black siyah 105, 113, 118, 124, 125
blackberry böğürtlen 53
blackcurrant siyah frenküzümü 53
bladder idrar torbası 138
blade bıçak 110
blank boş 127
blanket battaniye 27
bleach renk açma 30
bleed, to kanamak 139, 145
blind *(window)* kepenk 129
blister su toplaması 139
block, to tıkanmak 28
blood kan 142
blood pressure tansiyon 141, 142
blood transfusion kan nakli 144
blouse bulüz 116
blow-dry fönleme 30
blue mavi 105, 113
blusher allık 110
boat vapur 74
bobby pin pens 111
body vücut 138
body lotion vücut losyonu 110
boil çıban 139
boiled haşlama 40, 46, 51
boiled egg haşlanmış yumurta 38, 42
bone kemik 138
book kitap 12, 104
booking office bilet gişesi 19, 67
booklet *(of tickets)* karne 72
bookshop kitabevi 98, 104
boot çizme 118
born doğdu 150
botanical garden botanik bahçesi 81
botany botanik 83
bottle şişe 17, 56, 57, 58
bottle-opener şişe açacağı 106
bottom aşağı 145
bowel barsak 138
bow tie papyon 116
box kutu 120
boxing boks 89
boy erkek çocuğu 112, 128
bra sütyen 116
bracelet bilezik 121
braces *(suspenders)* pantalon askısı 116
brain *(food)* beyin 40, 46
braised pilâki 45
brake fren 78
brake fluid hidrolik yağı 75
brandy konyak/kanyak 58
bread ekmek 36,38,43,64, 120
break, to kırmak 139, 145; bozmak 29, 119
break down, to arızalanmak 78
breakdown arıza 78
breakdown van kurtarma aracı 78
breakfast kahvaltı 24, 38
breast meme 138
breathe, to nefes almak 142
bridge köprü 85
bring, to getirmek 13, 57, 95
British İngiliz 93
broiled *(Am.)* ızgara 46
broken bozuk 29, 119; kırık 123, 139, 140
brooch broş 121
brother erkek kardeş 93
brown kahverengi 113
bruise çürük 139
Brussels sprout Brüksel lahanası 49
bubble bath banyo köpüğü 110
bucket kova 106, 128
buckle toka 117
build, to inşa etmek 83
building bina 81, 83
building blocks/bricks inşaat kutusu 128
bulb ampul 28, 75, 119
Bulgaria Bulgaristan 146
burger köfte 46
burn yanık 139
burn out, to *(bulb)* yanmak 28
bus otobüs 18, 19, 65, 66, 72, 80
business iş 16, 131
business district ticaret merkezi 81
business trip iş seyahatı 93
bus station otogar 66
bus stop otobüs durağı 19, 72
busy meşgul 96
butane gas bütangaz 32, 106
butcher's kasap dükkânı 98
butter tereyağ 36, 38, 51, 64, 120
button düğme 29, 117
buy, to satın almak 82, 100, 104, 123

C

cabbage lâhana 49
cabin *(ship)* kamara 74
cable telgraf 133
cable car teleferik 74

cable release deklanşör 125
cake pasta 37, 64
cake shop pastane 98
calendar takvim 104
call *(phone)* görüşmesi 135, 136
call, to *(summon)* çağırmak 78, 79, 156; *(phone)* aramak 136
calm sakin 91
cambric patiska 114
camel deve 98
camel-hair devetüyü 114
camera fotoğraf makinesi 124, 125
camera case fotoğraf çantası 125
camera shop fotoğrafçı dükkânı 98
camp, to kamp yapmak 32
campbed kamp yatağı 106
camping kamping 32
camping equipment kamp malzemesi 106
camp site kamping yeri 32
can *(of peaches)* kutu 120
Canada Kanada 146
Canadian Kanadalı 93
cancel, to iptal etmek 65
candle mum 106
candy akide şekeri 126
can opener konserve açacağı 106
cap kasket 116
capital *(finance)* sermaye 131
car araba 19, 20, 26, 32, 75, 76, 78
carafe sürahi 56, 57
carat kırat 121
caravan karavan 32
carbon paper karbon kâğıdı 104
carburet(t)or karbüratör 78
card *(playing)* kağıt 93, *(business)* kart 131
card game iskambil oyunu 128
cardigan hırka 116
car hire araba kiralama 20
carp sazan 44
carpet halı 127
car park park yeri 77
car racing araba yarışı 89
car radio otomobil radyosu 119
car rental araba kiralama 20
carrot havuç 42, 49
carry, to taşımak 21
cart bagaj arabası 18, 71
carton *(of cigarettes)* karton 17, 126
cartridge *(camera)* kaset 124
cash, to bozdurmak 18, 130, 133
cash desk kasa 103, 155
cassette recorder teyp 119
cassette kaset 127
casserole tencerede pişmiş 46
castle şato 81
catalogue katalog 82
cathedral katedral 81
Catholic Katolik 84
cauliflower karnıbahar 49
caution dikkat 79, 155
cave mağara 81
caviar havyar 40
celery kereviz 42, 49
cemetery mezarlık 81
centre merkez 19, 21, 72, 76, 81
century yüzyıl 149
ceramic plate seramik tabak 127
ceramlic tiles seramik döşeme 127
certificate rapor 144
chain *(jewellery)* zincir 121
chair iskemle 106
chamber music oda müziği 128
champagne şampanya 56
change *(money)* üstü 62
change, to degiştirmek 61, 65, 75, 123; *(train)* aktarma yapmak 66, 68, 69, 72; *(money)* çevirmek 18, 130
charcoal odun kömürü 106
charge ücret 20, 32, 77, 90, 136
charge, to ücret almak 24, 124
cheap ucuz 14, 24, 101
cheaper daha ucuz 25, 101
check *(restaurant)* hesap 62
check, to kontrol etmek 75, 123; *(luggage)* teslim etmek 71
check-in *(airport)* bagaj kayıtı 65
check out, to hareket etmek 31
checkup *(medical)* sağlık kontrolu 142
cheers! şerefe! 58
cheese peynir 38, 42, 52, 63, 64, 120
chemist's eczane 98, 108
cheque çek 131
cherry kiraz 53
chess satranç 93
chess set satranç takımı 128
chest göğüs 138, 141
chestnut kestane 53
chewing gum çiklet 126
chick peas nohut 49
chicken tavuk 43, 48, 51, 63
chiffon şifon 114
child çocuk 24, 61, 82, 91, 93, 139, 150
children's doctor çocuk doktoru 137
chilli pepper kırmızı biber 52
China Çin 146

chilled soğutulmuş 56
chips patates kızartması 51; *(Am.)* çips 64
chocolate çukolata 38, 64, 120, 126
chop pirzola 46
chopped kıyılmış 51
Christmas Noel 152
chromium krom 122
church kilise 81, 84
cigar puro 126
cigarette sigara 17, 95, 126
cigarette case sigara tabakası 121, 126
cigarette holder sigara ağızlığı 126
cigarette lighter çakmak 121
cine camera film kamerası 124
cinema sinema 86, 96
circle *(theatre)* balkon 87
city şehir 81
city walls surlar 81
classical music klasik müzik 128
clean temiz 61
clean, to temizlemek 29, 76
cleansing cream temizleme kremi 110
cliff uçurum 85
clip iğne 121
cloakroom vestiyer 87
clock saat 121, 153
clock-radio uyandıran radyo 119
close, to kapanmak 11, 82, 108, 130, 132
closed kapalı 155
cloth kumaş 118
clothes elbiseler 29, 116
clothes peg çamaşır mandalı 106
clothing giyim 112
cloud bulut 94
coach *(bus)* şehirlerarası otobüs 66
coat manto 116; palto 116
coconut hindistancevizi 53
coffee kahve 38, 60
coffeehouse kahvehane 60
coin para 83
cold soğuk 14, 25, 38, 57, 61, 94, 155
cold *(illness)* nezle 108
collar yaka 117
collect call ödemeli arama 135
colour renk 103, 112, 119, 124, 125
colour chart renk katalogu 30
colour rinse şampuanla boyama 30
colour shampoo nüans verici boya 111
colour negative renkli fotoğraf filmi 124
colour slide renkli slayd filmi 124
comb tarak 111
come, to gelmek 35, 56, 95, 137, 144
comedy komedi 86
commission komisyon 130
compact disc kompakt disk 127
compartment kompartman 70
compass pusula 106
complaint şikayet 61
concert konser 88
concert hall konser salonu 81, 88
condom preservatif 109
conductor *(orchestra)* orkestra şefi 88
confirm, to konfirme etmek 65
confirmation konfirmasyon 23
congratulation kutlama 152
connection *(train)* bağlantı 65, 68
constipated kabız 140
consulate konsolosluk 156
contact lens kontakt lens 123
contagious bulaşıcı 142
contraceptive doğum kontrol ilacı 109
contract sözleşme 131
control kontrol 16
convent manastır 81
cookie bisküvi 64
cool box soğutma çantası 106
copper bakır 122
copperware bakır eşya 127
coral mercan 122
corduroy fitilli kadife 114
coriander kişniş 52
corkscrew tirbuşon 106
corn *(Am.)* mısır 43
corner köşe 21, 36, 77
corn plaster nasır için plaster 109
cost fiyat 20, 80, 131, 135, 136
cost, to tutmak 133
cot çocuk yatağı 24
cotton pamuk 114
cotton wool pamuk 109
cough öksürük 108, 141
cough drops öksürük şurubu 109
counter gişe 133
country memleket 93
countryside şehir dışında 85
courgette kabak 49, 50
course saha 90
court house mahkeme 81
court kort 90
crab pavurya 41, 44
cramp kramp 141
crayon mum boya 104
cream krema 43; *(cosmetic)* krem 110

creamed kremalı 51
crease resistant buruşmamak 114
credit card kredi kartı 20, 31, 62, 102, 130
crepe krep 114
crisps çips 64
crockery tabak–çanak 106, 107
cross haç 121
crossing *(by sea)* karşıya geçiş 74
crossroads kavşak 77
cruise vapur gezisi 74
crystal kristal 122, 127
cucumber hıyar 49
cuff link kol düğmesi 121
cuisine mutfak 34
cumin kimyon 52
cup fincan 36, 107
curler bigudi 111
currency para 129
currency exchange office kambiyo bürosu 18, 129
current akıntı 91
curve *(road)* viraj 79
customs gümrük 16, 102, 133
cut *(wound)* kesik 139
cut (off), to *(phone)* kesmek 30
cut glass kesme cam 122
cutlery çatal–bıçak takımı 106, 121
cycling bisiklete binmek 89
Cyprus kıbrıs 146
cystitis sistit 142

D

dairy mandıra 98
dance, to dans etmek 88, 96
danger tehlike 79, 155, 156
dangerous tehlikeli 79, 91
dark koyu 101, 113, 126; karanlık 25
date *(day)* tarih 25, 151; *(appointment)* buluşma 95; *(fruit)* hurma 53
daughter kız 93
day gün 16, 20, 24, 80, 90, 94, 142, 143, 151
daylight gün ışığı 124
day off tatil günü 151
death ölüm 155
decade on yıl 149
decaffeinated kafeinsiz 38
December Aralık 150
decision karar 25, 102
deck *(ship)* güverte 74
deck chair şezlong 91, 106
declare, to *(customs)* deklare etmek 17
deep derin 142
delay gecikme 69
delicatessen şarküteri 98
delicious nefis 62
deliver, to teslim etmek 102
delivery teslim 102
denim blucin kumaşı 114
Denmark Danimarka 146
dentist dişçi 98, 145
denture takma dişi 145
deodorant deodorant 110
department bölüm 83, 100
department store büyük mağaza 98
departure hareket 65
deposit depozito 20
dessert tatlı 37, 54
detour *(traffic)* başka yola verme 79
diabetic şeker hastalığı 141
diabetic şeker hastaları 37
dialling code telefon kodu 134
diamond elmas 122
diaper kundak 111
diarrhoea barsak bozuğu 140
diced doğranmış 51
dictionary sözlük 104
diesel motorin 75
diet perhiz 37
difficult zor 14
difficulty zorluk 28, 102, 141
digital dijital 122
dill dere otu 52
dining-car restoran vagon 68, 71
dining room yemek salonu 27
dinner akşam yemeği 94
direct direkt 65
direct to, to yol göstermek 13
direction yön 76
director *(theatre)* rejisör 86
directory *(phone)* telefon rehberi 134
disabled sakat 82
discotheque diskotek 88, 96
discount tenzilat 131
disease hastalık 142
dish yemek 36, 42
disinfectant dezenfektan 109
dislocate, to çıkarmak 140
display case camekân 100
dissatisfied memnun olmamak 103
diversion *(traffic)* başka yola verme 79
dizzy baş dönmesi 140
doctor doktor 79, 137, 144, 145, 156
doctor's office muayenehane 137

dog köpek 155
doll oyuncak bebek 128
dollar dolar 18, 102, 130
double duble 58
double bed çift yatak 23
double room çift yataklı oda 19, 23, 74
down aşağıda 15
downstairs aşağı katta 15
downtown şehir merkezi 81
dozen düzine 149
drawing pin raptiye 104
dress elbise 116
dressing gown sabahlık 116
dried fruit kuru meyva 53, 64
drink içki 58, 59, 61, 95
drink, to içmek 35, 36, 37, 143
drinking water içme suyu 32, 155
drip, to *(tap)* damlamak 28
drive, to kullanmak 21, 76
driving licence ehliyet 20, 79
drop *(liquid)* şurup 109
drugstore eczane 98
dry kuru 30, 110, 111
dry cleaner's kuru temizleyici 29, 98
dry shampoo kuru şampuan 111
dull hafif 140
dummy emzik 111
during esnasında 15
duty *(customs)* gümrük 17
dye boyamak 30, 111

E

ear kulak 138
earache kulak ağrısı 141
ear drops kulak damlası 109
early erken 14, 31
earlier daha erken 145
earring küpe 121
east doğu 77
Easter Paskalya 152
easy kolay 14
eat, to yemek yemek 36, 37, 71
eat out, to restoran'a gitmek 33
economics ekonomi 83
economy *(ticket)* turist mevki 65
eel yılan balığı 44
egg yumurta 38, 42, 64, 120
eggplant patlıcan 49
eight sekiz 35, 96, 147
eighteen on sekiz 147
eighth sekizinci 149
eighty seksen 148
elastic bandage esnek sargı 109
Elastoplast plaster 109
electric toothbrush elektrikli diş fırçası 119
electrical appliance elektrik alet 119
electrical goods shop elektrikçi dükkânı 98
electricity elektrik 32
electronic game elektronik oyun 128
elevator asansör 27, 100
eleven on bir 147
embarkation iskele 74
embassy büyükelçilik 156
embroidery el işi 127
emerald zümrüt 122
emergency tehlikeli durum 155
emergency exit imdat çıkışı 27, 99, 155
emery board manikür takımı 110
empty boş 14
enamel mineli 122
end son 150
engaged *(phone)* meşgul 136
engagement ring nişan yüzüğü 122
engine *(car)* motor 78
England İngilitere 146
English İngilizce 12, 16, 80, 82, 84; *(person)* İngiliz 104, 105, 126
enjoy, to hoşlanmak 62, 92, 96
enjoyable hoş 31
enjoy oneself, to hoşlanmak 96
enlarge, to büyütmek 126
enough yeter 15
entrance giriş 67, 82, 99, 155
entrance fee giriş ücreti 155
envelope mektup zarfı 27, 104
equipment takım 91; malzeme 106
eraser silgi 104
escalator yürüyen merdiven 100
estimate *(cost)* tahmin 78, 131
Europe Avrupa 146
evening akşam 35, 87, 95, 96, 151, 153
evening dress gece elbisesi 88, 116
everything herşey 31, 62
exchange, to değiştirmek 103
exchange rate kambiyo kuru 18, 130
excluding hariç 24
excursion gezinti 80
excuse, to affetmek 11, 70, 153
exercise book defter 105
exhaust pipe egzoz 78
exhibition sergi 81
exit çıkış 67, 99, 155

expect, to beklemek 130
expenses masraflar 131
expensive pahalı 14, 19, 21, 101
export ihraç 131
exposure *(photography)* poz 124
exposure counter poz sayar 125
express *(mail)* ekspres 133
expression tabir 100
expressway otoyol 76
extension cord/lead uzatma kordonu 119
extra *(additional)* daha 24, 27
eye göz 138, 139
eyebrow pencil kaş kalemi 110
eye drops göz damlası 109
eye liner göz kalemi 110
eye shadow far 110
eyesight göz 123
eye specialist göz doktoru 137

F
fabric *(cloth)* kumaş 113
face yüz 138
face pack yüz maskesi 30
face powder pudra 110
factory fabrika 81
fair fuar 81
fall *(autumn)* sonbahar 150
fall, to düşmek 139
family aile 93, 144
fan vantilâtör 28
fan belt v-kayışı 75
far uzak 11, 14, 100
fare yolculuk 66
farm çiftlik 85
fast *(film)* yüksek hızlı 124
fat *(meat)* yağ 37
father baba 93
faucet musluk 28
fava bean bakla 49
February Şubat 150
fee *(doctor)* ücret 82, 144
feeding bottle biberon 111
feel, to *(physical state)* hissetmek 140, 142, 143
felt keçe 114
felt-tip pen keçe kalem 105
ferry araba vapuru 74
fever ateş 140
few az 14; *(a)* birkaç 14, 15, 16, 24, 80
field tarla 85
fifteen on beş 147
fifth beşinci 149
fifty elli 147
fig incir 53
fill in, to doldurmak 26, 133, 144
fillet fileto 46
filling *(tooth)* dolgu 145
filling station benzin istasyonu 75
film film 24, 86
film winder film sarıcı 125
filter filtre 125
filter-tipped filtreli 126
find, to bulmak 11, 27, 76, 100, 137
fine iyi 10, 25, 92
fine arts güzel sanatlar 83
fine grain ince grenli 124
finer daha ince 113
finger parmak 138
Finland Finlandiya 146
fire yandın 156
first ilk 66, 68, 72, 77, 92, 142, 149
first-aid kit ilk yardım kutusu 106
first class birinci mevki 65, 69, 70
first name ad 25
fish balık 44
fish, to balık avlamak 90
fishing balık avlamak 90
fishing tackle olta 106
fishmonger's balıkçı dükkânı 98
fit, to uymak 115
fitting room giyinme kabini 115
five beş 58, 147
fix, to tamir etmek 145
fizzy *(mineral water)* gazlı 59
flannel flânel 114
flash *(photography)* flaş 125
flash attachment flaş 125
flash cube flaş kübü 125
flashlight cep feneri 106
flash gun flaş 125
flat düz 118
flat tyre lâstik patlağı 78
flea market bit pazarı 81
flight uçuş 65
flippers palet 128
floor kat 27
floor show atraksiyon 88
florist's çiçekçi dükkânı 98
flour un 37, 43
flower çiçek 85
flu grip 142
fog sis 94
folding chair portatif iskemle 106
folding table portatif masa 106

folk music half müziği 128
follow, to takip etmek 77
food yemek 35, 37, 61
food box yiğecek kutusu 106
food poisoning zehirlenme 142
foot ayak 138
football futbol 89
footpath yol 85
for için 15
forbid, to yasak etmek 32, 155
forecast rapor 94
forest orman 85
forget, to unutmak 61
fork çatal 36, 61, 107
form *(document)* form 26, 133, 144
fortnight iki hafta 151
fortress kale 81
forty kırk 147
foundation cream fondöten kremi 110
fountain çeşme 81
fountain pen dolmakalem 105
four dört 35, 147
fourteen on dört 147
fourth dördüncü 149
frame *(glasses)* çerçeve 123
France Fransa 146
free *(vacant)* serbest 14, 80, 82, 96
french fries patates kızartması 51
fresh taze 52, 61
Friday Cuma 29, 87, 151
fried tavada kızarmış 45, 46, 51
friend arkadaş 93, 95
fringe kâkül 30
from -den/dan 15
front ön taraf 23, 69, 75, 145
frost don 94
fruit meyva 53
fruit juice meyva suyu 37, 38, 59
frying pan tava 106
full dolu 14
full board tam pansiyon 24
full insurance tam sigorta 20
furniture mobilya 83
furrier's kürkçü dükkânı 98

G

gabardine gabardin 114
gallery galeri 81, 98
game oyun 128; *(food)* av hayvanları 48
garage garaj 26, 78
garden bahçe 85
gardens park
garlic sarmısak 52
gas gaz 156
gasoline benzin 75, 78
gastritis gastrit 142
gate büyük kapı 81
gauze gazlı bez 109
gem değerli taş 121
general genel 27, 100, 108, 112, 129, 137, 142
general delivery post restant 133
general practitioner dahiliyeci 137
genitals cinsel organlar 138
gentleman bay 155
geology jeoloji 83
Germany Almanya 146
get, to bulmak 19, 21, 32, 35, 72; *(fetch)* almak 11, 108; *(go)* gitmek 19, 66, 76, 85, 89, 100
get off, to inmek 72
get to, to varmak 70
get up, to kalkmak 144
get back, to geri almak 102
gherkin turşu 64
gift *(present)* hediye 98
gift shop hediye dükkânı 98
gin cin 58
gin and tonic cin-tonik 58
girdle korse 116
girl kız çocuğu 112, 128
give, to vermek 13, 75, 123, 126, 130, 131, 136, 140, 143, 145
give way, to *(traffic)* öncelik vermek 79
glass bardak 36, 56, 57, 58, 61; kadeh 58
glasses gözlük 123
gloomy karanlık 84
glossy parlak 116
glove eldiven 116
glue zamk 105
go, to gitmek 21, 72, 73, 77, 96, 142
go away, to gitmek 156
go out, to çıkmak 96
gold altın 121, 122
golden dore 113
gold plated altın kaplama 122
golf golf 90
golf course golf sahası 90
good iyi 14
good-bye allahaısmarladık 10; güle güle 10
gooseberry bektaşı üzümü 53
gram gram 120
grammar book gramer kitabı 105

DICTIONARY Sözlük

grape üzüm 53, 64
grapefruit greyfrut 38, 59
grapefruit juice greyfrut suyu 38, 59
gray gri 113
graze sıyrık 139
greasy yağlı 30, 110, 111
Great Britain Büyük Britanya 146
Greece Yunanistan 146
green yeşil 42, 49, 113
green bean yeşil fasülye 49
greengrocer's manav 98
green salad yeşil salata 42
greeting selam 10, 152
grey gri 113
grey mullet kefal 44
grilled ızgara 45, 46, 51
grocer's bakkal dükkânı 98, 120
group grup 82
guest house pansiyon 19, 22
guide rehber 80, 155
guidebook rehber kitabı 82, 104, 105
gum *(teeth)* diş eti 145
gynaecologist jinekolog 137

H

hair saç 30, 111
hairbrush saç fırçası 111
haircut saç kesmek 30
hairdresser's kuvaför 30, 99
hair dryer saç kurutma makinesı 119
hairgrip pens 111
hair lotion saç losyonu 111
hair pin firkete 111
hair slide saç tokası 111
hairspray sprey 30, 111
half *(adj)* yarım 56, 80, 120, 149
half *(noun)* yarım 149
half an hour yarım saat 153
half board yarım pansiyon 24
hall *(large room)* salon 88
hall porter kapıcı 26
ham jambon 38
ham and eggs jambon ve yumurta 38
hammer çekiç 106
hammock hamak 106
hand el 138, 139
handbag *(purse)* el çantası 116, 156
hand cream el kremi 110
handicrafts el sanatları 83
handkerchief mendil 116
handmade el işi 113
hand washable el ile yıkamak 114

hanger askı 27
happy kutlu olsun 152
harbour liman 81
hard sert 123
hard-boiled *(egg)* çok pişmiş 38
hardware store nalbur 98
hare tavşan 48
hat şapka 116
hayfever saman nezlesi 108
hazelnut fındık 52, 53
head baş 46, 138, 139
headache baş ağrısı 141
headphone(s) kulaklık 119
head waiter şef garson 61
health insurance sağlık sigortası 144
health insurance form sağlık sigorta formu 144
heart kalp 138
heart attack kalp krizi 141
heat, to ısıtmak 90
heating ısıtma 23, 28
heavy ağır 14, 101
heel ökçe 118
helicopter helikopter 74
hello! merhaba! 10; *(phone)* alo! 135
help yardım 156
help! imdat! 156
help, to yardım etmek 13, 21, 71, 100, 103
herbs otlar 52
here burada 12; işte 16
high yüksek 84, 141
high season mevsim içi 150
hill tepe 85
hire kiralama 20, 119
hire, to kiralamak 19, 74, 90, 91
history tarih 83
hitchhike, to otostop yapmak 74
hold on! *(phone)* bekleyin! 136
hole delik 29
holiday izin 16, 151
holidays tatil 151
home ev 96
home address ev adresi 31
home town mahalle 25
honey bal 38
horseback riding ata binmek 89
horse racing at yarışı 89
hospital hastane 99, 142, 144
hot sıcak 14, 25, 28, 38, 94, 155
hot dog sosis 64
hotel otel 19, 21, 22, 26, 30, 80, 96, 102
hotel guide otel listesi 19

hotel reservation otel rezervasyonu 19
hot water sıcak su 23
hot-water bottle termofor 27
hour saat 80, 90, 137
house ev 83, 85
how nasıl 11
how far ne uzaklıkta 11, 76, 85
how long ne kadar zaman 11
how many kaç 11
how much ne kadar 11
hundred yüz 148
Hungary Macaristan 146
hungry, to be acıkmak 13, 35
hunt, to hayvan avlamak 90
hunting hayvan avlama 90
hurry *(to be in a)* acele etmek 21, 36
hurt, to acımak 139, 140, 142, 145; *(oneself)* yaralanmak 139
husband koca 93
hydrofoil deniz otobüsü 74

I

ice buz 58
icecream dondurma 64
ice cube buz kübü 27
ice pack soğutma torbası 106
icon ikon 127
ill hasta 140, 156
Iceland Islanda 146
illness hastalık 140
important önemli 13
import ithal 131
imported ithal malı 113
impressive etkileyici 84
in içinde 15
include, to dahil olmak 24
included dahil 20, 31, 32, 62, 80
India Hindistan 146
indigestion hazımsızlık 141
indoor *(swimming pool)* kapalı hava 90
inexpensive pahalı olmayan 35, 124
infect, to mikrop kapmak 140
infection mikrop kapma 140
inflamation iltihabı 142
inflation enflasyon 131
inflation rate enflasyon oranı 131
influenza grip 142
information office danışma bürosu 67, 155
injection iğne 140, 142, 143, 144
injured yaralı 79, 139
injury yara 139
ink mürekkep 105
inland yurt içi 132
insect bite böcek sokması 108, 139
insect repellent böceklerden korunmak için ilaç 109
inside içerde 15
instead yerine 37
instrumental music enstrümantal müzik 128
insurance sigorta 20
insurance company sigorta şirketi 79
interest faiz 131
interested, to be ilgilenmek 83
interesting ilginç 84
international yurt dışı 133, 134
interpreter tercüman 131
intersection kavşak 77
introduce, to tanıştırmak 92
introduction *(social)* tanışmak 92
investment yatırım 131
invitation davet 94
invite, to davet etmek 94
invoice fatura 131
iodine tentürdiyod 109
Iraq Irak 146
Ireland Irlanda 146
Iran Iran 146
Irish Irlandalı 93
iron *(laundry)* ütü 119
iron, to ütülemek 29
ironmonger's nalbur 99
Italy Italya 146
ivory fildişi 122

J

jacket ceket 116, 117
jade yeşim 122
jam reçel 38, 120
jam, to sıkışmak 28, 125
January Ocak 150
Japan Japonya 146
jar kavanoz 120
jaundice sarılık 142
jaw çene 138
jazz caz 128
jeans blucin 116
jersey kazak 116
jewel mücevher 121
jewel box mücevher kutusu 121
jeweller's kuyumcu 121
jewellery kuyumcu 99

DICTIONARY

Sözlük

joint eklem 138
Jordan Ürdün 146
journey yolculuk 66
juice meyve suyu 59
July Temmuz 150
jumper *(sweater)* kazak 116
June Haziran 150
just *(only)* sadece 54, 100

K
kerosene gazyağı 106
kettle elektrikli çaydanlık 119
key anahtar 27
kidney böbrek 46, 138
kilo(gram) kilo 120
kilometre kilometre 20
king-size uzun 126
kind *(type)* tür 46, 140
kiosk büfe 126
kitchen mutfak 36
knee diz 138
kneesocks uzun çorap 116
knife bıçak 36, 61, 107
knock, to kapıyı çalmak 155
know, to bilmek 16, 24, 96, 114

L
label etiket 105
lace dantel 114
lady bayan 155
lake göl 81, 85, 90
lamb kuzu 40, 46
lamp lamba 20, 106, 119
landmark görüş 85
landscape çevre 92
lantern fener 106
large büyük 20, 101, 134
last son 14, 66, 68, 72; geçen 151
last name soyad 25
late geç 14
later sonra 10, 136
laugh, to gülmek 95
laundry *(place)* çamasırhane 29, 99; *(clothes)* çamaşır 29
laundry service çamaşır servisi 23
laxative müshil 109
leap year artık yıl 149
leather deri 114, 118, 127
leave alone, to rahat bırakmak 96
leave, to hareket etmek 31, 68, 69, 74, 80, 153; gitmek 95; *(deposit)* bırakmak 20, 26, 156
leek prasa 49
Lebanon Lübnan 146
left sol 21, 69, 77
left-luggage office bagaj deposu 71
leg bacak 138
lemon limon 37, 38, 53, 59, 64
lemonade limonata 59
lens *(glasses)* cam 123; *(camera)* objektif 125
lens cap objektif kapağı 125
lentil mercimek 43, 49
less daha az 15
lesson ders 91
let, to *(hire out)* kiralamak 23, 155
letter mektup 132
letter box posta kutusu 132
lettuce marul 42, 49
library kütüphane 81, 99
licence *(permit)* ehliyet 20, 79
lie down, to uzanmak 142
life belt cankurtaran simidi 74
life boat cankurtaran sandalı 74
life jacket cankurtaran yeleği 74
lifeguard yüzme öğretmeni 91
lift asansör 27, 100, 155
ligament bağ 138
light hafif 14, 54, 56, 101; *(colour)* açık 101, 113, 126
light ışık 28, 124; *(cigarette)* ateş 95
lighter çakmak 126
lighter fluid benzinli çakmak 126
lighter gas gazlı çakmak 126
light meter pozometre 125
light music hafif müzik 128
lightning şimşek 94
like, to *(want)* istemek 13, 20, 23; *(take pleasure)* beğenmek 25, 61, 92, 102
lime misket limonu 53
line hat 136
linen *(cloth)* keten 114
lip dudak 138
lipsalve dudak kremi 110
lipstick ruj 110
liqueur likör 58
listen, to dinlemek 128
litre litre 56, 75, 120
little (a) biraz 14
live, to yaşamak 83
liver karaciğer 138
lobster istakoz 40, 44

local yerli 36, 58
long uzun 61, 116, 117
long-sighted hipermetrop 123
look, to bakmak 36, 100, 123, 139
look for, to aramak 13
look out! dikkat! 156
loose *(clothes)* bol 116
lose, to kaybetmek 123, 145, 156
loss kayıp 131
lost *(to be)* kaybolmak 13, 156
lost and found office kayıp eşya bürosu 67, 156
lost property office kayıp eşya bürosu 67, 156
lot *(a)* çok 14, 92
lotion losyon 110
loud *(voice)* yüksek 135
lovely nefis 94
low düşük 141
lower aşağıda 69
low season mevsim dışı 150
luck şans 152
luggage bagaj 17, 18, 21, 26, 31, 71
luggage trolley bagaj arabası 18, 71
lump *(bump)* yumru 139
lunch öğle yemeği 35, 80, 94
Luxembourg Lüksemburg 146
lung akciğer 138

M

macaroni makarna 51
machine makina 114
mackerel uskumru 44
magazine dergi 105
magnificent dağanüstü 84
maid oda temizlikçisi 26
mail posta 28, 133
mailbox posta kutusu 133
main asıl 100
make, to yapmak 114
make up, to *(prepare)* hazırlamak 28, 71
make-up makyaj 110
make-up remover pad makyaj pamuğu 110
mallet çekiç 106
man erkek 115, 156
mango mango 53
manager müdür 26
manicure manikür 30
many çok 14
map harita 76, 105
March Mart 150
marinated salamura 45
market pazar 81, 99
marmalade portakal reçeli 38
mascara rimel 110
married evli 93
marrow sakızkabağı 49
mass *(church)* ayin 84
match kıbrıt 106, 126; *(sport)* maç 89
match, to *(colour)* uymak 112
matinée ilk oyun 87
mattress hava yatağı 106
mature *(cheese)* eski 52
mauve leylak rengi 113
May Mayıs 150
mayonnaise mayonez 45
meadow çayır 85
meal yemek 24, 34, 143
mean, to demek 11, 26
measles kızamık 142
measure, to ölçmek 114
meat et 46, 61
meatball köfte 46
mechanic araba tamircisi 78
mechanical pencil mekanik kurşun kalem 105
medical certificate sağlık raporu 144
medicine tıp 83; *(drug)* ilaç 143
medium *(meat)* orta 20, 46, 56
medium-sized normal 134
meet, to boluşmak 96
meerschaum pipe lületaşı pipo 127
melon kavun 53
memorial anıt 81
mend, to yamamak 74
menthol *(cigarettes)* mentollü 126
menu menü 36, 37, 39, 40
merry neşeli 152
message mesaj 28, 136
methylated spirits ispirto 106
metre metre 112
mezzanine *(theatre)* balkon 87
middle orta 69, 87, 150
midnight gece yarısı 153
mild hafif 126
mileage kilometre ücreti 20
milk süt 38, 59, 64, 120
milkshake frape 54, 59
milliard milyar 148
million milyon 148
minced meat kıyma 46, 51, 63
mineral water maden suyu 59
minister *(religion)* protestan rahip 84
mint nane 52

minute dakika 12, 21, 40, 69, 153
mirror ayna 115, 123
miscellaneous çeşit 127
Miss bayan 10
miss, to eksik olmak 29, 61
mistake hata 31, 61, 62, 102
mixed salad karışık salata 42
modified American plan yarım pansiyon 24
moisturizing cream nemlen dirici krem 110
monastery manastır 81
Monday Pazartesi 151
money para 130, 156
money order havale 133
month ay 16, 141, 150
monument âbide 81
moon ay 94
moped küçük motosiklet 74
more daha 15, 27
morning sabah 31, 143, 151, 153
Morocco Fas 146
mortgage ipotek 131
mosque cami 81, 84
mosquito net cibinlik 106
mother anne 93
motorcycle motosiklet 74
motorboat motorbot 91
motorway otoyol 76
mountaineering dağcılık 89
mountain dağ 84, 85
moustache bıyık 31
mouth ağız 138, 142
mouthwash gargara 109
move, to hareket etmek 139
movie film 24, 86
movie camera film kamerası 124
movies sinema 86, 96
Mr. bay 10
Mrs. bayan 10
much çok 10, 14
mug bardak 107
mulberry dut 53
muscle adele 138
museum müze 81
mushroom mantar 42, 49
music müzik 83
music box müzik kutusu 121
musical müzikal 86
mussel midye 41, 44
must *(have to)* gerek 142
mustard hardal 37, 52, 64, 120
mutton stew düğün eti 46
myself kendim 120

N
nail *(human)* tır 110
nail brush tırnak fırçası 110
nail clippers tırnak makası 110
nail file madeni tırnak törpüsü 110
nail polish tırnak cilâsı 110
nail polish remover aseton 110
nail scissors tırnak makası 110
name ad 23, 35, 79, 92, 131, 133, 136
napkin peçete 36
nappy kundak 111
narrow dar 118
nationality tabiyet 25; millet 92
natural history tabiyat bilgisi 83
nauseous bulantı 140
near yakın 14, 15, 19, 32, 84
nearby yakında 22, 77
nearest en yakın 75, 78, 90, 104, 108, 129, 132, 134
neat *(drink)* sek 58
neck boyun 30, 138
necklace kolye 121
need, to lazım olmak 29, 118, 133, 137
needle iğne 27
negative negatif 125
nephew erkek yeğen 93
nerve sinir 138
nervous sinir 138
nervous system sinir sistemi 138
Netherlands Hollanda 146
never hiç 15
new yeni 14, 86, 118
newsagent's gazeteci 99
newspaper gazete 104, 105
newsstand bayi 19, 67, 99, 104
New Year yeni yıl 152
New Zealand Yeni Zelanda 146
next gelecek 14, 21, 66, 68, 72, 74, 76, 77, 151
next time gelecek sefere 95
next to yanında 15, 77
nice *(beautiful)* güzel 94
niece kız yeğen 93
night gece 143, 151
nightclub gece klübü 88
night cream gece kremi 110
nightdress gecelik 116
nine dokuz 147
nineteen on dokuz 147
ninety doksan 148
ninth dokuzuncu 149
no hayır 10

noisy gürültülü 25
nonalcoholic alkolsüz 59
none hiç biri 15
nonsmoker sigara içilmeyen 68
noodle erişte 43
noon öğle 31
normal normal 30, 110
north kuzey 77
North America Kuzey Amerika 146
nose burun 138
nosebleed burun kanaması 141
nose drops burun damlası 109
not değil 15
notebook not defteri 105
note paper mektup kâğıdı 105
nothing hiç birşey 15, 17
notice *(sign)* uyarı 155
notify, to bildirmek 144
November Kasim 150
now şimdi 15
number numara 25, 26, 65, 69, 134, 136
nurse hastabakıcı 144
nut fındık 64
nutmeg ufak hindistancevizi 52

O
occupation meslek 25
occupied meşgul 14, 155
October Ekim 150
office büro 67; *(ticket)* gişe 19, 67
oil yağ 37, 75
oily *(greasy)* yağlı 30, 111
old eski 14; ihtiyar 14
old town eski şehir 81
olive zeytin 38, 41
olive oil zeytinyağ 52
omelet omlet 42
on üstünde 15
once bir kez 149
one bir 64, 101, 147
one-way *(ticket)* gidiş 69
on foot yürüyerek 66, 76, 85
onion soğan 49
only sadece 15, 24, 80, 87
on time zamanında 68
onyx oniks 122
open açık 14, 82, 108, 155
open, to açmak 11, 17, 130, 132, 142
open-air açık hava 90
opera opera 88
opera house opera binası 81, 88
operation ameliyat 144
operator santral memuru 134
operetta operet 88
opposite karşısı 77
optician gözlükçü 99, 123
or veya 15, 143
orally ağız yolu ile 143
orange *(colour)* portakal rengi 113
orange *(fruit)* portakal 53, 59
orange juice portakal suyu 38, 64
orchestra orkestra 88; *(seats)* salon 87
orchestral music orkestra müziği 128
order *(goods, meal)* ısmarlama 102
order, to *(goods, meal)* ısmarlamak 36, 61, 102, 103
ornithology ornitoloji 83
other başka 17, 58, 74, 101
out of order bozuk 136
out of stock kalmadı 103
outlet *(electric)* priz 27
outside dışarıda 15, 36
oval oval 101
overalls tulum 116
overdone çok pişmiş 61
overheat, to *(engine)* ısınmak 78
overnight *(stay)* bir gece 24
overtake, to geçmek 79
owe, to borçlu olmak 144
oyster istiridye 44

P
pacifier emzik 111
packet paket 120, 126, 133
page *(hotel)* belboy 26
pail kova 106, 128
pain ağrı 140, 141, 143, 144
painkiller ağrı kesicisi 140, 143
paint, to *(tablo)* yapmak 83
paintbox boya kutusu 105
painter ressam 83
painting resim 83
pair çift 116, 117, 149
palace saray 81
palpitation çarpıntı 141
panties külot 116
pants *(trousers)* pantalon 116
panty girdle korse 116
panty hose külotlu çorap 116
paper kâğıt 105
paperback cep kitabı 105
paperclip ataş 105
paper napkin kağıt peçete 105, 106

paprika kırmızı biber 49
paraffin *(fuel)* gazyağı 106
parcel paket 132
pardon efendim 11
park park 72, 81
parka anorak 116
park, to park etmek 26, 77
parking park 79, 77
parliament parlamento 81
parsley maydanoz 42, 52
partridge çil 48
party *(social gathering)* parti 95
pass *(mountain)* geçit 85
pass, to *(car)* geçmek 16, 70
passport pasaport 16, 17, 25, 26, 156
passport photo vesikalık fotoğraf 124
pass through, to transit geçmek 16
pasta hamur işleri 51
paste *(glue)* yapıştırıcı 105
pastry tatlı 64
pastry shop pastane 99
patch, to *(clothes)* yamamak 29
path patika 85
patient hasta 144
pay, to ödemek 17, 31, 62, 102, 136
payment ödeme 131
pea bezelye 43, 49
peach şeftali 53, 120
peak tepe 85
peanut amerikan fıstığı 53
pear armut 53
pearl inci 122
pedestrian yaya 79
peg *(tent)* kazık 107
pen kalem 105
pencil kurşun kalem 105
pencil sharpener kalemtıraş 105
pendant pandantif 121
penicillin penisilin 143
penknife çakı 106
pensioner emekli 82
pepper biber 50, 64
per cent yüzde 131, 149
per day günlük 32
perform, to *(theatre)* oynamak 86
perfume parfüm 110
perhaps belki 15
per hour saatlık 77
period *(monthly)* aybaşı 141
period pains aybaşı ağrıları 141
permanent wave perma 30
permit ruhsatı 90
per night bir gecelik 24
per person bir kişi için 32
person kişi 32
personal özel 17
personal/person-to-person call ihbarlı aramak 135
per week bir haftalık 24
petrol benzin 75, 78
pewter kalay 122
pheasant sülün 48
photo fotoğraf 125
photocopy fotokopi 131
photographer fotoğrafçı 99
photography fotoğraf 124
phrase deyim 12
pick up, to *(person)* almak 80, 96
picnic piknik 63
picnic basket piknik sepeti 106
picture tablo 83; *(photo)* fotoğraf 82
pie börek 64
piece parça 120
pike turna 44
pill doğum kontrol hapı 141
pillow yastık 27, 107
pin iğne 121
pine kernels çam fıstığı 52
pineapple ananas 53, 59
pink pembe 113
pipe pipo 126
pipe cleaner pipo temizleyen 126
pipe tobacco pipo tütünü 126
pipe tool pipo takımı 126
pistachio fıstık 52
place yer 25, 76
place of birth doğum yeri 25
plaice pisi 44
plane uçak 65
planetarium rasathane 81
plaster *(cast)* alçi 140
plastic plastik 107
plastic bag plastik torba 107
plate tabak 36, 51, 107
platform *(station)* peron 67, 68, 69, 70
platinum platin 122
play *(theatre)* oyun 86
play, to oynamak 86, 88, 93; *(music)* çalmak 88
playground oyun alanı 32
playing card oyun kâğıdı 105
please lütfen 10
plimsolls tenis ayakkabısı 118
plug *(electric)* fiş 29, 119
plum erik 53
pneumonia zatürree 142
poached haşlama 45
pocket cep 104, 117

pocket calculator hesap makinesi 105
pocket watch cep saatı 121
point, to *(show)* göstermek 12
poison zehir 109, 156
poisoning zehirlenmek 142
Poland Polonya 146
pole *(ski)* kayak sopası 91
police polis 78, 156
police station karakol 99, 156
polish *(nail)* boya 118
pomegranate nar 53
pond küçük göl 85
politics politika 83
pop music pop müzik 128
poplin poplin 114
pork domuz 46
port liman 75; *(wine)* porto 58
portable portatif 119
porter hamal 18, 26, 71
portion porsiyon 37, 54, 61
post *(letters)* posta 28, 133
post, to postalamak 28
postage stamp posta pulu 28, 126, 132
postcard kartpostal 105, 126, 132
poste restante post restant 133
post office postane 99, 132
potato patates 49, 51
pottery çömlekçilik 83
poultry kümes hayvanları 48
pound *(money)* sterlin 18, 102, 130
powder pudra 110
powder compact pudriyer 122
prawn(s) karides 44
prayer mat namaz seccâdesi 127
prefer, to tercih etmek 49
preference tercih 101
pregnant hamile 141
premium *(gasoline)* süper 75
prepare, to hazırlamak 28, 60, 108
prescription reçete 108, 143
press, to *(iron)* ütülemek 29
press stud çıtçıt 117
pretty sevimli 84
price fiyat 24, 131
priest katolik rahip 84
print *(photo)* baskı 125
private özel 91, 155
process, to *(photo)* banyo etmek 124
profit kâr 131
programme program 87
propelling pencil yedek kalem içi 105
Protestant protestan 84
provide, to bulmak 131
prune kuru erik 53
public holiday millî bayram 152
pudding muhallebi 54
pull, to çekmek 155
pullover kazak 117
purchase satın alma 131
pure saf 114
purple mor 113
push, to *(door/button)* itmek 155
put, to kaymak 24, 140
puzzle puzzle 128
pyjamas pijama 117

Q

quail bıldırcın 48
quality kalite 103, 113
quantity miktar 14, 103
quarter dörtte bir 149
quarter of an hour çeyrek 153
quartz kuars 122
question soru 11
quick çabuk 14, 137
quickly çabuk 36, 79, 156
quince ayva 53
quiet sakin 23

R

rabbi haham 84
race course/track hipodrom 90
racket *(sport)* raket 90
radiator *(car)* radyatör 78
radio *(set)* radyo 23, 28, 119
radish turp 49
railway station tren istasyon 21, 66
rain yağmur 94
rain, to yağmur yağmak 94
raincoat yağmurluk 117
raisin üzüm 52
rangefinder telemetre 125
raki rakı 57
rare *(meat)* çiğ 61
rash isilik 139
raspberry ahududu 53
ravioli mantı 51
rate *(price)* oran 131
raw çiğ 45
razor tıraş makinesi 110
razor blade tıraş bıçağı 110
read, to okumak 40
reading lamp başucu lambası 27

ready hazır 29, 31, 36, 118, 123, 125, 145
real gerçek 118, 121
rear arka 75
receipt makbuz 103, 144
reception resepsiyon 23
receptionist resepsiyon şefi 26
recommend, to tavsiye etmek 35, 36, 40, 43, 48, 49, 54, 80, 86, 88, 137, 145
record *(disc)* plak 127, 128
record player pikap 119
rectangular dikdörtgen 101
red kırmızı 56, 105, 113
red mullet barbunya 44
reduction indirim 24, 82
refill *(pen)* yedek (kalem) 105
refund parayı geri almak 103
regards selamlar 152
register, to *(luggage)* teslim etmek 71
registered mail taahhütlü 133
registration kayıt 25
registration form kayıt formu 25
regular *(petrol)* normal 75
religion din 83
religious service ibadet 84
rent, to kiralamak 20, 74, 90, 155
rental kiralama 20
repair tamir 125
repair, to tamir etmek 29, 118, 119, 121, 123, 145
repeat, to tekrar etmek 12
report, to *(a theft)* ihbar etmek 156
reservation rezervasyon 19, 23, 65, 69
reservations office rezervasyon bürosu 67
reserve, to ayırmak 19, 35, 87, 155; rezerve etmek 23
restaurant restoran 19, 32, 33, 35, 67
return *(ticket)* gidiş–dönüş 65, 69
return, to *(give back)* geri vermek 103
reverse the charges, to ödemeli aramak 135
rheumatism romatizma 141
rhubarb ravent 53
rib kaburga kemiği 138
ribbon şeridi 105
rice pilav 51
right sağ 21, 69, 77; *(cornet)* doğru 11, 14, 70
ring *(on finger)* yüzük 122
ring, to *(doorbell)* zili çalmak 155
river nehir 85, 90
road yol 76, 77, 85
road assistance yol yardım 78
road map karayolları haritası 105
road sign trafik işaretleri 79
roasted kızarmış 46, 51
roast beef sığır kızartması 46
roll *(bread)* küçük ekmek 38, 64
roller skate tekerlekli paten 128
roll film makara film 124
roll up, to sivamak 142
room oda 19, 23, 24, 25, 26, 27, 28, 56; *(space)* yer 32
room service oda servisi 23
rope halat 107
rosary tespih 122
rouge allık 110
round yuvarlak 101
round *(golf)* maç 90
roundtrip *(ticket)* gidiş–dönüş 69
route yol 73
rowing boat kayık 91
rubber *(material)* kauçuk 118; *(eraser)* silgi 105
ruby yâkut 122
rucksack sırt çantası 107
ruin harabe 81
ruler *(for measuring)* cetver 105
rum rom 58
running water lavabo 23

S

safe *(not dangerous)* emniyetli 91
safe kasa 26
safety pin çengelli iğne 110
sailing boat yelkenli kayık 91
salad salata 42, 49, 53
salami salam 64, 120
sale *(bargains)* indirimli satışlar 100
sales tax Katma Değer Vergisi (KDV) 24, 102
salmon som balığı 44
salt tuz 37, 38, 52, 64
salty tuzlu 61
same aynı 118
samovar semaver 127
sandy kumlu 90
sandal sandalet 118
sandwich sandviç 64
sanitary towel/napkin adet bezi 109
sapphire safir 122
sardine sardalya 41, 44
satin saten 114
Saturday Cumartesi 89, 151

saucepan tencere 107
saucer fincan tabak 107
sausage sosis 64
sauteed tavasi 45
scarf atkıı 117
scarlet kızıl 113
scenic route güzel manzaralı yol 83
school okul 79
scissors makas 107
Scotland Iskoçya 146
screwdriver tornavida 106
sculptor heykeltraş 83
sculpture heykeltraşlık 83
sea deniz 23, 85, 91
sea bass levrek 44
seafood deniz hayvanları 44
season mevsim 40, 42, 48, 150
seasoning baharat 37
seat yer 69, 70, 87
second *(clock)* saniye 153
second ikinci 77, 149
second class ikinci mevki 69, 70
second-hand kullanılmış 104
second-hand shop eskici dükkânı 99
secretary sekreter 27, 131
section bölüm 141
see, to görmek 25, 26, 87, 90, 96, 121, 132
sell, to satmak 100
send, to göndermek 26, 78, 102, 103, 132, 133; çekmek 133
sentence cümle 12
separately ayrı 62
September Eylül 150
service servis 24, 62; *(religion)* ayin 84
serviette peçete 36
sesame susam 52
setting lotion saç sertleştirici 111
seven yedi 70, 147
seventeen on yedi 147
seventh yedinci 149
seventy yetmiş 148
sew, to dikmek 29
shade *(colour)* ton 112
shampoo şampuan 30, 111
shampoo and set mizampli 30
shape biçin 103
share *(finance)* hisse senedi 131
shave, to tıraş olmak 31
shaver tıraş makinesı 27, 119
shaving brush tıraş fırçası 111
shaving cream tıraş kremi 111
shelf raf 120
sherry şeri 58
ship gemi 74
shirt gömlek 117
shivery titreme 140
shoe ayakkabı 118
shoelace ayakkabı bağı 118
shoemaker's kunduracı 99
shoe polish ayakkabı boyası 118
shoe shop ayakkabı mağazası 99
shop dükkân 98
shopping alışveriş 32
shopping area alışveriş merkezi 82, 100
shopping centre alışveriş merkezi 99
short kısa 30, 116, 117
shorts şort 117
short-sighted miyop 123
shoulder omuz 138
shovel kürek 128
show şov 88
show, to göstermek 13, 76, 86, 100, 101, 119, 124
shower duş 23, 32
shut kapalı 14
shutter *(camera)* obtüratör 125
side kenar 30
sideboards/burns favori 31
sightseeing tour şehir turu 80
sign *(notice)* levha 79, 155
sign, to imzalamak 26
signature imza 25
signet ring mühürlü yüzük 122
silk ipek 114
silver *(colour)* gümüş rengi 113, 121
silver gümüş 113, 122
silver-plated gümüş kaplama 122
silverware gümüş çatal–bıçak–kaşık 122
simple basit 124
since beri 15, 150
sing, to şarkı söylemek 88
single *(not married)* bekâr 93
single *(ticket)* gidiş 65, 69
single room tek yataklı oda 19, 23, 74
sister kız kardeş 93
sit, to oturmak 95
six altı 147
sixteen on altı 147
sixth altıncı 149
sixty atmış 147
size *(clothes)* beden 114; *(format)* büyüklük 124
ski kayak 91
ski, to kayak kaymak 91
ski boot kayak ayakkabısı 91

skiing kayak kaymak 89
skiing equipment kayak takımı 91
skin cilt 110, 138
skirt etek 117
sky gök 94
sleepy yorgun 143
sleep, to uyumak 70, 144
sleeping bag uyku tulumu 107
sleeping-car yataklı vagon 68, 69, 70
sleeping pill uyku ilacı 109, 143
sleeve kol 117, 142
sleeveless kolsuz 117
slice *(ham)* dilim 120
slide *(photo)* slayd 124
slip iç eteklik 117
slipper terlik 118
slow yavaş 14, 21, 135
slow down, to yavaşlamak 79
slowly yavaş 12
small küçük 14
smoke, to sigara içmek 36, 95
smoked füme 40, 41, 45
smoker sigara içilen 68
snack hafif yemek 35, 63
snack bar snack bar 67
snap fastener çıtçıt 117
sneakers tenis ayakkabısı 118
snorkel şnorkel 128
snow kar 94
snow, to kar 94
snuff enfiye 126
soap sabun 27, 111
soccer futbol 89
sock erkek çorabı 117
socket *(outlet)* priz 27
soda soda 58, 59
soft drink alkolsuz içki 64
soft yumuşak 123
soft-boiled *(egg)* az pişmiş 28
sold out *(theatre)* hepsi saltıldı 87
sole taban 118; *(fish)* dil balığı 44
soloist solist 88
some bir az
someone birisini 95
something birşey 29, 36, 54, 108, 112, 139
somewhere herhangi biryerde 86
son oğul 93
soon yakında 15
sore *(painful)* ağrı 145
sore throat boğaz ağrısı 141
sorry özür dilerim 11, 16, 87
sort *(kind)* tür 86, 120
soup çorba 43, 63
sour ekşi 61
south güney 77
South America Güney Amerika 146
souvenir hatıra 127
spade kürek 128
Spain İspanya 146
spare tyre yedek lâstiği 75
sparking plug buji 75
sparkling *(wine)* köpüklü 56
spark plug buji 75
speak, to konuşmak 135; bilmek 12, 16, 80, 84, 134, 137
speaker *(loudspeaker)* hoparlör 119
special özel 37
special delivery expres 133
staff personel 26
stain leke 29
stainless steel paslanmaz çelik 107, 122
stalls *(theatre)* salon 87
stamp *(postage)* posta pulu 28, 126, 132, 133
staple tel raptiye 105
star yıldız 58, 94
start, to başlamak 80
starter *(appetizer)* antre 40
station *(train)* istasyon 19, 66, 70, 73
stationer's kirtasiye dükkânı 99, 104
statue heykel 82
stay seyahat 92
stay, to kalmak 16, 24, 26, 93, 142
steak biftek 46
steal, to çalmak 156
steamed buğulama 45
stew haşlama 46
stewed yahni 46, 51
stiff neck tutuk boyun 141
still *(mineral water)* sade 59
sting, to sokmak 139
stitch, to *(clothes)* dikmek 29, 118
stock exchange borsa 82
stocking çorap 117
stomach mide 138
stomach ache mide ağrısı 141
stools abdest 142
stop *(bus)* durak 72
stop! dur! 79
stop, to durmak 21, 66, 68, 70, 156
stop thief! hırsızı yakalayın! 156
store *(shop)* mağaza 98
straight ahead doğru 21, 77
strange tuhaf 84
strawberry çilek 53

street sokak 25, 77
street map şehir planı 19, 105
string bean çali 49
string sicim 105
strong sert 126, 143
student oğrenci 82, 93
study, to okumak 93
stuffed dolma 45, 46, 50, 51
sturdy sağlam 101
sturgeon mersin balığı 41, 44
subway *(rail)* metro 73
suede süet 114, 118, 127
sugar şeker 37, 64
suit *(man)* erkek elbisesi 117; *(woman's)* tayyör 117
suitcase bavul 18
summer yaz 150
sun güneş 94
sunburn güneş yanığı 108
Sunday Pazar 82, 151
sunglasses güneş gözlüğü 123
sunshade *(beach)* güneş şemsiyesi 91
sunstroke güneş çarpması 141
sun-tan cream güneş kremi 111
sun-tan oil güneş yağı 111
super *(petrol)* süper 75
supermarket süpermarket 99
supplement *(ticket)* fark 69
suppository fitil 109
surgery *(consulting room)* muayenehane 137
surname soyadı 25
suspenders *(Am.)* pantalon askısı 117
swallow, to yutmak 143
sweater kazak 117
sweatshirt koton kazak 117
Sweden İsveç 146
sweet *(food)* tatlı 56, 57, 61
sweet *(candy)* akide şekeri 126
sweet shop şekerci dükkânı 99
sweet corn mısır 49
sweet pepper tatlı biber 49
sweetener sakarin 37
swell, to şişirmek 139
swim, to yüzmek 90, 91
swimming yüzmek 89
swimming pool yüzme havuzu 32, 90
swimming trunks erkek mayosu 117
swimsuit mayo 117
switch elektrik düğmesi 29
switchboard operator santral memuresi 26
Switzerland İsviçre 146
swollen şiş 139
swordfish kılıç balığı 40, 44
synagogue sinagog 84
synthetic sentetik 114
Syria Suriye 146

T

table masa 35, 36, 107
tablet tablet 109
tailor's erkek terzisi 99
take, to almak 18, 25, 102, 136, 143
take away, to *(carry)* götürmek 18, 21, 66, 96, 102, 103
take off, to *(plane)* kalkmak 65
take out, to çekmek 145
talcum powder talk pudrası 111
tampon tampon 109
tangerine mandalina 53
tap *(water)* musluk 28
tart turta 54
tax vergi 32, 102
taxi taksi 18, 19, 21, 31, 66
tea çay 38, 59, 64, 120
team takım 89
tear, to yırtmak 140
tearoom pastane 99
teaspoon çay kaşığı 107, 143
telegram telegraf 133
telegraph office postane 99
telephone telefon 28, 78, 79
telephone, to telefon etmek 134
telephone booth telefon kulübesi 134
telephone call telefon 136
telephone directory telefon rehberi 134
telephone number telefon numarası 96
telephoto lens teleobjektif 125
television *(set)* televizyon 23, 28, 119
telex telex 133
telex, to telex çekmek 130
tell, to söylemek 13, 72, 76, 135, 136, 153
temperature ısı 56, 90; *(fever)* derece 140
temple tapınak 82
ten on 21, 112, 147
tendon kiriş 138
tennis tenis 89, 90
tennis court tenis kort 90
tennis racket tenis raket 90
tent çadır 32, 107
tenth onuncu 149

tent peg çadır kazıkları 107
tent pole çadır direği 107
term *(word)* terim 131
terrace teras 36
tetanus tetanoz 140
thank you teşekkür ederim 10, 37, 62, 92, 95
that şu 11, 12, 18, 61, 70, 100, 156
theatre tiyatro 82, 86
theft hırsızlık 156
then *(after that)* sonra 15
there orada 14, 69, 77; oraya 100, 142
thermometer derece 109, 144
these bu 29
thief hırsız 156
thigh but 138
think, to düşünmek 93; *(believe)* sanmak 31, 70, 102
third üçte bir 149
third üçüncü 149
thirsty, to be susamak 13, 35
thirteen on üç 147
thirty otuz 147
this bu 11
those şunlar 64, 120
thousand bin 148
thread iplik 27
three üç 73, 141, 147, 149
throat boğaz 138
throat lozenge boğaz pastili 109
through içinden 15
through train ekspres tren 68, 69
thumb başparmak 138
thumbtack raptiye 105
thunder gök gürültüsü 94
thunderstorm fırtına 94
Thursday perşembe 30, 151
thyme kekik 52
ticket bilet 65, 69, 72, 74, 87, 88
ticket office bilet gişesi 67
tide met 91
tie kravat 117
tie clip kravat iğnesi 122
tie pin kravat iğnesi 122
tight *(clothes)* dar 116
tights külotlu çorap 117
time zaman 68, 80; *(clock)* saat 65, 68, 80, 84, 87, 95, 108; *(occasion)* kez 142, 143
timetable tren tarifesi 68
tin *(can)* kutu 120
tinfoil alüminyum kâğıdı 107
tin opener konserve açacağı 107
tint nüans verici boya 111
tinted renkli 123
tire lâstik 75, 76
tired, to be yorgun olmak 13
tissue *(handkerchief)* kâğıt mendil 111
toast kızarmış ekmek 38
tobacco tütün 126
tobacconist's tütün satıcısı 99
today bugün 29, 94, 151
toe ayakparmağı 138
toilet *(lavatory)* tuvalet 23, 27, 32, 37, 67
toilet paper tuvalet kağıdı 111
toiletry güzellik malzemesi 110
toilet water kolonya 111
token jeton 133
tomato domates 42, 43, 49, 50, 51, 59, 64
tomato juice domates suyu 59
tomb mezar 82
tomorrow yarın 29, 35, 94, 96, 137, 151
tongue dil 40, 138
tonic water tonik 59
tonight bu akşam 29, 86, 87, 88, 96
tonsils bademcikler 138
too -de/da 15
tooth diş 145
toothache diş ağrısı 145
toothbrush diş fırçası 111
toothpaste diş macunu 111
top üst 30, 145
topaz topaz 122
torch *(flashlight)* cep feneri 107
torn yırtık 140
touch, to dokunmak 155
tough *(meat)* sert 61
tour tur 80
tourist office turizm bürosu 19, 67, 80
tourist tax turist vergisi 32
towards doğru 15
towel havlu 127
towelling havlu kumaş 114
tower kule 82
town şehir 19, 21, 72, 76, 88
town hall belediye binası 82
tow truck kurtarma aracı 78
toy oyuncak 128
toy shop oyuncakçı dükkânı 99
tracing paper kopya kâğıdı 105
tracksuit eşofman 117
traffic trafik 76
traffic light trafik ışıkları 77
trailer karavan 32

train tren 66, 67, 68, 70
tranquillizer sakinleştirici 109, 143
transformer transformatör 119
translate, to tercüme etmek 12
translator çevirmen 155
transport araç 74
travel, to seyahat etmek 92
travel agency seyahat acentası 99
travel guide rehber kitabı 105
traveller's cheque traveller's çek 18, 62, 102, 130
travel sickness yol tutması 108
treatment tedavi 143
tree ağaç 85
tremendous heybetli 84
trim, to *(beard)* kısaltmak 31
tripe işkembe 63
trip yolcu 152
trolley araba 18, 71
trousers pantalon 117
trout alabalık 44
try, to denemek 115, 136; tatmak 35, 58
T-shirt tişort 117
tube tüp 120
Tuesday Salı 87, 151
tumbler bardak 107
tuna ton 41, 44
tunny ton 41, 44
turbot kalkan 44
Turkey Türkiye 146
turkey hindi 48
Turkish *(language)* Türkçe 11, 12
Turkish Türk 38
Turkish delight lokum 127
turn, to *(change direction)* dönmek 21, 77
turnip şalgam 49
turquoise türkuvaz 113
turquoise zümrüt 122
turtleneck dik yakalı 117
tweezers cımbız 111
twelve on iki 147
twenty yirmi 147
twice iki kez 149
twin bed iki yatak 23
two iki 23, 73, 87, 141, 147
typewriter yazı makinesi 27
typing paper daktilo kâğıdı 105
tyre lâstik 75, 76

U
ugly çirkin 14, 84
ulcer ülser 141
umbrella şemsiye 117
uncle amca 93; dayı 93
unconscious bayılmak 139
under altında 15
underdone *(meat)* az pişmiş 46, 61
underground *(railway)* metro 73
underpants don 117
undershirt fanilâ 117
understand, to anlamak 12, 101
undress, to soyunmak 142
United States Amerika Birleşik Devletleri 146
university üniversite 82
until kadar 15
up yukarı 15
upper yukarıda 69
upset stomach mide bozulması 108
upstairs yukarı katta 15, 69
urgent acele 13, 133, 145
urine idrar 142
use ihtiyaç 17
use, to kullanmak 78, 134
useful önemli 15

V
vacancy boş 23
vacant boş 155
vacation tatil 151
vaccinate, to aşılanmak 140
vacuum flask termos 107
vaginal infection dölyolu mikrop kapması 141
valley vâdi 85
value değer 131
value-added tax Katma Değer Vergisi (KDV) 24, 102
VAT *(sales tax)* KDV 24, 102
veal dana 46
vegetable sebze 43, 49
vegetable store manav 99
vegetarian etsiz yemek 37
vein damar 138
velvet kadife 114
velveteen ince fitilli kadife 114
venereal disease zührevi hastalık 142
vermicelli erişte 51
vermouth vermut 58
very çok 10, 15, 31, 145
vest fanilâ 117; *(Am.)* yelek 117
veterinarian veteriner 99
video cassette video kaset 119, 124, 127

video camera video kamerası 124
video recorder video 119
view manzara 23, 25
village köy 76, 85
vinegar sirke 37
vine leaves yaprak 50
vineyard bağ 85
visit ziyaret 92
visit, to gezmek 84
visiting hours ziyaret saatları 144
vitamin pills vitamin 109
V-neck V-yakalı 117
vodka votka 58
volleyball voleybol 89
voltage voltaj 27, 119
vomit, to kusmak 140

W

waist bel 142
waistcoat yelek 117
wait, to beklemek 21, 40, 95, 108
waiter garson 26, 36
waiting room bekleme salonu 67
waitress kadın garson 26, 36
wake, to uyandırmak 27, 71
Wales Galler ülkesi 146
walk, to yürümek 74
wall sur 85
wallet para cüzdanı 156
walnut ceviz 52, 53
want, to *(wish)* istemek 13, 20, 30, 57, 72, 156
warm sıcak 94
wash, to yıkamak 29
wash basin lavabo 28
washing powder çamaşır tozu 107
washing-up liquid bulaşık deterjanı 107
watch saat 121, 122
watchmaker's saatçi 99, 121
watchstrap kol saati kayışı 122
water su 28, 38, 58, 59, 75, 90
watercress roka 49
waterfall şelâle 85
water flask matara 107
watermelon karpuz 53
water pipe nargile 50, 127
waterproof *(watch)* su geçirmez 122
water ski deniz kayağı 91
wave dalga 91
way yol 76
weather hava 94
weather forecast hava raporu 94
wedding ring alyans 122
Wednesday Carşamba 151
week hafta 16, 20, 24, 80, 92, 151
weekday hafta içi 151
weekend hafta sonu 20, 151
well *(healthy)* iyi 10, 115
well-done *(meat)* iyi pişmiş 46
west batı 77
what ne 11, 13
wheel tekerlek 78
when ne zaman 11
where nerede 11
which hangi 11
whisky viski 17, 58
white beyaz 56, 113, 124
who kim 11
whole bütün 143
why neden 11
wide bol 118
wide-angle lens geniş açılı objektif 125
wife karı 93
wig peruk 111
wild boar yabani domuz 48
wind rüzgar 94
window pencere 28, 36; *(shop)* vitrin 100, 112
windscreen/shield ön cam 76
wine şarap 56, 57, 61
wine merchant's şarap tüccarı 99
winter kış 91, 150
winter sports kış sporları 91
wiper cam sileceği 76
wish kutlama 152
with ile 15, 69
withdraw, to *(bank)* çekmek 130
without -siz/sız 15
woman kadın 115, 141, 156
wonderful fevkalâde 96
wood *(forest)* orman 85
wood alcohol ispirto 107
woodcock çulluk 48
wool yün 114
word kelime 12, 15, 133
work, to *(function)* çalışmak 28, 119
working day iş günü 151
worse daha kötü 14
worsted kamgarn 114
worry beads tespih 127
wound yara 139
wrap, to sarmak 103
wrestling güreş 89, 90
wrinkle resistant buruşmaz 114
wristwatch kol saati 122

write, to yazmak 12, 101
writing pad bloknot 105
writing-paper yazi kâğıdi 27
wrong yanlış 14, 77, 136

X
X-ray *(photo)* röntgen 140

Y
year yıl 92, 141, 149
yellow sarı 113
yes evet 10, 92
yesterday dün 151
yet henüz 15, 16, 24
yoghurt yoğurt 38, 42, 54, 64
young genç 14
youth hostel gençlik yurdu 22, 32

Z
zero sıfır 147
zip(per) fermuar 117
zoo hayvanat bahçesi 82
zoology zooloji 83
zucchini kabak 49

Türkçe fihrist

BLACK SEA
GEORGIA
BULGARI
Edirne
Samsun
İstanbul
SEA OF MARMARA
İzmit
Trabzon
Kars
Bursa
Erzurum
Sivas
ANKARA
Eskişehir
TURKEY
Van Gölü
Van
Elâzığ
Manisa
Kayseri
İzmir
Malatya
Diyarbakır
Denizli
Konya
Mardin
Bodrum
AEGEAN SEA
Marmaris
Antalya
Adana
Gaziantep
Mersin
Antakya
IRAQ
SYRIA
CYPRUS
MEDITERRANEAN SEA